Christian Living

Seven Days a Week

A Topical Concordance of the Bible

Christian Living

Seven Days a Week

A Topical Concordance

of the Bible

Jack McInturff

Library of Congress Control Number:		2007904163
ISBN:	Hardcover	978-1-4257-7730-2
	Softcover	978-1-4257-7707-4

This book was printed in the United States of America.

To order additional copies of this book, contact:
Xlibris Corporation
1-888-795-4274
www.Xlibris.com
Orders@Xlibris.com
36731

Introduction

A question that each person who is a Christian deals with on a daily basis is, what does it really mean to be a Christian? There is a section in this book that deals specifically with that, entitled "Being a Christian." However, the real question is how to live this life seven days a week. It is easy to go to church with other believers and really get into listening to the message, singing the songs, praying and worshipping God. Some of the songs really lift your spirits, and you are up on that mountaintop. However, how much of that can you carry outside the doors, and how much should be? For example, if I am very emotional in my worship on Sunday, I cannot show that same emotion at my job on Monday. I can express it in other ways. I can have a cheerful and helpful attitude toward those around me. One song says in its refrain, "I'll live for you every day." And another says, "I will lift your name on high." That is the question: How are you going to live for Jesus every day? How will you lift His name on high? In order to be faithful, this is exactly what we must do. We must let Him live in us daily and in our living show honor and respect to Him.

This subject is so broad that I am not going to attempt to go into all the implications of this daily Christian living in this book. Hopefully, I can deal with this some more at another time. Instead, I am going to approach this subject from the standpoint of a topical concordance of the Bible.

Christian living is simply *living* your life as a follower of Jesus Christ. The key here is living. It should be living in a manner that attracts people to Christ and does not turn them away from Him. Since each of us is different, there is no one pattern or mold. It begins with who you are. Then as you live life, you attempt to live and be (for life involves doing and being) it in obedience to God. For one person, they may become a missionary in a foreign country, and for another, it may mean to be a faithful and loving wife to her husband and a loving and caring mother to her children. Christians come in all sizes, shapes, and forms. There are the rich and the poor, the young and the old, the very intelligent and the mentally handicapped, male and female, all races. Christ has called all.

Some people will express their faith in an intellectual manner and others in a very emotional manner. Some have many talents and some have few. Thus, with such a diversity, you cannot lay down a model and say this is the Christian way. In addition to this, Christian living is a growing process.

Christian living involves problems, beliefs, attitudes, and everything that makes up living. It is really a relationship. Christianity has a philosophy, but it is not a philosophy. It has a body of teachings, but it does not consist of those teachings. The Christian faith is really your relationship with Jesus Christ, who is our Lord and Savior. It is this and only this. The teachings, actions, and everything else are an outgrowth of this relationship.

Therefore, since daily Christian living involves problems and beliefs, I have commented on different topics and given Bible references. The Bible version used throughout this book is the New International Version. It is hoped that this will be beneficial in your Christian walk. In the topical section, the words in parenthesis that are in capital letters refer to other subject entries. The references are not complete but are merely suggestive. The Bible is the real guide for Christian living. Each person needs to look to the Bible for the answers that he or she needs.

I want to add a note here. In these writings and in all things, the reader should test them and see if they are correct according to scripture. In any sermons, religious writings, and any written material (including this one), do not take the writer or speaker's word for it, but see if it is true to the scripture. Scripture or scriptures here refers to the Old and New Testament only and not to other books.

These topics are aimed at both Christians and non-Christians. They are a few of the things that we have to deal with, and some important beliefs, as you strive to walk the Christian walk or as you search for some meaning as to what it means to be a Christian.

For we Christians, unfortunately, do not always act in a Christian manner; but that is because we are human. I hope this strengthens your faith if you are a Christian. If you are a non-Christian but are searching for truth, I pray that Jesus Christ our Lord and Savior will meet you as you read. If you are seeking truth, there is only one place to find it. Jesus said in John 8:32, *"Seek the truth and the truth will set you free."* In addition, in John 14:6, He says, *"I am the way, the truth, and the life. No one comes to the Father except through me."*

Computers are an important part of our world today. A common saying in the computer world is "garbage in, garbage out." This simply means that if you give your computer bad data, then you will get bad results. The human mind is an amazing computer. If you give it bad data, then you will get bad information from it, just like any computer. Therefore, in order for the mind to work properly, you need to give it the best data that you can. In other words, put good data in and you will get good data out. You cannot expect to get the right answer to a problem if you do not have all of the facts and if you do not feed it the right information. Therefore, instead of putting in garbage, you must put in good data, and the Bible is one of the best sources of good data. To live the Christian life means to give it a good diet of scripture.

This applies to life in general. Just as a machine, an automobile, and a number of other things have an operation manual for safety, maintenance, and operation, so also we human beings need an operational manual; and the Bible is one very important source. It is amazing how many people think that they can write their own manual (you can't) and then wonder why they have so many problems. Of course, part of the problem is that there are a number of things that are demanding our attention: business and other people, just to mention two.

The Bible is a great source for inspiration and strength, but not if you just read it and it remains just words. Be open, be receptive, be expectant, study the scripture, meditate upon it, and let its message sink into you. Let that message be a vital part of you. Head knowledge is not enough. It must define you. Then you are living the Christian life. God speaks to us from scripture for it is God's word. This is not an occasional practice, but an everyday practice. Your mind needs good food just as your body does. I do hope this book will help you, and I pray for God to bless you. For anything that you gain from this book, give thanks to God. He is the one that deserves the praise.

Jack McInturff

Topical Concordance

Bible abbreviations:

Act	Acts	Jud	Judges
Amos	Amos	1,2 K	1,2 Kings
1,2 Ch	1,2 Chronicles	Lam	Lamentations
Col	Colossians	Lev	Leviticus
1,2 Cor	1,2 Corinthians	Lk	Luke
Dan	Daniel	Mal	Malachi
Deut	Deuteronomy	Mic	Micah
Ecc	Ecclesiastes	Mk	Mark
Eph	Ephesians	Mt	Matthew
Est	Esther	Nah	Nahum
Ex	Exodus	Neh	Nehemiah
Ezek	Ezekiel	Num	Numbers
Ezra	Ezra	Ob	Obadiah
Gal	Galatians	1,2 Pet	1,2 Peter
Gen	Genesis	Phm	Philemon
Hab	Habakkuk	Phil	Philippians
Hag	Haggai	Prov	Proverbs
Heb	Hebrews	Ps	Psalms
Hos	Hosea	Rev	Revelation
Is	Isaiah	Rom	Romans
Jas	James	Ruth	Ruth
Jer	Jeremiah	1,2 Sam	1,2 Samuel
Jn	John	Song	Song of Solomon
1,2,3 Jn	1,2,3 John	1,2 Th	1,2 Thessalonians
Job	Job	1,2 Tim	1,2 Timothy
Joel	Joel	Tit	Titus

Jon	Jonah	Zech	Zechariah
Josh	Joshua	Zeph	Zephaniah
Jude	Jude		

Contents of Topical Concordance

Contents (continued)

Contents (continued)

Contents (continued)

Contents (continued)

Topics

ABANDON (Desertion, Loneliness)

Ex 2:11-25; 2 Ch 12:1-16;1 Sam 7:2-3; Ps 22; Job 2:1-13; Mt 27:46; Rom 8:35-39.

Have you ever felt abandoned or have you abandoned God? Jesus's disciples abandoned Him. Peter denied Jesus three times in the courtyard after He was arrested (Jn18:27). At the Cross, John was the only disciple who was there (Jn 19:26). They abandoned Him because they were afraid that they would be arrested and might be put to death or at least mocked. They believed that Jesus was the Messiah and would deliver His people, but He was being put to death. It is no wonder that they fled from Him. Everything seemed to be lost.

We feel abandoned when there does not seem to be anyone there to support us. We do not see our friends. Sometimes the problem is that we have abandoned and isolated ourselves. We have shut ourselves off from those who would help us. Friends are there, but in our hurt, we do not see them and we do not let them help us. We are feeling alone. Perhaps we have made a bad mistake, and in our mind, we wonder how anyone can love us. Sometimes it is true that there is no one there, and we are be attacked by our enemies. Psalms 27:1 and 4 have some good words for this. David writes, "The Lord is my light and salvation—whom shall I fear? The Lord is the stronghold of my life—of whom shall I be afraid?" And in verse 4, he writes, "One thing I ask of the Lord, that is what I seek; that I may dwell in the house of the Lord all the days of my life, to gaze upon the beauty of the Lord and to seek him in his temple." So trust in God and do not fear your enemies

Sometimes we abandon God just as the disciples did. We may grow discouraged and feel that God is not needed, that He is not interested, or is not capable of doing anything. It happens many times at the death of a loved one that a person questions if there is a God or if He cares because how could He let such a terrible thing happen. This is natural, and do not feel bad about feeling that way, but do not dwell on that attitude either. This is Satan speaking to the person. Satan is giving his old lie, which says, "God does not really care about you." Yes, we wonder how such a terrible thing could happen, but terrible things do happen, and that is an unpleasant fact. When we abandon God, the consequences are devastating because we are walking away from the solution that we are seeking and that we need. When a terrible thing happens that we do not understand, let this be a time that we cling to God that much more. Let us say, "O, God, I need thee!" **God is the answer and He is the only answer that will never fail**. Imprint that thought in your mind as deeply as you can. Let it be part of what you live by.

Do not give up when you feel forsaken. God never gives up on us. He never fails. Others may forsake us, but He does not, and He has said that He will be with us even to the end of the age (Mt 28:20). We need to trust God for He is faithful. The terrible burden of sin that Jesus bore on the Cross made Him feel forsaken and utter the agonizing words of the Twenty-second Psalm, "My God, my God, why has thou forsaken me?" But He found consolation in those words also. God is always with us even in those times when we do not feel His presence.

Fear may cause us to abandon God or feel that we are abandoned. Fear caused the disciples to forsake Jesus on the night that He was betrayed. However, we must not let fear rule us. In Him is the power to overcome all fears. As the hymn "Because He Lives" states, "Because He lives, I can face tomorrow because He lives all fear is gone. Because I know who holds the future, my life is worth the living just because He lives." That is the marvelous foundation of our faith: Because He Lives! Yes, because He lives, life is indeed worth the living.

Even in suffering, we are not abandoned although we may wonder where God is. We need to remember that God is a good God, and although we may not understand why something is happening to us, He is good and wants good for us, and He takes the worse seeming defeat and turns it into an amazing force for good. He does not send bad things upon us (as we have said, it is simply a part of life that bad things happen), but He does seek to use us in those bad situations. When my daughter was in the hospital recently, visitors and her mother were able to witness to her roommate by simply being themselves. They showed God's love by being themselves. They did not preach. The prayer that was said for Rebecca one day touched her roommate also. On the Cross, when it seemed the forces of evil had triumphed, God used this event for the salvation of the world. Trust in His power and love.

Satan will try to convince you otherwise, but hold firmly to that belief and Satan must flee from you.

ABILITIES (CRAFTSMANSHIP, Skills, Talents)

Ex 28:1-14; 35:10-19; Deut 32:48-33:29; Mt 13:12; 25:15; Lk 12:48; Act 6:2-4; Eph 4:4-7; 1 Pet 4:10-11.

Do not belittle your talents or gifts. Too often people look at a very talented person and feel that they themselves have very little talent or at least nothing important. In I Corinthians 12:19-26, Paul uses the picture of the body. The body is made up of different members. All are important. All are needed. You are important also regardless of your gift. God gives each of us special abilities, and they are all important. We need to use these abilities gladly, willingly and with joy, and use your gifts to the best of your ability. In using your gifts in this way, you are doing it unto the Lord. We must also seek to develop our skills, and as time progresses, you will obtain other skills. If that is the case, then use them wisely also.

Do not think too highly of yourself or put down another because of your skills. If you have many skills, then that is wonderful but much will be expected of you. You should encourage and strengthen the person who has lesser gifts so that each of you uses your skills to serve God.

ABORTION (IMAGE, LIFE, MURDER)

Gen 9:1-17; Jer 1:1-5; 2Ch 28:1-8; Ps 139:1-14.

Persons have worth in the sight of God. He knew you and planned for you even before you were born (Jer1:5). We must have as much respect for others and ourselves as our Maker has for all of us. We are made in the image of God.

Today children are sacrificed to the gods of economy, whim, and convenience just as surely as King Ahaz sacrificed to the pagan gods. Some say, "I (or we) cannot afford this child, this is a bad time, it will ruin my figure, and it will interfere with my career." People do not consider the child but only what effect that child will have upon them.

In Matthew (19:14), Jesus says for the little children to come unto Him. However, in order for them to come to Him, they must first be allowed to be born.

There is the question of cases where the mother would die if the child is born. Should an abortion be done in those cases? In some of those cases, I would say there is no question that the birth should be aborted because the child is not viable either. In other situations, I will leave that up to the couple.

Pray about it; think about it long and hard, do not let it be a snap decision, and consider all the factors that are involved. Rape is another example. Do not hold it against the baby that something bad happened to you. Let that child be a blessing. If you need to give it up for adoption because there is too much pain involved, then take that route. Give the baby to a family that can and wants to give loving care.

ABUNDANCE (BLESSING, MATERIALISM, WEALTH)

Deut 8:10-20; Mk 10:17-31; Lk 12:13-21; Jn 10:1-21.

It is easy to feel that your abundance is the result of your own effort and cleverness in times of plenty. However, we need to remember that any abundance is the result of God's blessings on us. He expects us to be faithful managers of our blessings.

Sometimes that very abundance can cause a person to feel that they are independent from God. Sometimes wealth and material possessions and blessings are used to fill an emptiness that a person may experience, instead of reliance upon God.

There is another kind of abundance—the abundant life. Let us rejoice in this abundance and see that all our abundance is used for God's glory. This abundant or eternal life is more precious than all the world's treasures. In Matthew 13:45-46, Jesus compares the Kingdom of Heaven with a merchant who finds a pearl of great price, and he sells everything he has in order to possess it. This is how precious it is. It needs to be number one in your life.

ACCEPTANCE (AFFIRMATION, ENCOURAGEMENT, Support)

Ex 34:1-17; Jud 11:1-11; Mt 20:15; Mk 8:27-38; Lk 2:8-20; 4:16-30; 9:1-9; 12:48; Jn 1:1-18; Act 11:8; Rom 5:1-11; 15:1-13; Heb 6:18-19.

God accepts us just as we are. That is something that we need—acceptance. He accepts those who in faith turn to Him. Therefore, in the same manner, we need to show God's forgiving and redeeming love, which is in Christ Jesus. Not accepting others cheats us of the benefits of fellowship with that person. We are both less. It is true that some people are not that easy to accept, but we still need to accept them. We are accepting the person but not necessarily their lifestyle.

Sometimes you will not be accepted because of your faith, but do not let that be a reason that you reject someone. Remain true to God. We cannot reject anyone since God freely offers His fellowship to all. We may and should reject certain lifestyles, but we must accept that person so they can find a lifestyle that is pleasing to God.

Acceptance of the world's ways and standards is dangerous for it may be contrary to God's will. Be sure that what you accept is in keeping with God's word and will.

ACCOMPLISHMENTS (Achievements, EFFORTS, SUCCESS)

Gen 1:1-31; 11:1-9; Ezra 3:11-12; Ecc 1:1-11; Jud 15:1-20; Mk 10:35-45; Lk 10:1-24; Rom 3:21-31; Phil 3:1-6; 1Pet 2:1-12.

God felt good about His accomplishments. When He looked at what He had created, He said it was good (Gen 1:31). We should feel good about our accomplishments too. Of course, this is only true if our accomplishments are pleasing to God.

Our ultimate value must be in pleasing God and not in our accomplishments. Success is transitory, but God is eternal.

Achievements, no matter how good, are wrong if they are not in agreement with the will of God. In addition, none of our achievements diminishes our dependence upon Him.

Our achievements should be an expression of our thankfulness to God, and must be done in the right attitude. A good accomplishment done with the wrong attitude is sinful. The apostle Paul points this out in I Corinthians 13:1-3.

ACTIONS (DOING, EFFORTS, WORK)

Gen 15:1-6; Ex 14:5-18;1 Sam 7:1-17; Est 4:1-17; Mt 5:13-20; Lk 3:1-18; Jas 1:19-27.

Actions must accompany faith. Faith leads to action. God expects us to express our faith by our actions, and God works through faithful people.

Children imitate their parents and their peers in their actions. Therefore, parents must watch their own actions and that of the child's peers, so that their children imitate the proper actions.

Prayer and action must go together. For example, if I pray, "Hallowed be thy name," then I must act in a manner that shows that His Name is hallowed to me. We must do what is right. True repentance is shown in action. Our words and actions must back one another up. The song "Amazing Love" has the words, "In all I do I honor you." Let that characterize our life. Let us honor God in deed and action.

We need to remember that thoughts precede actions. Therefore, we must have good thoughts in order to have good actions.

ADMISSION (see CONFESSION, TRUTH)

ADORATION (see PRAISE, WORSHIP)

ADULTERY (CHASTITY, MARRIAGE, Prostitution, SEX, Sexual immorality)
Deut 22:29-29; Lev 20:10; Prov 6:24-33; Is 1:21-31; Hos 1:1-11; Mt 5:27-32; Lk 16:16-18; Jn 8:1-11.

Adultery was a serious sin and punishable by death. Lust is one form of adultery. Wrong thoughts must be corrected before they become sinful actions and involve others. Look at what happened to David and Bathsheba (2 Sam 11). What began as lust ended in the murder of Uriah. Jesus accepted the person while rejecting the sin. In John 8:3-7 is the account of a woman caught in the act of adultery (it is interesting that only the woman was brought). The law said that she should be stoned to death. Jesus did not say the law was wrong. It wasn't, and sin is punishable by death, but instead, He said, "Whoever among you is without sin cast the first stone." None did for they knew that they were sinners. Jesus forgave the woman. This is what she needed. She needed forgiveness, not death.

Serving other gods and not being faithful to God is a form of spiritual adultery. Those other gods can be materialism, money, power, and a number of things. Let us be faithful.

ADVERSITY (see CONFLICTS, OPPOSITION)

ADVICE (Counsel, DIRECTION, HELP)
Num 13:1-14:19;1 K 12:1-15; Prov 1:1-9, 24-33; 6:20-24; 9:9; 10:1-21; 11:14; 12:15; 15:22; 19:20; 20:18; 24:6; Job 5:8-27; 18:1-19:6.

When receiving advice, the person giving it must be evaluated as well as the advice that is being given. Is that person qualified to give advice? Is the advice good? Does the person follow the advice that he or she is giving? We need to keep God's standards in mind. Follow the word of God. Good advice is given out of love. It is based upon facts.

The adviser must be trustworthy. When we give advice, let us do it humbly, and let us receive it with thanks.

AFFIRMATION (ACCEPTANCE, ENCOURAGEMENT, Support)
Lk 14:7-14; Act 20:32; 1 Cor 1:4-9; 8:1; 1 Th 5:8-11; I Jn 4:7-21.

Genuine affirmation needs to be given to Christians and non-Christians. We build each other up in love, just as each of us needs to receive affirmation. This validates that we are a person of worth. We also need to give affirmation to others.

Look for the positive that is in another. Help them to see the positive. Help them to see their worth in the eyes of God. Remind them that God loved them so much He gave His Son for them.

AFRAID (see FEAR)

ALONE (LONELINESS, Privacy, Solitude)
Mt 14:22-36; Lk 5:12-16.
Quiet time was important to Jesus, and it should be to us. This was a time for communing with the Father, for replenishment of the soul, for receiving the strength needed to face life's demands and problems, for recharging. We need to use this time for getting closer to God and concentrating upon a renewed oneness with God. Let it be a blessed time. Then come away with a renewed sense of direction, purpose, and meaning for your life. Pour out your concerns honestly, but also listen for God to speak to you. It should be all of this, but we should not feel lonely when we are alone. You do not have to be. You are not alone. God is with you.

AMBITION (DESIRES, MOTIVES)
Ex 7:1-14; Num. 16:1-40; Jud 9:1-20;2 Sam 5:6-12; Mt 4:8-10; 16:26; 23:5-12; Mk 9:33-37; 10:36-39; 2 Cor 5:11-21; 1 Jn 2:16.
Ambition is good, providing it is in keeping with God's will and providing you do not do the wrong things to promote your ambition. The wrong kind of ambition is destructive to others and to you. It can put our plans ahead of God's plans. It can also emphasize the wrong priorities.

We need always to measure our ambitions with God's standards. Another important thing to remember about ambition is that parents must not impose their ambitions onto their child. This is done in several ways. Perhaps the parents want a child to be active in sports, just like they were, but the child does not have athletic ability or interest in that sport. Sometimes children are shoved into the television or movie business or a beauty pageant. The child may not have an interest but is doing it to please the parents. Still another example is that the child may want to go into a profession very much different from his parents' even though he or she comes from a long line of bakers, farmers, lawyers, etc.

Let the child pursue his or her ambition, not yours, and be proud of the child's decision provided it is something that God blesses and the person can bless others in that endeavor.

ANGER (Dislike, HATRED)

Gen 4:1-16; 16:6; 19:24; 27:1-41; Num. 22:20-23; 25:10-11; 1 Sam 11:6;2 Sam 6:6-7; 1K 21:4; Est 3:5-6; Ps 30:5; 37:8-9; Mt 5:21-26; Mk 3:5; 11:15-19; Jn 2:15-16; 4:1; Rom 1:18-32; 2:1; 2 Cor 2:11; Gal 4:16; Eph 4:26-27; 6:4; Jas 1:19-20; 3:1-12.

There is good and bad anger. Anger that is not under control can lead to sin. There are many causes of anger, but the wrong kind is destructive and can eat away at a person. It can destroy relationships so that they can never be mended.

One deadly weapon of anger is the tongue. We need to be careful of what we say, especially in anger. Think twice before you speak. In addition, maybe even a third time. Words spoken in anger can really hurt a person and damage a relationship.

There is a proper anger. Jesus showed anger in the cleansing of the temples (Mt 21:13). There is the anger against sin. We should get angry about sin and not ignore it. Petty things, we can ignore. Do not make a big deal about them.

Anger prevents us from pleasing God.

When we get angry with someone, let us get over that anger quickly and mend that broken relationship. We cannot love God as long as we are angry with our brother (1Jn 4:20).

ANSWERS (COMFORT, GUIDANCE, Response)

Dan 2:1-49;1 Cor 13:1-13; Jas 1:1-8.

We need to expect positive answers from God when we are asking for His guidance. We will get His guidance although the answer we get may be different from what we expect. In addition, the answer may not be the one that we like.

We can't expect all of the answers; some things must be taken on faith.

God has also said He would grant us wisdom.

We expect answers and need answers, but we must seek those answers in an appropriate way and in reliable sources. Is the answer from a reliable source? Is it in keeping with God's word?

ANXIETY (see WORRY)

APATHY (see COMPLACENCY)

APPEARANCE (IMAGE, IMPRESSION)

1 Sam 16:1-13; Mt 9:9-12; 15:1-20;2 Cor 11:1-15.

Appearance is important and reflects your attitudes about yourself and others. However, it must not be the basis by which we judge a person. Part of our appearance is an attempt to fit in with others. We want to be accepted, so we dress a certain way. We want to create a certain impression about ourselves so we dress in a certain manner. God looks upon a person's heart and not on the outward appearance. In the same manner, we need to look beyond the outward appearance.

We need to look at the world around us, others, and ourselves from God's viewpoint. How attractive are we on the inside? Is God's love evident in us? Is a person attracted to Jesus Christ because of your lifestyle?

We need to be careful so that we are not taken in by appearances. They can be deceiving. Our own appearance should not deceive others. We must be genuine and reflect who we really are. If you love Christ, then let that be evident in who you are.

APPROVAL (ACCEPTANCE, RESPECT)

Jud 18:1-31; Jn 5:31-47; Act 14:8-2; Rom 2:1-16.

Approval is important—God's approval and approval from others. We should be giving approval to one another, for this is one way of building each other up (1 Th 5:11). Of course, we can only give approval to actions when they are in keeping with God's will, but we can still give approval to a person. There is a difference between the person and their deed.

Just as we want and need approval from others, so also this cannot be the yardstick by which we base our actions. We must not do something simply to try to please other people. We must always strive to please God. This is the most important approval. Our approval is from hearing those words of our Lord, *"Well done, good and faithful servant"* (Mt 25:21).

ARGUMENTS (ANGER, DISAGREEMENT)

Prov 15:1-9; 26:17-28; Phil 2:12-18; Tit 3:1-11.

We have disagreements and different opinions, and that is good, but we must not let these differences become divisive. We must be united in Christ.

Self-control is important to prevent arguments. Speak in a soft voice. Anger uses harsh words and a rising voice, but do not respond in the same manner.

While an argument between others is occurring, you must wait until they have had a chance to cool off before you can try to mend the broken relationship. Otherwise, maybe both of them will turn against you.

ARMOR (spiritual)

See Eph 6:8-10.

ASSURANCE (CONFIDENCE, HOPE)

Ex 4:1-1; 13:17-22; Lk 18:18-30; 21:5-19; Rom 6:1-14.

We need assurance and hope, but this must be based upon God and not the false gods of wealth, fame, etc. This false assurance can lead us away from God.

True assurance is based upon God's promises and His word. It is based upon Christ's resurrection and God's care for us. Sometimes people want the assurance that they are going to heaven. The answer to that is in their relationship to Christ. If they have accepted Him as Lord and Savior of their life, and I don't mean a lip-service acceptance of Him but a genuine surrender to God, then we have Jesus's assurance in John 14:2 that He goes to prepare a place for us in His Father's house so that we can be there with Him.

ATTITUDE (EMOTION, FEELING)

Gen 4:1-16; 39:1-23; Ex 14:1-14; Ruth 2:1-12; Rom 6:1-14.

We have positive and negative attitudes. Negative attitudes can cause us to turn away from God. Wrong attitudes can also cause bad decisions. They can cause broken relationships with family, friends, and others.

Positive attitudes allow God to work through us. We need to measure our attitudes with Christ. Are they in keeping with His spirit? Of course, sometimes we are going to have bad attitudes, for that is just part of being human, but we need to try to get rid of these bad attitudes as quickly as possible because they just tear you down. It is downright unhealthy if they are prolonged.

AVARICE (see GREED)

BARRIERS (CHALLENGES, Obstacles, PROBLEMS)

Deut 1:19-36; Jud 3:1-6; Mt 8:5-13; 27:45-56; Jn 4:1-26; Rom 8:38-39.

There are many barriers between God and man, and man and man—pride, doubt, money, race, language, time, distance.

We must not let barriers separate us from God and other people. We must always be ready to share God's redeeming love. For in Christ, He has broken down the wall of division between men and God (see Eph 2:14).

A strong marriage should not have barriers. Man and wife must be willing to share with one another. It is not easy, but they must really be willing to share with that person. Parents should not have a barrier between them and their children. Let your children know you and love you. You need it and they do too. Of course, this sharing must always be done in a caring manner and not forced upon someone or dumped upon someone. It is sad when a person (probably when he or she has grown up) says, "I never knew my father or my mother. I couldn't get close to them."

We must strive to overcome the barriers we encounter and let them show our dependence upon God. We need His strength to face those barriers. As Paul says that there is absolutely nothing now or forever that can separate us from the love of God, which is in Christ Jesus (Rom 8:38-39).

He has already overcome the greatest barrier—the barrier between man and God.

BELIEF (FAITH, TRUST)

Gen 15:1-6; Deut 27: 1-10; Rom 10:5-13; Jas 2:14-24. See concordance for complete references under believes, belief, etc.

All of us have beliefs. The human needs certain beliefs in order to operate. For example, I believe that I must do certain things in order to stay alive. Thus, no one can say that he or she does not believe. It is simply a matter of what they do believe. We could state further that those beliefs must eventually be accepted on faith. No matter how long a line of logic you take, you will get to a point where you will have to say that is just the way it is.

Our beliefs come to us in a variety of ways. They are what we have been told by teachers, parents, and others so that we come to a point that they are simply accepted. Some of these beliefs are good and some are bad. Some are true and some are false.

The beliefs that I want to concentrate on here are religious beliefs. These beliefs must be a confession of the heart and not mere lip service. These beliefs involve action but are more than action.

Example: I believe in God. This must involve my total being. It should be reflected in my lifestyle and affect all my decisions and actions. In other words, if I truly believe in God, then I will show it in my life. Yet after all of this is said, there is a point at which I must stop doing and believe. He must work in my life.

Our Christian beliefs must be firmly rooted in the Bible. That is their test. In addition, these beliefs must become a part of your inner self if they are to have any effect upon you.

BELIEVERS

Job 1:1-12; Rom 1-17; Col 3:11-17; Jas 1:2-16. See concordance for complete references.

There are distinctive characteristics of a believer. The believer has taken the name of Christ. Therefore, Christ like traits should be evident in that person's life: peace, love, mercy, forgiveness. What that really means is that that person has accepted and trusted Jesus Christ as Lord and Savior. Your faith is based upon a relationship with God. It is not ritual or buildings, but only your relationship to God.

The way believers treat each other and other people is another characteristic. This again is an imitation of Jesus Christ. There should be a genuine living out of His teachings in your everyday life. Often the way is difficult, and that is why it is even more important to rely upon God. However, the reward is eternal life. The reward is all of those things that you really want.

BIGOTRY (see PREJUDICE)

CHANGE (DIFFERENCE, Improvement)
Gen 44:1-34; Num 10:11-36; Josh 11:16-23; Mt 3:1-12; 15:1-20; Lk 7:18-35; Jn 4:27-42; 8:1-11;2 Cor 5:11-21.

There are good changes and bad changes. There are all kinds of changes: physical changes (growth, aging), social changes, spiritual changes, and financial changes, just to mention a few. People can and do change. Usually this is gradual. However, there are dramatic changes also. In fact, this is what the Christian faith is completely about. Conversion is a change of direction—a change from walking away from God to a turning toward God. It is a change that God brings about in us from being His enemy to being His child.

The conversion of the apostle Paul from a persecutor of the Christian faith to a great evangelist was a tremendous change (see Acts 9). God can help us to face changes. In His mercy, God waits for us to change.

God works to change people from the inside. He removes the heart of stone and replaces it with a heart of flesh (Ezek 11:19). This inward change should be evidenced by outward action.

The first step in change is to repent of your sin. Then the next step is to walk day by day in faith with the Risen Lord, letting Him guide your actions and decisions, looking to Him for the guidance that you need. Seek Him in prayer. Prayer does change things. Pray with expectation and belief.

I would like to add a couple of thoughts here. It is easy to say that we should change our thinking about certain matters, but it is not that easy to do. New Year's resolutions do not last very long. What is the problem? The apostle Paul had that problem too (see Rom 7:19). Our mind has two levels: the conscious and the subconscious. If you want real change, then you must change on the subconscious level. In other words, you have to reprogram your inner computer to a new way of thinking. Visualize your goal and express it in positive terms, not negative terms. Athletes do this all the time to improve their performance. Instead of saying, "I do not want to be a liar," say, "I tell the truth all the time." The first statement simply reinforces the lying, so you will continue to lie. The second statement says that you are a truthful person and so you will act on that level, provided you have gotten this into your subconscious.

CHARACTER (Personality)

Gen 22:1-14; 1 Sam 16:1-13; Ps 57:7; 112:7-8; Prov 13:1-6; 22:1; 24:21-22; Is 3:9; Mt 5:43-48; 10:22; 13:19; Mk 1:1-13; Rom 5:1-11;2 Th 2:15; 3:3; 2Tim 3:1-5; Jas 1:25.

We all want to have good character. Parents want their children to have good, strong character. We like to be around people of good character and want to emulate them. The perfect model for this character is Jesus Christ. We should emulate Him. We will fall short, but we still need to try to live like Jesus.

Some good character traits are honesty, loyalty, integrity, compassion, mercy, love, courage, faithfulness, humility, patience, reliability, trustworthiness, and unselfishness, just to mention a few.

When looking at character, we need to follow God's standards and not the world's standards. What may appear pleasing and desirable may not actually be pleasing and desirable. Challenges, temptations, suffering, and problems can help develop character.

CHASTITY (ADULTERY)

Ex 20:14; Job 31:1; Prov 5:15-19; 6:24-25; 7:1-5; 31:3; Mt 5:28; Act 15:20; 1 Cor 7:1-2, 7-9, 25; Eph 5:3; Col 3:5; 1 Th 4:3.

Sexual purity is an important virtue. Unfortunately, today many people look down on this virtue. The number of young people that abstain from sex before marriage is a minority. Too many young girls believe the lie that boys and even men will say, "If you love me you would have sex with me." That person simply wants his way. If he really loved you, he would not try to force you to do something you think is wrong. To those that can maintain chastity without sinning by lusting or having affairs, then this is a noble calling. However, if this puts too much temptation on you and is keeping you from serving God, then by all means marry and have a fruitful life in this manner.

CHILDREN (FAMILY)

Gen 17:16, 20; 28:3; 29:32-35; 30:1; Ex 20:1-20; 21:15-17; 22:22-23; Lev 19:3, 32; Deut 5:16; 6:1-25; 21:18-21; 27:16; Job 29:12; Ps 10:14-18;

27:10; 68:5; 107:38; 113:9; 127:3; 146:9; 148:12; Prov 1:8-9; 4:1-4, 10-11, 20-22; 6:20-25; 10:1; 13:1; 15:5, 20; 17:6; 19:26; 20:20; 22:15; 23:22; 28:7,24; 30:11, 17; Jer 20:15; 49:11; Ezek 22:7; Hos 14:3; Mt 15:4; 18:2-6; Mk 9:36-37; Lk 18:1-17; Jn 1:1-13; Rom 8:1-17; Eph 6:1-4;1 Tim 4:1-16; 1 Jn 3:1-10.

Parents must be godly examples to their children in word and in deed. Teaching them and bringing them up to know the Lord so they will be able to make their own decision to follow and serve Him. This is an awesome responsibility. Parents are also to be patient with their children.

Children are to obey and honor their parents. This is one of the commandments (Ex 20:12). Of course, this is assuming the parents are not teaching them to go against God's will or are not abusive or anything of this sort. Parents are to emulate the Heavenly Father. They are to love their children (Col 3:20). It is sad when a child does not know what it means to have a loving mother or father.

To all who accept Jesus and receive Him has been given the gift of being born into the family of God (Jn 1:12). We are children of the King. We are to be *childlike* in our faith but not childish.

CHOICES (DECISIONS, ACTIONS)

Prov 1:1-19; 13:1-6; Mt 9:9-13; Jn 5:16-30.

Every day we are faced with choices. How do we make the right ones? What do you use to make your decisions?

Just as Jesus identified with the Father and made His choices in the light of His Father's will, so we must identify with Jesus and do His will for us. What would Jesus have us do in this situation is a question we must always raise in our minds, not what is convenient or popular or easy.

Again, we need to be aware that the attractive solution or popular decision may not be the correct one and can lead us into sin.

We need to look at the long-term effect and not just the immediate result, and we need to remember that the correct choice may be difficult and very costly. Jesus went to the Cross and that was a very difficult choice and it cost Him His life.

Pray for guidance as you make your decisions.

CIRCUMSTANCES (Environment, Situation)

1 Sam 17:1-58; 2Ch 32:1-23; Est 4:1-17; Jas 1:1-18

How do you take your circumstances? Are they something to be endured? All of us have heard someone say, "I'm just a victim of circumstances." Do you feel that way sometimes? We are told to trust God no matter how dire the situation may appear. We are to work in that situation, but we are also to trust in God to work in and through that situation.

Christians are not promised rosy circumstances. On the contrary, you may be placed in difficult situations simply because you are a believer. We see that in the Bible and we see it each day. Jesus also warned His disciples that just as the world (those who do not believe in Him) will hate and persecute Him, they will also hate and persecute His followers (Jn 15:18). However, let circumstances also remind us of our dependence upon God and also remember that Jesus said that He has overcome the world (Jn 16:33).

CITIZENSHIP (GOVERNMENT)

Ex 22:28; Num 27:20; Ezra 6:10; 7:26; Prov 16:14-15; 24:21; Ecc 8:2-3; 10:4, 20; Jer 29:7; Mt 17:24-27; Rom 13:1-14; Col 1:1-14; 1Tim 2:1-2; Tit 3:1; I Pet 2:13-17; Rev 21:15-27.

We are citizens of two realms: the earthly and the heavenly. We are expected to be responsible earthly citizens even though we are only residing here temporarily. There are different viewpoints about how this citizenship should be carried out, but the important point is to find the way that you feel you should serve. Don't belittle another person if their viewpoint is different. Be a good, responsible citizen.

Our heavenly citizenship brings eternal benefits and immediate ones. Be sure to have a healthy balance between the two citizenships. Do not be guilty of being so heavenly minded that you are no earthly good.

COMFORT (HELP)

Gen 12:1-9; Job 16:1-22; Is 40:1-11; Jn 14:16-17; 15:26; 16:7-14; Lk 12:1-12; 2 Cor 1:3-11.

There is more than one aspect of comfort. We all want to be comfortable, but sometimes we ignore or are disobedient to God in order to get our comfort. Therefore, we should always ask, how much does our comfort cost us? Am I willing to pay the price to get it? Is that comfort at the expense of someone else? Should I pay the price for my comfort or is that price too high?

If we do not want to get uncomfortable, we may be unwilling to serve God because sometimes God asks us or puts us in uncomfortable situations.

Moses is one of many examples. How comfortable do you think it was for him to oppose pharaoh?

There is positive comfort also. We, as Christians, must give comfort to each other and to others (1 Th 5:11). Give comfort by a word, a deed or an action. Share a burden; whatever the situation calls for. Jesus told us to feed the hungry, clothe the naked, give drink to the thirsty, visit those that are sick or in prison (Mt 25:35).

God comforts also and helps us to face our trials. He has promised and has sent the Comforter (Jn 14:26).

COMMITMENT (FAITHFULNESS)
Josh 24:14-27; Ps 37:1-39; Mt 8:18-27; Lk 16:16-18; Rom 5:1-11.

God expects a complete commitment to Him. This involves your total being: heart, mind, and soul. It must be a consistent commitment that is evidenced by your entire lifestyle. It is a lifelong matter.

Christ committed Himself to us first. He gave Himself for us while we were yet sinners, even enemies of God.

To commit yourself to God or to anyone involves trust. There are many important commitments that must be made; however, too often people do not want to get involved, to be committed.

COMMUNICATION (see CONVERSATION)

COMMUNION (see LORD'S SUPPER)

COMPARISONS (Measurement, MOTIVES)
Gen 31:1-16; Jn 21:15-25;2 Cor 10:1-18.

Comparisons are necessary and needed for growth, but they can be destructive when they are used to puff you up and belittle someone else. What measurements are you using? Are they Christian? Why and what are you measuring?

One wrong kind of comparison can make us jealous. This is a comparison of what someone else has to what we have. The only thing wrong with this is if you have the feeling that that person does not deserve it. "Why does he or she have this or have that? Why does he or she get all of the breaks?" We are not to be envious. Be glad that that person does get breaks and does have nice things provided that they are not at the expense of someone else.

Another wrong kind of comparison can discourage us. "What is wrong with me? I can't do anything right." This is a comparison of yourself to someone else. The only thing wrong with this is the conclusion that you cannot do anything right. Do not be so hard on yourself and learn from your mistakes.

A word here to parents is that we must remember that comparing one child to another can really hurt and have a lasting effect upon that child. It can damage the way a person looks at himself or herself. "I'm dumb. I'm fat." It can also build resentment between siblings. Instead, give words that build your child up so he or she has respect for himself or herself.

We must always compare to God's standards. If we are faithful to those standards, we have no ground to boast and no need to feel frustrated by others' accomplishments. Also, when we strive in this manner, God works with us to accomplish those goals.

COMPASSION (CARING, UNDERSTANDING, LOVE)

2 K 4:1, 32-36; Job 6:1-30; Lam 3:1-66; Mk 2:1-12; 5:36-42; Jn 1:13; 8:7.

We are to exercise compassion just as Christ demonstrated His great compassion. We are to meet the needs of each other by word and deed. Jesus gave compassion to His disciples. He told them to love one another (Jn 13:34). Then again, scripture tells us that if we say that we love God but hate our brother, then we are liars (see 1Jn 4:20).

God shows His compassion for us by meeting our needs. His greatest example was the gift of His Son for our sins.

COMPLACENCY (Apathy)

Is 32:9-20; Joel 1:1-20; Mal 2:1-12; Rev 3:14-22.

We become complacent when we have a wrong sense of security. "Everything is fine. I don't need God. I don't need to obey Him."

We can become self-satisfied and blind to our sin because of our material abundance. Complacency can lead to a half-hearted following of God. God detests this, but the Holy Spirit can rekindle the love of God in a person.

COMPLAINING (Discontent, Griping)

Ex 16:1-10; Num 11:1-17; Phil 2:12-18.

There are numerous examples of Israel complaining to God. The whole Old Testament history shows one cycle after another of rebelling against God and falling away and then repenting. We are no better. We also complain about other people, our circumstances, and many other things.

Complaining is one way of dealing with stress. But it is not the best. Too much complaining is unhealthy. To a certain extent, complaining is helpful and even necessary because there are certain times that we need to complain in order for a situation to be corrected, but to dwell on our complaints is very unhealthy. We need to look for God's help in a situation and not for an easy or fast exit.

Instead of complaining to one another, we need to take our problems to God. Ask His direction in dealing with the situation.

Sometimes we complain because we focus on what we don't have instead of what we do have. We need to be thankful for the countless blessings that God has so freely given to us. Sometimes, complaining is the result of not trusting God.

Complaining is harmful to ourselves and to our relationships with others. Do you enjoy being around a constant complainer? It also repels others from Christ if you claim to be a Christian, and they see nothing but complaints from you.

CONCEIT

Prov 3:5; 12:15; 23:4; 26:5, 12, 16; 28:11; Is 5:21; Jer 9:23; Lk 18:11-12; Rom 1:22; 11:25.

We are to trust in God and not puff ourselves up. Conceit is a form of foolishness and can lead to destruction (Prov 16:18).

We are conceited when we use the wrong standards. When we look at Christ, we have nothing to be conceited about. We have no grounds upon which to boast. The apostle Paul had considerable credentials by which he could boast but he considered them rubbish when he compared them to knowing the Living Christ (see Phil 3:4-8). So, in the same manner, we have nothing to boast of. You may be smarter, stronger, richer, or more talented than someone else, but compared to Christ, you are nothing.

CONFESSION (Admission, TRUTH)

2 Sam 12:1-14; Neh 9:1-38; Mt 7:21-23; 10:32-33; Jn 1:15-18; 12:42-43; Act 18:5; 19:4-5; Rom 10:9-11; Jas 5:13-20; 1 Jn 1:1-10; 2:4; 4:2-3, 15.

Confession is essential in a person's life. If a person would receive forgiveness, then there must be a confession of sin (1 Jn 1:9-10).

There must be confession to God and confession to one another so that the broken relationships can be restored.

Confession is not easy, and some people do not make it easy, but it still needs to be done. May you always be a person who is willing to accept true confession and then extend forgiveness. And may you be ready to confess your sins and errors.

Confession is essential for fellowship and true worship (Mt 5:23-24).

CONFLICTS (OPPOSITION, Adversity)

Josh 22:9-34; 2 Sam 3:1-39; Jas 4:1-12.

It is important to hear one another out. Often conflicts can be avoided by listening to each other and not making wrong assumptions. Try to work out differences. See if there are any goals that would unite you—goals that are more important than any petty differences.

Sometimes conflicts can be avoided by remembering the source of the conflict. Is it a reliable source? Is it a beneficial or evil source?

Sometimes conflict is inevitable. You must stand up for what you believe. We must also let the will of God be at work in conflicts, for He can accomplish great things if we allow Him to work. Be sure not to get angry. Love the other person even though you disagree with the person. If the conflict cannot be resolved then let us part as friends.

CONFUSION (Disorder, PROBLEMS)

Deut 22:13-30; Mk 7:1-13; Rom 7:7-25.

Confusion can come when we try to follow our own path instead of God's way. The Pharisees had countless man-made laws that were added to God's laws, and this added to the confusion of the people, for more and more rules had to be made to explain the rules that were laid down. For example, what constituted work had to be spelled out in detail so people would not be involved in work on the Sabbath.

People can be confused when they don't know God's word. This is the way false teachers lead people astray.

Our sinful nature causes conflict and confusion within us. Sexual sin can cause a breakdown in relationships and confusion.

Do you want to know what to believe? You must study the Bible. What does it say? What does it actually say? Jesus said that He is the truth, the way, and the Life (Jn 14:6).

CONSCIENCE (GUIDANCE, GUILT)

Prov 28:1, 13-18; Job 27:6; Jon 1:1-17; Mt 6:22-23; 27:3-5; Act 2:37; 23:1; 24:16; Rom 2:14-15; 9:1; 14:1-23; 1Cor 10:27-31; 2 Cor 1:12; 4:2; 5:11; 1 Tim 1:5, 12-20; Tit 1:15; Heb 10:22, 26-27; 13:18; 1 Pet 2:19; 3:16, 21.

We must rely upon God's standard to gauge our actions and not our conscience. Sometimes we can become so hardened that our conscience does not speak to us.

We need to be sensitive to the feelings of others, but we must adhere to the things that are fundamental. However, in matters of a difference of opinions, let us be tolerant of our differences and do so in love.

We must avoid those things that the scriptures tell us are wrong, but there are a number of matters on which we must rely upon our conscience.

Thus, we need to be well trained in our faith. We need to read and develop ourselves so that our conscience is made stronger. In other words, we are feeding things to our mind so that our conscience has a good strong basis just as our body needs strong bones.

CONSEQUENCES (EFFECTS, RESULTS)

Gen 3:1-24;2 Sam 12:1-14;1 Ch 21:1-30.

Every act has its consequences. We need to consider those consequences before we act. Are they harmful? Just who will be affected?

One consequence of sin is that very often, we involve others in our sin and so it spreads in wider and wider circles. Still another problem is that one sin can lead to another and to another like the ripples in a pool. Sometimes the sins get greater. David and Bathsheba is an example (2 Sam 11). What began as a passion between two people ended in the murder of Bathsheba's husband.

We need to remember that even though we are forgiven of a sin, we still have to live with the consequences of that sin. If, in anger, I permanently injure someone and that person forgives me, the consequences of my action still remain. In this example, the person is permanently injured in some way. Still another example is that a drunken driver may kill someone. Even if the drunken driver is forgiven, the driver has to live with the knowledge that he or she killed someone, and that someone is still dead.

CONSISTENCY (Dependability)

Ruth 2:1-23; 1 Sam 31:1-13;1 K 11:1-13; Neh 5:9; Ps 33:1-22; 125:1-5; Prov 29: 15-21; Mt 6:24; Rom 14:22; 1 Cor 10:21.

God expects us to be consistent in our obedience, our faithfulness, and in our follow-through on our promises, for He is consistent. His word and truth are eternal.

Consistency in good qualities is important for good character. A person with consistency is dependable, is reliable, and is someone you can trust.

Consistency helps us to stand firm and not be shaken. If you trust in God, you will not be swayed by the fashions that come and go.

Consistency is important in parenting. The child needs to know what to expect from his or her parents.

One area that we take for granted is in the consistency of the laws of nature. The laws remain the same and we can count on them. This is also true in all of God's laws. What He says is wrong yesterday is wrong today. Unfortunately, many people who take the consistency of the natural laws for granted do not want to do that with His other laws. They want to make their own laws.

CONTENTMENT (HAPPINESS, JOY)

Gen 33:1-20; Ex 20:1-21; Ps 37:7, 16; 131:1-3; Prov 14:14; 15:13, 30; 16:8; 17:1, 22; 30:8; Ecc 2:24; 4:6; 5:12; 9:7-9; Mt 6:19-24; Lk 3:14; 1 Cor 7:20-24; Gal 5:26; Phil 4:10-23; 1 Tim 6:3-10.

What is the basis of your contentment, joy, or happiness? People seek it in various ways, but there is only one way that is lasting and eternal. It must grow out of a trust in God. It stems from having God's perspective. It is like Jesus's parable of a house built on sand. When the storms came, it was washed away. But the house founded on rock is one that is founded on God's word and is able to withstand any storms (see Mt 7:24).

Bitterness, covetousness, and materialism are barriers to contentment. Again, a couple of parables of Jesus illustrate the folly of trying to obtain contentment by material means. In one, a rich man has many possessions, so he tears down the old barns and builds new ones to store his possessions, but God says that this very night, his soul will be demanded of him; therefore, someone else will benefit from all of this treasure (see Lk 12:15-21).

In still another one in Matthew 6:19-21, Jesus tells us not to lay up material treasures for these can be stolen, corrupted, etc., but to lay up treasures in heaven for these cannot be stolen or corrupted for where your treasure is there your heart will be also. Then finally in Luke 9:25, He says, what shall it profit a man if he gains the whole world yet loses his very soul?

CONVERSATION (Communication, Discussion)

Col 4:2-6; Jas 1:19-27; 3:1-18.

Communication is very important, both in what is communicated and how it is communicated.

When we communicate our faith with others, it must be done in a gracious, courteous, and loving manner if we would be effective. Certainly it can't be judgmental or condescending. Our conversation must be attractive and worthwhile.

Listening is an important skill in conversation. We need to hear the other person and not be thinking up answers to his or her objections. Very often a disagreement can be worked out if each person listens to the other, but if not, then at least their differences will be clear. Listening is also important because it shows a respect for the other person. We like a person to hear us out and give us a chance to speak instead of hogging the floor and talking nonstop. In the same manner, we need to listen to others.

Idle conversation is destructive—boasting, manipulating, gossiping, putting others down, lying, or flattering. A test of conversation is to ask yourself: Is this true? Is it necessary to say it? Is it kind? If you can't say yes to all three, then don't say it. Yes, sometimes we do have to say unkind things, but they should be said in a kind manner and with a kind spirit. It is done because it is necessary and is out of love for that person.

CONVERSION (Regeneration, REPENTANCE)

Ps 31:10; 38:1-8, 13-22; Is 6:5; Lam 1:20; Ezek 33:10; Lk 5:8; Jn 16:7-11; Act 2:37; 16:14; 29-30.

Conversion stems from a change of direction. A person must sense that they are going in the wrong direction, and then confess with the mouth so that they can receive the forgiveness of sins that God is offering to them 1 Jn 1:9-10). This sense of going in the wrong direction is really a response to God speaking to them. It is God who seeks us out. And conversion is the proper response that says, "Yes, I need thee, Lord."

CONVICTIONS (BELIEFS)

Dan 1:8-21; Act 21:18-27.

Sometimes conviction means that you have to stand alone. Down through the ages, many have had to do that, and many have even given their lives for their belief. Conviction is to choose right in the midst of wrong. It should involve thought and prayer and not be made impulsively or by whim. It should involve essentials, but do not be adamant on nonessentials. Also, make sure that your convictions are based on God's word. There is a big difference between having conviction and being stubborn.

CORRECTION (ADVICE, TEACHING)

1 Cor 1:4-9; 4:14-21; Gal 2:11-21; Heb 12:1-12.

Correction is necessary when there is a compromising of principles. It needs to be motivated by love and should be followed by affirmation. Correction of children is one example.

Following up the correction with affirmation is important in order to maintain good relations with the other person. Scripture is an important source for correction. In 2Timothy 3:16-17, it says, "All scripture is God-breathed and is useful for teaching, for rebuking, and training in righteousness so the man of God may be thoroughly equipped for every good work".

COURAGE (Boldness, TRUST)

Ex 1:15-22; Deut 7:19-21; 33:26-29; Est 4:15-16; Prov 28:1; Ezek 2:6; Lk 23:50-56; Jn 16:1-33; Act 4:23-31; 1 Cor 16:13; 2 Tim 1:7.

It takes courage to stand by your convictions. Courage enables you to take the risk to aid another who is in danger. It also means to be willing to risk your reputation to do what is right. The supreme example of courage involves being willing to risk your life in doing what is right.

We need to ask God for the strength and the trust that it takes to be courageous for Him. We need to lay claim to the resources of Christ so that we are able to receive the courage that it takes to live a life for Him. Philippians 4:13 says that we can accomplish all things through Christ who strengthens us.

COVETING (see JEALOUSY)

COWARDICE (Fear, COURAGE
Gen 3:12; Deut 32:30; Josh 7:5; 23:10; Jud 7:3; I Sam 13:6-7; Job 15:24; 18:11; Prov 28:1; 29:25; Mt 8:26; 26:55-56, 69-72; Jn 19:12, 16.

There are various kinds of cowardice and reasons for it. Cowardice is based on fear of something.

Cowardice is used to try to escape responsibility. Someone else is blamed. We fear the consequences so we lie. We do not stand up for the truth.

A coward listens to people instead of to God. Cowardice is excessive fear; therefore the antidote for it is to act with courage. Let the power of God work in your life.

We have said that cowardice is excessive fear, and that is the problem—because it is excessive. All of us have various fears. Some fears are foolish and others are real and important. The fear of wild animals is one fear that it would be foolish to ignore. The important thing to note is not to be controlled by fear. Take the necessary precautions and remember that God is greater than anything. What is your greatest fear? God is greater than that fear. Trust in Him. The First Letter of John 4:18 says that perfect love drives out fear.

CRAFTSMANSHIP (ABILITY)
Ex 31:1-11; Ps 19:1-14; 139:1-24; Jer 10:1-10; 18:1-12; Eph 2:1-10.

Skills are gifts from God. They should be enjoyed and made the best use of, but they certainly should not be worshipped. Nor should we worship others because of their skills. We can admire those skills and perhaps even strive to emulate them. That is one way to improve ourselves.

God is at work in our salvation. He alone saves. He is at work in creation.

We need to allow God to mold us into the kind of persons that He would have us to be. This is the only way that we can satisfy that longing in our souls.

CREATION

Gen 1:1-2:2; Ps 19:1-1-14; Rom 1:18-32; 8:18-27.

We learn about God and ourselves through creation. We learn that life is not an accident but the result of a loving and caring God. As we look at creation, we learn things about Him. We are also given a responsibility. We are caretakers (Gen 2:15). Sin caused creation to fall from its perfect state.

As we look at the wondrous creation, it shows the majesty of God. He created the heavens and the earth (Gen 1:1). There are various views about how this universe and life began. For some the universe was the result of some great cosmic explosion. This is the big bang theory. In this same line of non-creative thinking, Darwin proposed the theory that life developed on earth through a long process of evolution.

For some Christians, this is an important point to debate; and a person is a heretic or nonbeliever for holding a different view, just as other Christians would laugh at someone who holds on to a literal twenty-four-hour-day creation account. This has caused harm and still does. No one knows, and it really doesn't matter. What is important in the Creation story is the fact that **God created**. This is all the story really says. It says that in the beginning, God created (Gen 1:1). It mentions *day*, but this does not have to be a twenty-four-hour day. In other places in the Bible, the Hebrew word *YOM*, meaning *day*, means a long period of time. For example, in Psalm 90:4, it says, "For a thousand years in your sight are like a day that has just gone by or a watch in the night". Whether this was done in twenty-four hours or over a long period, it is God who created. If it was a twenty-four-hour day, then God did it. If it was a long period, then God was at work in this process, and He did it. If there was a big bang, then God caused the big bang. Let us stand united that it is God who created and is the Creator.

Still another important point to mention here is the difference between God's perspective and ours. We look at the vast distances of space or even the size of our own planet compared to ourselves and wonder, how can we be important? This is the human viewpoint, but God knows our frame and who we are, but He still loves us and regards us as having value. We are very precious to Him. How do I how? I know because of the price that He paid to redeem us. He gave His very Son for us (Jn 3:16).

CRIME (see SIN)

CRISIS (see PROBLEMS)

CRITICISM (JUDGMENT)
Deut 13:1-18; Num 12:1-16; Job 19:1-28; Mt 7:1-6; Lk 17:1-10; Gal 5:13-26.
There is constructive and destructive criticism. Constructive criticism is motivated by love, is based on fact, and is given to help. Constructive criticism builds up; it does not tear down. Even in rebuke, there is love and forgiveness; the aim is to restore and build up.
Destructive criticism is not based upon facts; it is based on side issues. It is not done out of love.
In criticism we need to look at our own motives instead of judging others. Are you really concerned to help, or are you jealous and want to belittle the other person?

CRYING (see SORROW)

CURIOSITY (QUESTIONS, Interest)
Mt 3:1-17; Jn 4:1-42.
Curiosity is important. Questioning is one way of getting at the truth. Curiosity is important in the scientific world. Scientific experimentation and research are based on the attempt to gain knowledge on various matters. Science is one attempt to answer curiosity. It is also important in our Christian faith.
It can lead to God. It can help others be led to God. What is there about that person's life that makes him or her do what they do can be a question that is evoked in a nonbeliever when they see a believer carry out a Christ-like life, especially in the midst of great trials. Hopefully, they may feel that they like what they see and would like that in their own life. They want the joy, peace, and love that come from knowing Jesus Christ.

DANGER (FEAR, Risk)
Est 4:1-5:2; Neh 4:1-23.
When there is danger, we must rely upon other Christians and upon God. We must use the resources that we have available to meet that danger.
Facing danger involves preparation. That preparation involves several things. Part of it is to have a general idea of how you would act in the face

of certain dangers. When that danger comes, you might act very differently. When you face that danger, decide what course should be taken, what things are important (by all means do not panic). Approach with confidence and trust in God's direction. The apostle Paul says in Romans 8:37-39 that we are more than conquerors of all things through Jesus Christ, and there is absolutely nothing that can separate us from the love of God, which is in Christ Jesus.

DARKNESS (EVIL, SIN)

Ps 43:1-5; 119:105-112; Jn 1:1-9; I Jn 1:1-10.

Darkness is used to represent sin and evil especially in John's writings. It is opposed to what is good and true, which is represented by light. It is defeated by depending upon God and His word.

DEATH

Gen 3:19; Num 16:30; Josh 23:14; 1 Sam 2:6; 2 Sam 1:23; 12:23; 14:14; Job 7:1, 8-10; 10:21; 14:5-20; 16:22; 18:14; 21:23-26, 32-33; 24:20; 27:8, 22-23; 36:12, 14, 20; 38:17; Ps 23:1-6; 31:5; 37:1-2, 9-10, 35-37; 49:15; 73:3-4, 17-18, 24; 78:50; 89:48; 92:7; 103:14-16; 104:29; 116:15; 143:3; 144:4; Prov 2:22; 5:22-23; 10:25-27; 11:7; 13:9; 14:32; 29:1, 16; Ecc 3:2, 19-21; 5:15; 7:1-2; 9:5-6, 10; 12:5-7; Hos 13:14; Mt 10:28; 20:20-28; Lk 2:29; 9:24-25; 12:20; 13:5; 16:22-28; Jn 9:4; 11:11; 12:20-36; Act 5:3-10; 7:59; Rom 5:12-21; 1 Cor 1:18-31; 15:21-26, 50-58; 2 Cor 1:9-10; Phil 1:20-24;1 Th 4:13-14; 2 Tim 4:6-8; Heb 2:14-15; 9:23-28; 11:13; Rev 1:18; 14:13; 20:12-13; 21:4.

Because of sin, death came into the world for all men. Thus, the question is not if I will die, for that is a certainty, but rather how and what my destination after death will be.

There have been various answers to this. Some feel that death is the end and there is nothing after death. Your body goes into the ground and turns back into the elements. Some believe in reincarnation—that after death a person returns in another form, depending upon the life that person lived.

For the Christian, just as surely as we will die in the same manner, death is not the end but a new beginning. Death is a culmination. It is a going home. It is the completion of a hope that has not been fulfilled yet. We really can't imagine what that life is like. If a person came from heaven to describe it to us, they could not describe it to us in language that would even begin to describe it. How would you describe color to a person who has been blind all of his life?

God alone is the source that can lead us through death to eternal life. Christ defeated death for us. It is His ransom for our sin that breaks the bondage of sin; for the wages of sin are death (Rom 6:23).

Because He rose from the dead, then we too can rise and be with Him, for that is His promise to all who have received Him as Lord and Savior. In John 14:1-2 is that great passage where Jesus tells His disciples, *"Trust in God; trust also in me. In my Father's house there are many rooms and I go there to prepare a place for you . . . so that you may be with me."*

In the light of all this, death is not to be feared by the Christian. Yes, we are sad because of the loss of loved ones, but we are also glad because their pain and suffering are gone and they are with the Lord. In Matthew 22:32, Jesus reminds His disciples that God is a God of the living and not the dead. All those that believe in Him and are with Him have life. They are not dead.

DEBTS (Borrowing, OBLIGATION)

Ex 22:25-26; Deut 24:6, 11-13; Neh 5:3; Job 22:6; 24:9; Prov 3:21-35; 11:15; 22:26; Mt 18:23-33; Rom 1:8-17; 13:8-14.

To Christ we owe the debt that can never be repaid. He died for our sins. The only thing that He expects from us in return is grateful obedience. We owe Him love.

We need to repay our earthly debts as promptly and as diligently as possible. One mark of our present culture is that we buy things on credit, which is all right if we exercise caution. Too often people are living from paycheck to paycheck because of their excess debt. Some people are drowning in debt.

Other debts that we have—obedience, love, and concern—need to be repaid as quickly as possible, also not in a legalistic manner but with a rejoicing spirit. When love is shown to us, let us respond with love and kindness because we want to and not because we have to.

DECEIT (DISHONESTY)

Ex 20:1-21; Josh 7:1-26; Jud 16:1-30; Job 15:35; Ps 119:118; Prov 11:18; 12:17; 24:28; 26:24-28; Is 53:9; Jer 8:5; 9:6; 17:9; Lk 8:16-18; Jn 8:42-47; Rom 3:13; 2 Cor 4:2; Eph 5:6; Col 2:8;1 Pet 2:1; 3:10; Rev 12:1-9.

The great deceiver is Satan; thus, when we deceive someone, we are following Satan.

Deception is folly. We cannot hide our sins from God. We can fool ourselves and fool others for a time, but our deception will be found out.

We must be honest with ourselves, with others, and with God. Being honest with God is simply a matter of confessing to Him what He already knows.

Sometimes the deception of one person can bring consequences upon a whole family, a large number of people, or even a nation.

Deception destroys your trustworthiness and hurts irreparably what you stand for. Your trustworthiness and reputation can be restored, but it will take dedication, hard work, and time. You will have to demonstrate that indeed you are trustworthy.

DECISIONS (ACTIONS, Choices)

Gen 2:15-25; 28:20-21; Deut 30:19; Josh 24:15; Jud 6:37-39; 16:21; 1 Sam 8:19-20; 13:11-12; I K 18:21; Neh 1:1-11; Ps 17:3; Prov 18:10-17; 21:2; Is 50:7; Hos 10:2; Mt 1:19; 6:24; 10:32; 16:26; 24:13; 25:23; 26:41; 27:24; Lk 9:59-62; 11:23; 23:13-25; Jn 3:16; 5:16-30; Act 1:12-13, 21-25; 11:23; 14:22; Rom 8:38-39; 1 Cor 15:58; 16:13; Gal 5:1; 6:9; Eph 6:13; Phil 1:27; Col 1:23; 2:6-7; 2 Th 2:15-17; 2 Tim 1:13-14; 3:14; Heb 3:6-8, 14; 11:24; 12:1; 13:9; Jas 1:2-8, 12, 25; 4:17; 1 Jn 2:24, 28; Rev 22:11.

We are faced with many decisions every day. We need to learn from our mistakes when we make wrong decisions. We also need to look to God for guidance in making our decisions so that they are helpful to us and to those around us.

Prayer is an important resource that we need to use as we make our decisions. This should be a first step in our decision process rather than a step that we take to get approval for a decision already made.

Decisions need to be made based on good information, so we get all of the facts. Be open to all sides of an issue. Be open to new ideas and suggestions. Do not let pride cloud your decisions.

Decisions have to be made no matter how difficult they may be. We cannot continue to waver between two opinions. Not deciding is a decision of its own.

DELAY (Pause, PROCRASTINATION)

Josh 18:1-10; 1 Sam 13:1-15.

There are good delays and bad delays as well as unavoidable ones. Do not let delays put you into a foul mood. Try to make the best of any situation in which you find yourself.

Sometimes delays are the result of disobedience to God. In other words, we know what we should do but delay in doing it. When we put off jobs, this is a poor stewardship of time. It also can be costly to the success of the project.

Delays can also be a test of our patience. God may delay an action because we are not ready or the time is not right for the action. Let us always look to Him not only for the strength to be patient when that is what is needed but also the strength to proceed when we may want to delay.

DENIAL (EXCUSE, Refuse)

Mt 26:69-75.

There are various pressures and temptations to deny Jesus. It is not always popular to follow Jesus. Even lip service is sometimes frowned upon, let alone to really follow Him. Denial can begin with mere confusion: What should I think? How should I act? But ultimately it can lead to a rejection of Christ. We need to remember that if we reject Jesus before men, then He will reject us before the Father unless we ask for forgiveness and profess Him as Lord and Savior (Mt 10:33).

We also need to remember that any arguments that you may feel are reasons to reject Him are really arguments that you received from Satan, the great Deceiver. Remember the story in the Garden of Eden, where Eve was tempted by the Serpent who is the Devil (see Gen 3:4)? The Devil stated, "You will not die." The sin was that man wanted to be God. The Devil implanted this thought in Adam and Eve—the great deception for which we have paid for throughout time.

DEPENDENCE (TRUST)

1 Ch 29:10-25; 2 Ch 1:3-11; Mk 9:14-29.

We want to be independent and that is good, but we also need to remember that we can only have a limited amount of independence and ultimately we are dependent upon others and most of all God. Independence from God is impossible and at the root of all sins. In the story of the Garden of Eden, this was the story of Adam and Eve. They really did not want to rely upon God. They wanted to rule.

God gives us all our basic necessities: air to breath, water to drink, sun to provide us with warmth, plants for food just to mention a few. We must rely upon Him for these things. He also gives us guidelines on how to live our lives. We cannot do as we please. There are man-made laws, but there are God-given laws too.

We need to trust in Him daily and keep in touch with Him through prayer for the guidance that we need. It is also important to remember that we are in the hands of a loving and caring God. He wants each of us to develop to our fullest potential.

DEPRESSION (DISCOURAGEMENT, Boredom, Sadness)

Jud 15:1-20; 1 K 19:1-9; Job 3:1-3; 17:13-16; Ps 42:1-11; Ps 77:7-9; Prov 13:12; Jer 8:20; Lam 5:22; Jon 2:2-4; Mic 7:1-2; Lk 13:27-28; 23:29-30.

There are various causes for depression. Sometimes it is because of exhaustion. It can also follow a success. In today's society, drugs can be the cause of depression. Sometimes it is a physical ailment.

What is the cure? One cure is to meditate upon God's word. Let His precious promises and resources fill your whole being. The word of God tells you that you are a being who is valuable in His eyes. You are loved (Jn 3:16). You are in the hands of a loving God of whom there is none greater. He is good and wants good for you. You might need some medication; however, even in these cases, do not think that the medication alone is the cure. It is not. You must combine it with treating the inner self.

Sometimes the cure that is needed is simply to have patience. You don't see the answer right now so you become depressed. Just wait, for the answer will come.

Also be confident. God has acted in the past, He acts now, and He will continue to act in the future. God will act.

The one thing that we must make sure is that we are living in the will of God because there is a time coming in which a great depression will come and there is no escape. That depression is for all those outside the grace of God—hope for them is gone. These people outside the grace of God are there because they have placed themselves there by their willful disobedience. They have chosen not to believe.

DESIRES (Goals, NEEDS, SIN)

Gen 29:1-30; Ps 17:1; 22:26; 24:6; 25:5; 37:4, 7, 9, 34; Ps 40:1, 8; 42:1-3; 62:1; 63:1, 8; 84:2; 97:1-12; 143:5; Jer 29:13; Mt 5:6, 27-30; Lk 10:42; Act 21:1-16; Gal 5:13-26; Phil 3:12-14; Heb 11:6.

We have many desires: physical, emotional, spiritual, social, sexual, etc. Don't feel bad about them—they are natural, but how they should be met and how they are met is where the problem comes in.

Some desires and goals demand time and investment for their realization. We need to make sure that our plans, goals, and desires are in keeping with God's will for us. We must look at goals from a short—and a long-range point of view. Which is this desire—long or short?

There will be conflicts sometimes. When this happens, the right choice is obedience to God. We need to look to God to help us settle conflicts and not just go our own way. Uncontrolled desires can lead to sin.

DESPAIR (GIVING UP, HOPELESSNESS)
Gen 48:1-22; Ex 14:1-14; Ps 40:1-17; Is 59:1-21, Joel 1:1-12; Rev 16:1-21.

We can reach a point where everything seems hopeless. Sometimes everything seems to be going wrong.

The worse despair is for a person to see the sin in their life and not know what to do about it. Fortunately God has done something about it. He has sent His Son Jesus that we might receive forgiveness for our sins, and be restored to right relationship with God. We, as Christians, when we see such people, are to point them toward Jesus. We do this out of love, not in self-righteousness or being judgmental. We are really saying, "Yes, I was lost too until I found Jesus."

In our times of hopelessness, let us turn afresh to God. Trust in God is the key element for overcoming despair. It will include patience, for the answer may not come as quickly as we would like it to come, or it may come in an unexpected way.

DETERMINATION (Concentration, PURPOSE)
1 Sam 7:3-17; Lk 9:51-56.

Determination is a needed characteristic for the Christian. He or she needs to be determined to obey God even if this is unpopular, would make the person unpopular, or is difficult. We must be determined to follow Jesus in spite of obstacles because there will be obstacles. There is a difference between being determined and being stubborn.

DIFFERENCES (Characteristics)
Gen 19:1-29; Lk 6:12-26; Rom 14:1-13

We are different, and we have differences of opinions. All of us feel that we would like to make a difference. Do you feel your life is making a difference? Do people see God in you?

A Christian's lifestyle and viewpoint are different from a non-Christian's lifestyle and viewpoint. This should not prevent a dialogue between the two; in fact, that is what we are called to do, but the Christian needs to express his or her views in a respectful, humble, loving manner, and not in self-righteous, heavy-handed condemnation. This would only alienate the other person.

In differences, we need to affirm one another. Hold true to important matters. Learn from one another.

Now differences in talents and ability should be looked upon as complimentary to one another. One person has one skill and another has a different one. Each is important and together one person can enrich another. Paul uses the analogy of the body, in which he says the body is made up of many parts but all are needed (see Rom 12:17ff).

Still another important point to remember is differences in worship. Each of us is different and therefore we worship God in different ways. Some people are very formal and intellectual and worship in that manner. Others are emotional and have emotion in their worship (see worship). The key is for you to express your gratitude, your praise to God, and allow Him to speak back to you in the way that is most meaningful to you.

Unfortunately, Christians often make fun of one another. "Look at those people—they are rolling in the aisles, leaping in the air, and just plain making a spectacle of themselves." "Those people look like they are at a funeral and no one would dare smile."

Any worship needs a balance. There should be the freedom to express the joy that comes from knowing the Lord. There should be good biblical teaching and application. Don't go pointing fingers. Don't criticize how another person worships God. Instead, thank God that that person is worshipping God. Find the way that suits your personality and that enables you to be enriched. It must be more than emotionalism, and it must be more than traditionalism or intellectualism. It is where the Living God can meet you, that you allow Him to meet you, for He will not storm your castle. He will knock and you need to open (Rev 3:20).

DIGNITY (WORTH)
Gen 1:1-31; Lev 26:1-13; I Sam 2:1-11.

The fact that God created us gives us dignity. However, the greatest thing that gives us dignity is that God, through His Son Jesus Christ, showed how precious we are by redeeming us. He died on the Cross for us.

Our jobs should have dignity also because we are serving God. A job has dignity when you have the proper attitude toward it and when you perform it in a dignified manner. You are a ditchdigger? No, you are one of God's ditchdiggers.

Take the most unglamorous profession that you can think of and do not let anyone belittle you for doing that. (However, do not settle for something that is below your abilities or a waste of your abilities. That is poor stewardship.)

Think of the unglamorous profession in this manner. It is royal service for one of the King of the universe's men or women that is performing the task.

DIRECTION (GUIDANCE)

Ps 25:1-22; Mt 2:1-12; Jn 12:12-19.

We need guidance, direction. Let us go to God for that guidance and direction. Read His word. Pray to Him. Talk to others. The direction that you get should be from a reliable source or you will go in the wrong direction. This is true of driving somewhere and more so spiritually.

Also, remember to ask the following in taking advice from the Bible or advice that people give you from the Bible: Is that what the Bible actually says? Is it a misquote? Is it something taken out of context?

To follow Jesus may mean that you have to go in an entirely different direction than what you expected, but still go. The more we walk with Him, the more we will know Him.

DISAGREEMENTS (ARGUMENTS)

Gen 13:1-18; Num 12:1-16; Mt 5:21-26.

In a disagreement, the real issue should be discussed instead of the minor details. Too often disagreements are over minor things. Disagreements should be settled as quickly as possible and in an amicable manner. Otherwise they will fester like a sore. Ephesians 4:26 says, "Do not let the sun go down while you are still angry."

Disagreements can cause broken relations if they are not mended. They can hamper progress toward a goal. They can make a person self-centered. Also, don't be known as a disagreeable person. We don't like that trait in our friends.

DISCIPLINE (CORRECTION)

1 K 1:1-8; Prov 13:18-25; 29:15-19;1 Cor 5:1-13; 2 Cor 2:5-11; Eph 6:1-4; Heb 12:1-13.

Children need limits in order to learn how to grow up to be responsible adults. Prov 22:6 says, "Train up a child in the way that he should go, and when he is old he will not depart from it." Proper discipline is an expression of parental love; it is an unavoidable responsibility. Some parents do not discipline their children. If you love your child, you will discipline him or her. You are doing that child a big disservice if you do not, for you are not preparing the child for the outside world. That child is going to have to obey certain rules, first in school and then later as he or she is growing up and at work. Discipline is more than punishment. It is instruction in right and wrong.

There is also discipline in the church. This discipline is with the aim in mind of maintaining Christ's standards in the church. The church and the individual need to make sure that the correct standards are being used. These standards are what Christ expects of His disciples. For the church, it does not mean imposing man-made rules but God's rules.

Discipline must always be exercised in love and not in pettiness or vengeance. It should involve the opportunity for confession by the wrongdoer and restoration.

A third type of discipline that is important and is needed is self-discipline. We should check daily our progress and discipline ourselves when we fall short.

DISCOURAGEMENT (DEPRESSION, Disappointment)

Ex 5:3; 9:1; 1 Sam 1:1-28; 17:28-32; 1 K 19:3, 10; Neh 4:1-14; Jn 12:37-38; Phil 1:12-30.

We become discouraged when we attempt something and it does not turn out the way we would like it to turn out, or your plans or intentions fall through. That happens sometimes even when you have given your best effort or done a lot of planning. How should we handle discouragement? Seeking God's help through prayer or scripture is certainly one very important way. Seeking out others is another good way. May each of us be the kind of person that another would feel comfortable to come to for encouragement and that they would receive the encouragement that they need, for we are to encourage one another (see I Th 5:11).

Let us trust God even in the most trying and discouraging situations. We need to remember that He can work through even the worse of situations. After all, God used the greatest crime in all of history, the murder of His Son on the Cross, to accomplish the greatest miracle of all times, the salvation of the world. Satan's victory was turned into his defeat.

DISEASE (see SICKNESS)

DISHONESTY (Lying, Cheating)

Gen 27:1-29; Lev 19:13, 35-36; Deut 25:13-16; 1 Sam 15:1-23; Ps 37:21; 50:18; 62:10; Prov 3:27-28; 11:1; 20:10, 14, 23-30; Jer 22:13; Hos 12:7; Amos 3:10; Zech 5:3; Mt 21:12; Lk 16:1-8; 1 Th 4:6; Jas 5:4.

How do you react to dishonesty? Are we dishonest? We all are sometimes. Some people are more dishonest than others. However, let us seek God's forgiveness when we are, and correct the situation as quickly as possible. Often a person is more interested in not getting caught than the act of being dishonest.

DISOBEDIENCE (SIN)

Gen 3:1-24; Num 14:11-12, 22-24; 20:1-13; 32:8-13; Deut 18:19; 28:15-20; 1 Sam 13:13; 2 Sam 12:9-10; 1 K 11:5-6, 11-12; 1 Ch 13:1-14; Mt 9:30.

Disobedience is one form of sin and involves the wrath of God. Disobedience can lead to other sins and it can harden you heart. Continual disobedience, the disobedience with no repentance, will cause God's wrath to fall upon that person. Yes, we are all disobedient, but we must repent of that sin and start afresh. That is what God is calling us to do (1 Jn 1:9).

Punishment of disobedience may be swift or over a period of time. The consequences of disobedience can be long lasting.

DIVORCE (see MARRIAGE)

DOUBT (CONFUSION, QUESTION)

Gen 3:1-24; 21:7; Num 11:1-35; Job 4:3-5; 23:1-17; 30:20; Ps 22:2; 31:22; 33:4; 42:5-6; 49:5; 73:13-17; Jer 8:18; 15:18; 45:3; Lam 3:8, 17-18; Mt 8:26; 11:4-6; 14:29-31; 17:14-23; Mk 4:38; 8:17-18; 16:10-11; Lk 1:18; 4:1-13; 7:18-35; Jn 3:18; 14:8-11; 20:23-28; Jas 1:6-8.

Everyone has doubts from time to time, and they can be good. Doubts can be a means for growth. Doubts can also be blind hardheartedness. Thus, don't be worried about doubting, but just doubt for the right reason, and use it as a means to grow in your faith and as a means for obtaining the truth. Christ says that He is the way, the truth, and the life (see Jn 14:6). Therefore, we do not have to worry about doubt. Honest doubt can only clear away untruth. A legitimate search for the truth will only lead to Jesus.

Bad doubts can weaken your trust in God. For example, a person asks, "Is that really wrong, or is that really bad?" These types of questions can lead a person away from God. Yes, you should ask why something is wrong, but look to God for the answer. If it is contrary to His will, then it is wrong.

Take your doubts to God. Look for answers. Be open to His leading. Meditate upon God's word. Pray. Trust Him.

When you have a doubt or question, begin at a point that is not in doubt and move from there to the matter you are questioning. It is a matter of laying a foundation.

Ask this question, for example: How can there be a God? If you believe in Jesus Christ, then you can begin at this point. Here was a live person that walked on this earth just like you and me. We can identify with Him. Jesus said to His disciples if you have seen me you have seen the Father (see Jn 14:9). Thus, you can move from a concrete person to the intangible, to the Living God. To understand God completely is beyond the comprehension of our finite minds. However, we do know Him in the limited way that we are able to understand.

DRINKING (Drugs, Drunkenness)

Gen 9:20-29; Prov 20:1; 21:17; 23:1-3, 21, 29-35; 25:16; 31:4-5; Is 5:11-12; Dan 1:8; Act 24:25; Rom 13:14; 14:21; 1 Cor 9:25-27; Eph 5:15-20; Phil 4:5; 1 Th 5:6-8; Tit 2:2; 2 Pet 1:5-6.

Is drinking a sin? Some people would say so, but since our Lord drank wine, we know it is not a sin. However, it can become one. It is the abuse of alcohol that is wrong. Drinking when it leads to drunkenness can lead to many negative consequences. A drunken driver killing someone is one example.

This is the problem with social drinking. It can begin very innocently and develop into a bad habit, a habit that is out of control and can lead to alcoholism.

The Bible is aware of the dangers of alcohol, and there are many warnings about abusive or excessive use of alcohol (Prov 20:1). Alcohol dulls the senses and releases inhibitions. Sometimes a person becomes very aggressive when he or she is drunk. Rapes, physical and sexual abuse are a couple of additional examples of actions under the influence of alcohol.

Alcohol can be a form of escape. A person can't deal with a problem, so he or she tries to find the solution in a bottle. Often the person drinks himself into a stupor.

A person must find himself in God. Drinking is one wrong way of trying to satisfy a hunger that God has placed in him (Ps 42:2). That hunger can only be satisfied by God. We need to be filled with the Holy Spirit. Let this be how we get our enjoyment. Let this be how we solve our problems.

Alcohol is a drug, like cigarettes and the many other kinds that people use (see Drugs). Drinking, even in moderation, can be harmful because it could lead another person to drink even if he cannot handle drinking in moderation, if at all. Let us not be the cause of someone's stumbling.

DRUGS

1 Cor 6:19.

Drugs are a big problem today in many ways. Of course there are legal drugs, which are necessary and are very beneficial, but these are sometimes abused too. The first problem is what the drug can do to your body and mind. Many drugs cause delusions, and this is why people take them; they take them for the "high," as an escape, but it is a deadly escape. These drugs destroy the body and the mind. In fact many suicides are the result of drugs. There are even famous people who supposedly had it all but died from an overdose of drugs. Untold numbers of people have been injured by drugs. Cigarettes are a matter of taking your money and putting a match to it. Also, it is unhealthy, unclean, and intrudes itself upon others. Does a smoker think I enjoy him or her blowing smoke in my face? In other drug habits, a person may rob or even kill in order to get the money for their habit. All drug habits ravage a person's body and mind.

Another problem is that because of their addictive nature, it takes more and more of the drug to have the same effect. Withdrawal pains of the drug are still another problem.

In addition to the physical and mental problems of the drug, there are other problems too. Drugs are very expensive, so people may resort to stealing in order to get the money for their habit. People will even steal from their loved ones. Or they may lie and say they need the money for something else when it is really for drugs. Sometimes people get involved in prostitution to pay for their drugs.

Why do people take drugs? As was said above, it is a form of escape. Just as a drunkard tries to find a solution in a bottle, the drug addict tries to escape his or her problems by taking a pill, smelling a vapor, or shooting up. Addicts are trying to satisfy a hunger that cannot be satisfied that way.

Personally, I have only had one experience with drugs myself. Yes, I have and still do take prescription drugs, but I have never taken an illegal drug. However, the one experience that I had was with a prescription drug. I don't know if they even still make this drug, but I went to Mayo Clinic and was given a new drug to see if it would control epilepsy better. My epilepsy was under good control, but they had some concern. I took a new drug, Xerontin. They did not keep me at the clinic for observation but sent me home, which was over two hundred miles away. Before too long, I started having delusions. I wasn't seeing things, but I was imagining different things. My wife could not handle me, so I was taken to Monmouth Hospital. I was given sedatives but they had no effect. From Monmouth, I was transported to Galesburg Research Hospital, to the psych ward. When I was first admitted, they thought that I was having delerium tremens, which I was but from a prescription drug instead of an illegal drug or alcohol., Delerium tremens is a delirium associated with excessive drinking and is characterized by trembling, sweating and hallucinating. Later they discovered that it was a reaction to the medication that I was given. The withdrawal was not painful. It was simply a matter of getting that drug out of my system, and once that was done I was in my right mind. That was bad enough for me, but many people go through a living hell because of their habit.

The answer to drugs is to seek the living God. He will lift you up and not let you down. He will feed that hunger in your soul. As 1 Corinthians 6:19 says, "Your body is a temple of the Holy Spirit." Thus, we should not defile it.

DUTY (OBLIGATION)

Deut 6:5; 10:12-13; Lev 19:18; Josh 22:5; 23:11; Ps 31:23; 23:26; Mt 4:10; 7:12; 12:50; 22:21, 36-37; 25:34-40; Lk 10:25-37; Jn 14:15; 15:14; Act 4:19-20; 5:29.

What are the duties of man to man and man to God? This is a question that each of us has to answer for ourselves daily. Jesus summed this duty up by saying that we are to love God and to love man (see Mt 22:37-39). This is not a lip service—that is not acceptable—but a total devotion to God and a genuine concern for other people.

God showed us what His love is like when He gave His Son for us (Jn 3:16). Each of us has to ask, do we really love God, and if so, how much? For myself, I know that I do not love Him as much as I should. I am selfish at times, like anyone else. Therefore, it is my prayer that each one of us, most definitely myself included, will strive to get to know and love Jesus better. And by knowing Jesus, we will know the Father. We also know that if that prayer is granted it is a result of the Holy Spirit at work in our life. We do that by reading and meditating on good books, the scripture, and fellowship with other Christians. Let all of this sink into your heart, mind, and soul. In I Corinthians 2:16, Paul writes that we are to have the mind of Christ.

EARTH (CREATION)

Gen 1:1-31; Job 38:1-39:30; Ps 8:1-9.

As was stated earlier, God created the heavens and the earth. He made these because He loves us. God is love (1Jn 4:8), and He wanted to share His love with us.

We are to be caretakers of His creation (Gen 1:26). We should do the things that we need to do in order to be good stewards of the earth, as well as of our time, talents, and abilities.

Let's take care of our natural resources. This is especially true today, as we consume more and more energy. Oil is the present resource that is being depleted and we have to pay heavily for that. New means are going to have to be developed.

Let's not be a throwaway society of litterbugs. Let's recycle and do whatever little things need to be done to protect our earth. The pollution and raping of our countryside are crimes, and all of this is done in the name of progress and for the almighty dollar.

In more than one place, I have seen a small wood torn down to build a shopping mall. Often there is not that much of a need for one there. It is simply another example of someone pursuing that mighty dollar.

ECONOMY (MONEY)

Prov 10:4; 21:17; 23:20-21; 31:27; Mt 14:20; 15:37; Mk 14:4.

How should we handle our money? We are to use it wisely and not for selfish indulgence and pleasure. It is sad that some people have so much money that they do not know what to do with it, so they spend it very foolishly. There are numerous things that they could do to benefit others. Happily, some wealthy people do many good things with their wealth. Praise the Lord for them! On the other hand, we are not to hoard it miserly and grasp on to every penny. There is a time to spend and a time to save. There are things to spend it on and things not to. Resources are to be used to meet needs.

EDIFICATION

Rom 14:19; 15:2; 1 Cor 8:1; 10:23; 14:3, 17, 26; 2 Cor 12:19; Eph 4:12, 29.

Edification is an important responsibility of the Christian. Edification is moral and spiritual enlightenment for the benefit of each person (1 Cor 14:16). The Christian is to build up the body of Christ. We support and encourage one another (1 Th 5:11). In testing things, we need to ask, does this thing build up or tear down? Our speech, conduct, worship, and all parts of our life need to be done with this in mind. By your word, deed, and action you are helping someone. You are giving them further insight into what it means to follow Jesus.

EDUCATION (Learning)

Deut 4:9; 6:1-9; Ps 78:1-8; Prov 22:6; Dan 1:3-5; Lk 11:52; Act 22:3.

Teaching our children is an important responsibility. The passing of the faith from one generation to another was vital to the people of Israel and is vital for each Christian (Deut 4:10). As it has often been said, the Christian faith is always one generation from extinction. If the next generation does not receive it then it is gone. However we know that this will not happen.

This teaching should be a natural part of the home. It is a repetition in word and deed of God at work in daily life. It should be more than informational (although that is important) but rather relational. Relationship is the heart of the Christian faith. Your relationship to Christ is the vital element, not your knowledge about Him. Children need teaching so that they have the proper foundation upon which to grow, mature, and make decisions.

How does your child know that you love him or her? You tell the child, but you show it in how you relate to that child. You talk with your child. You listen. You do deeds that show that you love. A dad might play catch with his son or daughter if the child likes that. A mother might cook with a daughter or son—again, if that is something fun for the child.

EFFECTIVENESS (ACCOMPLISHMENTS)
1 K 4:1-28; 2 K 1:1-18; Act 1:1-11.

To be effective in our living, there needs to be order. It is also based upon trust in God. There is a reliance upon God's power and timing. If we want to be effective in something, then we should make sure that we are doing something in the will of God and that we trust His timing and power to see that the task gets accomplished.

EFFORT (INVOLVEMENT, WORK)
Ex 36:1-38; Josh 23:1-16; Mt 7:7-12; Col 3:18-25.

To accomplish goals, there must be a pulling together, a uniting of efforts. To be obedient to God takes effort; it is not an easy task. The Cross is one example. Jesus was obedient even to death on a cross. Jesus says we are to bear our cross (Lk 14:27).

Another important question to ask about any task is, is it worth the effort? Let's make sure that we are doing tasks that are worth the effort that goes into doing them. Is the task in God's will?

EGO (Self)
Jud 15:1-20; 1 Sam 15:1-35; Mt 3:1-17.

How should we regard our ego? It is unhealthy to have too much emphasis on your ego, but it is also unhealthy to have too low self-esteem.

Sometimes we do not give God the credit and boast of our achievements. "I did this." We do not stop and think that God gives us the ability to do things, gives us the food we eat, the air we breathe. You simply did what God has given you the ability to do.

Another problem is the concern about other people's opinions. We puff ourselves up or are deflated by what others think. The important thing is, how faithful are we to God? Are we walking with Him? Are we following His will? If so, then we do not need to fear anyone. There is no one greater than God. Yes, to follow Him may cause you to be unpopular and even mistreated, but they did that to Jesus also (Jn 16:33). There is no greater joy than to hear those words of the Master: "Well done, my good and faithful servant" (see Mt 25:21).

The antidote for low self-esteem is to remember that you are loved by the King of the universe. You are worth very much in His eyes. You may not be handsome or pretty, strong or smart, but that doesn't matter. Accept Jesus and you will be a child of the King.

EMBARRASSMENT (SHAME)

Gen 2:18-25; Num 22:21-36; Mt 14:1-12; Rom 1:8-17;1 Th 2:11-12.

Sometimes embarrassment is the result of sin. We don't want others or God to know certain things. We are embarrassed. Sin can also result from trying to avoid embarrassment. For example, to avoid the truth, a person may lie or blame another.

Are you embarrassed to be a Christian in a particular situation? If so, your faith is not genuine, or at least certainly very weak. You need to correct that attitude as quickly as possible. This type of embarrassment ruins your witness; it reflects badly on the Christian faith. Our faith must be so strong that we can never be embarrassed by it. Our own actions may embarrass us and be an embarrassment to the Christian faith, but the Christian faith should never be an embarrassment to us. Paul declares in Romans 1:16 that he is not ashamed of the gospel of Jesus Christ. Let that be our declaration also.

EMOTIONS (FEELINGS)

Gen 1:1-31; Num 14:1-45; Jud 11:1-40; Ezra 3:1-13; Jn 11:32-35.

Emotions are a part of being a human. It is important to express your emotions whether you are a man or woman. In the past, it has often been felt that it is unmanly for a man to show emotions such as crying, but this is not true. The Son of God wept (see Lk 19:11). The shortest verse in the Bible is just two words, "Jesus wept" (Jn 11:35). By expressing our emotions, we are able to identify with God our Creator.

Emotions bring richness to life; they give it color. How drab life would be without emotions. Just think of some of our emotions: joy, sorrow, love, hatred, compassion, to mention a few.

While it is important to express feelings, it is also important that they be under control and that we are not ruled by them. Uncontrolled emotions can lead to bad decisions and rash promises, for our emotions color how we look at something. They can lead to various sins. So do not be rash. All of us have had the experience where something looks entirely different the next day, and that is because we are looking with a different set of emotions. We may even say, "Why did I get so upset about that?"

True worship involves our total being: heart, mind, and soul. It involves a full range of emotions: joy to sorrow. Just as emotionalism only in worship is wrong (it is one-dimensional), so, too, pure intellectualism in worship is wrong, for it too is only one-dimensional. As has just been said, worship must involve your total being.

EMPLOYMENT (DIGNITY, WORK)

Lev 25:6; Deut 5:14; 15:18; 24:14-15; Josh 1:1-9; Ps 1:1-6; 92:1-15; Prov 22:16; 25:11-15; 29:21; Ecc 3:1-13; Jer 22:13; Mal 3:5; Mt 10:10; 20:1-2; Lk 10:7; 15:15-16; 2 Cor 8:1-15; Eph 6:5-9; Phil 3:7-21; Col 4:1; Jas 5:4; Tit 2:1-15.

Work should be done in a manner that is pleasing to God and offered up to Him as our reasonable and acceptable service. Both employer and employee have that responsibility.

Often work is hated. It may be repetitious, tedious, seemingly meaningless, stressful, and a variety of other things. It is not looked upon as a chance to serve God. At work, there are many temptations, for you may be working for a non-Christian employer and company. Many of your fellow workers may not be Christians. There may be discrimination, lying, cheating, laziness, and many other unpleasant things.

For the Christian, it is important that you serve God in your position whether you are a top executive or a janitor. Do your best. Be trustworthy. You are doing it for God, so rejoice. Do not degrade yourself or let others degrade you because of your job (see Dignity). In all that you do, strive to help others.

ENCOURAGEMENT (Motivation, FELLOWSHIP)

Josh 24:1-15; Act 14:1-28; Rom 1:8-17; 1 Th 3:6-13; 4:13-18; 5:1-28; 2 Tim 1:1-18; Phil 17-19; Heb 12:1; 1 Pet 1:1-13.

Where do we go for encouragement? Do you give encouragement?

God's faithfulness in the past is a source of encouragement. We have seen what He has already done; we simply need to remember His faithfulness and trust in Him to lift us up.

In the same manner, we need to lift others up. Be a source of strength for them. Help point the way toward God's love by demonstrating it in our deeds and actions. Let them see God working in and through you.

Another means of encouragement is to look to God's word. Study and live it. Rely upon the precious promises that it gives.

When we encourage others, then that can be a source of encouragement for ourselves. And still another important source is prayer. We can give and receive encouragement by prayer.

ENDURANCE (PATIENCE, STRENGTH)

Ps 37:24; Prov 4:18; Hos 12:6; Mt 10:16-42; Lk 22:31-32; Jn 8:31-32; Act 14:21-22; 1 Cor 15:1-2, 58; 16:13; Gal 6:9; Col 1:10, 22-23; 1 Th 3:8, 13; 5:21; 2 Th 3:13; 2 Tim 3:14; 4:1-8; Tit 1:9; Heb 2:1; 3:1-6; 4:14; 6:1, 11-12; 10:23, 35-36; 12:1; 2 Pet 1:10-11; Rev 14:1-20; 21:7; 22:11

Endurance takes preparation. One must be prepared in order to have the resources and strength at hand to withstand trials and temptations.

Endurance is a sign of your faith. It shows how firmly you believe. Do you believe because it is convenient, easy, or profitable? Would you be willing to give your life for your faith? In the past many have, and even today there are people that have to give their life for their faith.

If we stand firm, then we are more than compensated by our reward.

ENEMIES (Opponents)

Ex 23:1-9; 1 Sam 18:1-30; Prov 24:17-18; 25:21-22; Mt 5:21-26, 43-48; Lk 6:27-35; Rom 12:14; 1 Jn 2:1-11.

Jesus gives us those words to love our enemies (Mt 5:44). This truly demonstrates a transformed life. The type of love he calls for here is volitional. It does not mean to have a warm, fuzzy feeling. Instead we are called to act for the benefit of that person—to do good to your enemies. We don't like what they are doing to us, but do good for them even if they are persecuting you. This is exactly what Jesus did for each of us. While we were still sinners (and enemies of God), Christ died for us (see Rom 5:8), and on the Cross, He said, *"Father, forgive them, for they do not know what they are doing"* (Lk 23:34).

Bickering and pettiness between people can begin with disagreements and grow until it becomes enmity. Something very small can become very large.

We are warned that hatred can get in our way of worshipping. In Matthew 5:23, we are told to settle the matter with our adversary first and then present our gift to God. We cannot love God if we have hate for another (I Jn 4:20).

To repeat what was said above, the love that Jesus is commanding here is a sincere desire of goodwill for the other person. It is wanting the best for that person. It is not the emotional type that we commonly think of. It is a matter of the will rather than feelings. It is a decision to act in a certain way.

ENVYING (JEALOUSY)

Deut 5:1-33; 1 K 21:1-29; Job 5:2-3; Ps 37:1, 7; 49:16; 73:3; 112:10; Prov 3:31; 14:30; 23:17; 24:1; 27:4; Ecc 4:4; Sol 8:6; Ezek 35:11; Rom 13:13; 1 Cor 3:3; 2 Cor 12:20; Gal 5:19-26; 1 Tim 6:4; Jas 3:14-16; 5:9; 1 Pet 2:1.

Envying another's property, possessions, and things of this sort makes a person unhappy, but also can lead to other sins, such as adultery or even murder. The story of David and Bathsheba illustrates this very well (2Sam 11:1-17).

We need to trust in God. Serve Him and seek Him and the other things that we have need of will come (Mt 6:33).

EQUALITY (Fairness)

Gal 3:28; Eph 2:11-22; Phm 1:1-25.

In today's world, there is injustice and inequality. Where can you find equality? That true equality only comes in Jesus Christ. In Christ we are one, as it says in Colossians 3:11. He breaks down all barriers. He calls all to Himself: male and female, rich and poor, free and slave, the strong and the weak, those of all races.

This is why it is important that if we would claim the name of Jesus, then we must not be guilty of any prejudice of any kind. Christ accepts and loves. We must accept and love.

The Cross is the great equalizer because here the barriers between man and man were destroyed and also the barrier between God and man. We can all equally come to God.

ESCAPE (SECURITY)

Ex 14:1-31; 1 K 22:29-40; Is 16:1-14; Jon 1:1-17.

With problems and temptations, we often want to escape. We certainly want to avoid them, but they can't always be avoided. We think, "I can't handle this," and so we run. There may even be a small pathetic plea to God before one runs. But was it a sincere plea, or was it something more like, "I don't know where you are, or if you even care, but I've had it. I'm gone."

There are many different ways in which people try to escape: drugs, sex, drinking, pleasures, materialism, gambling, and suicide, to mention a few.

Are you running from something? Where are you running to? Everyone is running for the same reason. Problems and temptations build up and we get to a point where we can't handle them; there is a hunger there. There is a need. If that hunger and need can be satisfied, then the problems and temptations will take care of themselves. The hunger that you are feeling is the need for God. In John 6:35, Jesus says that He is the bread of life and that those who come to Him will never be hungry or thirsty. Jesus is saying that fellowship with Him will satisfy the hunger and thirst that our soul feels.

We cannot run away from God. Jonah tried. Psalms 139:7-12 says that we cannot flee from God's presence, for wherever we go, God is there. Instead, God is the source that we need to run to. He can supply the strength that you need. He gives us the strength that is needed to face our trials and problems. In Philippians 4:13, Paul makes this assertion: "I can do everything through him who strengthens me." As we have just mentioned, it is the hunger for God that each of us needs. We need to love and to be loved. The satisfaction that we need is from a genuine relationship with Jesus Christ. *Doing religious ritual and works are not what is needed*, but rather **a deep relationship with the Living Savior.** That is what is needed and is the only thing that will satisfy your longing.

Seek out other believers who can give you the support that you need. Pray and read God's word. Trust Him because He has already overcome the world (Jn 16:33).

ETERNAL LIFE (HEAVEN, SALVATION)

Ps 21:4; 39:5-6; 95:11; 133:3; Is 32:1-20; Dan 12:2; Mt 7:13-14, 21-23; 10:39; 16:26; 19:16-21, 27, 29; 22:11-12, 29-32; 25:46; Lk 18:18-30; 20:34-35; Jn 3:1-21; 4:14; 5:24-25, 29, 39-40, 47; 6:60-71; 7:38; 10:10, 27-28; 12:23-25, 50; 14:1-3; 17:1-26; 20:22; Act 13:46-48; Rom 2:7; 5:21; 6:22-23; 1 Cor 15:53-54; 2 Cor 5:1-10; Gal 6:8; 1 Tim 1:16; 4:8; 6:12; 2 Tim 2:11-13; Tit 1:2; 3:7; 1 Jn 5:1-12; Jude 21; Rev 1:18; 3:5; 21:1-4.

What is eternal life? Often it is thought of as life without end, but that could be hell for it makes a difference in what that life is. It is life without end, but it is a life with God. It is completely different from this life. There is no sickness, sorrow, death, sin, or evil.

This eternal life begins right now. It is a quality of life and not just a quantity. It involves a peace that passes all understanding. In John 17:3, eternal life is defined this way, "*Now this is eternal life: that they may know you, the one true God, and Jesus Christ, whom you have sent.*" Thus, eternal life is based upon an intimate knowledge of the Living God and His Son Jesus Christ. This knowledge is not a factual knowledge but rather a relationship. It is the knowledge of a person; it is a relationship with that person.

Eternal life begins when we receive the Lord Jesus Christ as our Lord and Savior. It is looked for by many people in many different places, but it can only be found in Jesus Christ.

It is nothing that we earn or deserve. It is a free gift from God. It comes from trusting in God.

ETERNAL PUNISHMENT (see HELL)

EVIL (SIN)

Gen 3:1-24; Ex 2:1-10; 23:2, 32; Num 16:26; Jud 9:1-57; 2 Sam 23:6-7; 1 Ch 4:9-10; 2 Ch 19:2; Job 21:1-34; Ps 1:1; 26:4-5; 28:3; 101:4; 119:115; 139:19; 141:4; Prov 1:10-11, 14-15; 4:14-15; 12:11; 24:1; 29:24; Jer 15:17; Hab 2:1-20; Lk 9:37-45; Rom 16:17; 1 Cor 6:14-15; Eph 6:10-20; 1 Tim 6:5; 2 Tim 3:4-5.

Why is there evil? We really don't know why, but we just know that there is evil. It is frustrating and irritating to see evil prevail. There are a couple of things that we need to remember. The first is that God acts in His time and He has made it very clear that His way will prevail and not evil. The second is that we commit evil, so it is good that He gives us time to repent of that evil. Still another thing is that we are not to return evil with evil.

EXAMPLE (Demonstrating, Modeling)

Gen 26:1-35; Lev 18:2-3; 11:44; 19:2; 20:23; 1 Ch 8:9-13; 10:6; 2 Ch 30:7; Prov 22:24; Jer 16:12; Ezek 20:18; Hos 4:9; 5:5; Zech 1:4; Mt 4:1-11; 5:48; 23:1-3; Mk 10:43-45; Rom 15:2-7; 1 Cor 8:9-13; 10:6; Eph 4:17; Phil 4:9; Col 3:13; 1 Th 1:6-7; 1 Tim 4:12; Tit 2:7; Heb 12:1-13; Jas 5:11; 1 Pet 2:11-17; 5:3; 1 Jn 2:6; 3 Jn 1:11; Rev 3:21.

All around us, there are many different kinds of examples. What kind of an example are you? You are one, whether you want to be or not.

As parents, we are examples to our children. They see what we do and assume that it is right behavior even if we say it isn't. There is the saying, "Do as I say and not as I do." But this doesn't work. There is the other saying, "Monkey see. Monkey do." Children do as we do and not as we say. If our actions are different from our teaching, then that is teaching them that our words don't mean very much. We need to make sure that we are the right kind of examples for our children (Prov 22:6).

Both word and deed are important as examples, but they must back each other up. They must be consistent; otherwise, what is seen is hypocrisy. This is true, not only of parents with their children, but with all of us. We don't think very highly of a person that says one thing and does another.

The example that we need to follow is Jesus. He showed us what it means to please God. He showed us life as it is supposed to be—how to live as a human being. Let others see the love of God, which is in Christ Jesus, shining in and through your life by your example in word and deed. This was evident in Jesus's life. He lived what He taught. He embodied His teachings.

We need to set the right kind of examples. We need to live so people are attracted to Jesus and not repelled. All of us have heard the statement, "If that is what it means to be a Christian, then I don't want anything to do with it." This is truly sad.

As was said earlier, there are many examples in the world today. Especially, children want to imitate certain idols such as movie stars or music singers, but also they might imitate other youth. This makes it imperative that the Christian set the correct example. We are like a living letter. This is the only gospel that some people read. What are people reading when they look at you?

EXCUSES (Explaining)

Gen 3:12; Ex 3:1-18; 32:22-23; Deut 30:11-14; Mt 11:20-30; Mk 7:1-37; Lk 9:59-62; 14:18-20; Act 24:25; Rom 2:1; 7:7-25; Jas 1:1-27.

Making excuses is part of being human, but it does not make it right. We use it as a means to escape blame or to avoid responsibility. There are reasons for doing or not doing something. Reasons are legitimate.

Sometimes excuses are made to avoid serving God. Moses tried to use excuses to get out of the mission that God had for him—"I am a poor speaker"—but God did not accept them. We too make excuses of why we should not serve, but God does not accept those excuses either. Are you using excuses to try to avoid serving God or making the best use of your time, talents, money, and abilities?

In the same manner, we must not use excuses to avoid helping others. This is what we are called to do in the name of Christ. We are to minister to the needs of one another. We are to show love. We are to perform acts of mercy.

EXPECTATIONS (HOPES)

Deut 10:12-22; Mk 9:1-13; Jn 6:16-21; Rom 1:8-17.

What do you expect out of life? Some people think that life owes them. What do you expect of yourself? Examine yourself realistically. Check out your strengths and weaknesses, your goals. You have talents. You have time and opportunities. Make the most of them.

As a person seeks God, they can become frustrated in the attempt by trying various man-made ways. But He has told us what He expects. Micah 6:8 answers the question of what God expects of us, "To act justly and to love mercy and to walk humbly with your God." Then, in Matthew 22:37-39, it says to love the Lord thy God with all your heart, mind, soul, and strength, and to love your neighbor as yourself.

Sometimes we try to limit God by expecting Him to act in a certain way. God acts in His own way—just as Jesus as the Messiah was different to the Jews than what they were expecting. Because we believe in God, we need to have big expectations. We need to have big dreams. All things are possible with God (Mt 19:26).

EXPEDIENCY (Useful)
1 Cor 6:12; 8:8-13; 9:19-23; 10:23, 27-31.

The philosophy of some people is to do whatever is most expedient. Paul corrects this attitude in 1 Corinthians 6:12, where he states that not all things are beneficial, not all things are helpful. We must watch our actions lest they lead someone to sin, lest they be offensive. The key is to ask, is this thing helpful? Does this honor God?

FAILURE (Defeat, MISTAKES)
Josh 8:1-29; 1 Sam 10:22; Is 42:23; Mt 1:1-17; Lk 22:54-62.

We need to learn from our mistakes. Failure should keep us humble. It also can make us helpful because we can identify with others and encourage them when they make mistakes.

Our failures should remind us of our need for God and our need for others. Don't bemoan your failure, but *let it make you stronger*. Yes, some of our errors are foolish and stupid, and we may say, "Boy, am I stupid? I can't do anything right." The error may be foolish and stupid, but that doesn't mean that you are foolish and stupid, and it doesn't mean that you can't do anything right. Don't become bitter either. Lean on God. A mistake means that you are one step closer to the right answer because you have eliminated one wrong possibility. All scientific successes came after many failures. And in the end, the only real failure is to stop trying.

FAITH (BELIEF, CONFIDENCE, TRUST)
Gen 12:10; 15:6; 16:1-16; 50:24; Ex 14:1-31; Num 20:3-5; Deut 1:22; Josh 14:6-12; Jud 3:5-7; 6:25-30; 1 Sam 3:8-9; 2 K 4:6; 6:16-17; 7:1-10;

13:4-6; 19:31; 2 Ch 16:9; Est 4:16; Job 1:1, 9, 20-22; 2:10; Ps 5:11; 7:1; 11:1-4; 16:1-11; 18:1-3, 18; 25:1-5, 15, 20; 27:14; 33:18-22; 51:12; 64:10; 84:5, 12; 91:1-2; 119:125; 125:1; 144:2; Dan 3:16-18; Mt 3:1-17; 6:25-34; 9:22; 14:22-33; Mk 9:14-29; 11:22; Lk 8:48-50; 17:1-10; 24:1-12; Jn 11:25-27; Rom 5:1-11; 14:1-23; 1 Cor 4:1-21; Heb 10:19-39; 11:1-40; Jas 2:1, 18, 21-24; 5:20. (See a concordance for a complete reference on this topic)

What is faith? What is strong faith? What weakens faith?

To some, faith is a crutch and they would scoff at it. Yet these same people act on faith every day and don't even know it. They have faith in the physical laws of the universe. But just because they have been true in the past doesn't mean they will continue to be true. We just assume that they will. So don't tell me that you don't have faith.

Faith to others is a blind, wishful hope. That is not biblical faith. Faith is an intellectual assent to some proposition, but for the Christian it is much more than this. Yes, this intellectual assent is important, but real faith involves the total being. It is a *commitment* to God of your heart, mind, soul, and strength. It is a trust.

Sometimes we grow impatient with God and try to "help" Him fulfill His promises. This is true today and even true in the Bible. In Genesis 16:1-4, Abraham had been promised a son by God, but when his wife, Sarai, was barren, they did not think that promise could be kept without some "help"; therefore, she gave him Hagar, her servant, so that a son could be born. The result of this distrust, this lack of faith, is seen in the animosity between the descendants of the two sons of Abraham—between the Israelites and Arabs. When we take matters into our own hands, we cause problems that would not be there if we had simply trusted.

God acts in His own time and will not be forced. He will accomplish all that He says He will.

Faith is weakened when we listen to the wrong voices and begin to trust others instead of God. Sometimes, as has just been noted, our impatience can weaken our faith. Lack of knowledge of the Bible is a big source of weakened faith. We listen or read something that is supposedly scriptural but actually is a distortion of the truth.

In order for faith to be productive it must be more than words; it must be evidenced by a changed life.

Strong faith endures. The lion's den (as in the example of Daniel) and the fiery furnace (see Dan 3) are two examples of ones that risked their lives for their faith. This was the faith that dared to risk everything—even life itself. Many of us will not be called on to have to take that risk (but we must be willing to do so); however, there are many down through the ages that have, and even today there are many that have to die for their faith.

FALSEHOOD (Deceit, LYING)

Lev 19:11-12, 16; Job 27:4; 36:4; Ps 5:6-9; 10:7; 31:18; 34:13; 36:3; 50:19; 62:4; 63:11; 101:5-7; 109:2; 116:11; 120:2-4; 144:8-11; Prov 3:3; 6:12-19; 10:9-18, 31; 12:17-22; 17:4-7; Mt 6:12; 26:69-74; Jn 8:44-45; Act 5:1-9;1 Tim 4:2; 1 Pet 3:16; Rev 21:8.

Lies can begin in a seemingly harmless manner. There is the so-called white lie. A person might say, "I didn't lie; I just didn't tell everything." This is what is called a half-truth.

You put lies in their proper perspective when you remember that the devil is the father of lies. Thus, if you are telling lies, then you are following Satan.

Lies hurt relationships. They break trustworthiness. Trust has been violated. You don't trust someone who has lied to you. The person who lied did not have the trust in you to tell you the truth. If a non-Christian sees a Christian lie, then that hurts that person's testimony.

FAMILY (CHILDREN, HOME, PARENTS)

Gen 2:23-24; 18:19; 37:1-11; Ex 10:1-29; 34:1-35; Deut 6:1-25; 11:19-20; Josh 24:15; Prov 15:17; 19:13; 21:9, 19; Mt 12:46-50; Lk 2:41-52; Act 16:1-5; Rom 2:17-29; 1 Cor 17:10; 11:3, 7-9; Eph 3:14-21; 5:22-24; 6:1-4; Col 3:18; I Pet 3:1, 6.

There are many problems in a family. Favoritism can be very disruptive to family unity. The child that is in disfavor may go to all kinds of actions to try to win favor or might do disruptive acts since that is what he or she feels is expected from him or her. Favoritism can cause rebellion. The favored child may feel that too much is expected from him or her.

Sins of the parents can have consequences that are passed down through several generations. Alcoholism, abuse, and greed are just three examples of this. One consequence is that the child indulges in the same sin. An alcoholic child may stem from alcoholic parents. A child that is abused may become an abuser. Another consequence is the disruption in the home caused by the parent. Perhaps the parents get divorced, or maybe there is financial turmoil.

Anther problem in the family is work. One or both parents may work so much that the family is neglected. Supposedly, the work is done to provide for the family's needs when in reality it satisfies the ego of the worker. For the Christian, you must not neglect your family no matter how important your work is. Nor should you let materialism drive your home so that the family is neglected.

Parents, by word and deed, need to teach their children the principles of the faith. The effect of parental teaching is pointed out in this quote by an anonymous author, "What a parent says to a child is not heard by the world, but it will be heard by posterity." This is a sobering thought with much truth.

The children need to see the love of God at work in their parents' lives. It must be real, or the children will be soured on the faith and regard it as a mockery. God must be seen as important and vital to the life of the family. This means there must be a consistent living of the faith, and not just a talking of it.

In the family, each member is honored and is of value. There must be love and respect for one another. The parents are not to abuse their authority, and the children are to obey their parents out of love (Col 3:20-21).

In addition to our earthly family, we are part of a spiritual family. The church is part of this family. Hence, we regard all of the members as a family. We should have familial (of, or relating to a family) love and concern for one another. In a family we do not have to pretend to be something that we aren't.

Because of our faith, we share in God as our heavenly Father. As part of His family, we need to have a strong love for God and for one another. This family is eternal.

FASTING

2 Ch 20:1-30; Ezra 8:21-23; Dan 10:2-3; Joel 1:14; Zech 8:19; Mt 6:16-18; 9:14-15; Act 9:8; 27:9, 33-34.

Fasting is a spiritual discipline. Sometimes it is done in connection with prayer and sometimes it is in connection with repentance. Fasting helps a person with concentration. There are many different kinds. Sometimes it is a complete abstinence from food and water. Then sometimes there is just an abstinence from food.

FEAR (Afraid)

Gen 15:1-21; 21:7; 32:9-12; 46:3-4; Ex 2:7-8; 4:1; 14:10-11; 20:1-26; Deut 1:22; 2:25; 10:12-22; Josh 1:1-18; Jud 7:10-11; 1 Sam 14:6;1 Ch 11:12-14; 28:20; Neh 2:1-20; Job 28:28; Ps 25:1-22; 27:1; Prov 29:25; Mk 4:38-40; 6:49-50; Lk 9:24-25; 12:4-5; Jn 6:18-19; 7:13; 12:42-43; Act 5:17-18; 2 Tim 1:6-7.

There are many kinds of fears. One important fear is of God. This is appropriate. How can we not fear Him when we think of His majesty, of His power, of His justice?

Fearing God is recognizing Him as the Holy, Almighty, Righteous, All-knowing, and All-powerful God. He is the One with no beginning and no end.

But fear of God is not a terror of Him. He does not want us to follow Him out of fear but out of love for God is love (1 Jn 4:8). We are called to obey Him, to love Him.

There are many other things that we fear. What do *you* fear? Why do you fear it?

Some fears are healthy and are for our protection. For example, you fear wild animals and you fear them for good reason. You fear violating certain physical laws because you know you could be hurt or even killed. We should fear violating God's moral laws also, but many don't see any danger in that.

As we said, fear of God is appropriate, and so we must not let the fear of man prevent us from serving God. Some people are so concerned about what others will think or say that they become more interested in pleasing man than in pleasing God.

There are various irrational fears too such as fear of heights. You don't have to have this fear if you take sensible precautions. Walking a tightrope is dangerous. I don't have any more of a fear of heights than most people, but I don't plan to try to walk a tightrope. Fear of heights is good if it keeps you from taking foolish chances. Be sensible.

Please God and you will find the power to overcome all of your fears. Just place yourself in His hands. There is no greater power than God. If I am acting, doing, and thinking in keeping with the will of God, then I don't need to be concerned about others. He gives us the power to accomplish things that we could not accomplish on our own. Can't speak before a group of people? If God wants you to, then He will give you the courage to do it.

FEELINGS (EMOTIONS)

Job 6:1-7:21; Ezek 3:1-27; Jn 11:17-36; Rom 12:9-21; Gal 5:1-26.

We need to express our feelings honestly to God and to one another. Let your feelings be made known. To stifle your emotions is unhealthy and can cause all sorts of problems. Yet we should not be burdensome either and go around dumping our emotions on people. Balance is what is needed. Don't stifle your emotions but don't constantly impose them upon others. We, as Christians, need to care for one another just as God cares for us (1 Th 5:11). Repeatedly, we are told to have love for one another (see Gospel of John and epistles of John).

We need to act in spite of our feelings. Sometimes we do not feel like doing God's will, or helping others, or worshipping God, but we must do it anyway. If someone has hurt you, do not take your anger out on that person, but in love forgive and help that person. Emotions and feelings are important but they can also be very fickle.

FELLOWSHIP (FRIENDSHIP, Warmth)

Gen 3:1-24; Lev 26:12; Num 16:26; Ezra 10:11; Ps 1:1; Prov 1:10-15; 4:14-15; 9:6; 14:7; Mt 17:4; 18:17, 20; Mk 9:37; Lk 22:32; 24:32; Jn 6:53; 13:34; 14:20-23; 15:4-7, 12; 17:21-26; Act 1:14; 2:1, 42-46; 17:4; 20:13-38; Rom 1:12; 7:4; 8:1, 10, 17; 12:5; 15:1-7; 16:17; 1 Cor 12:12-13, 27; 2 Cor 6:14-17; 13:11; Gal 6:2; Eph 5:11; Phil 1:1-11; 2:1-2; Col 2:2; 3:16; 1 Th 4:18; 5:11, 14; 2 Th 3:6, 14-15; Heb 2:11; 3:13; 10:1-39; 1 Pet 3:8-9; 1 Jn 1:3-7; 3:6, 14, 24; 4:7-13; 5:12, 20; 2 Jn 1:9; Rev 3:20.

Fellowship is an abused word. What is it? It is certainly much more than a warm, fuzzy feeling. Biblical fellowship is a mutual sharing of the faith and of friendship. It is a bonding that is based upon the love of Christ.

God wants to have fellowship with us. That is why we were created. He wants us to share our thoughts, deeds, and actions with Him. Fellowship draws us together and strengthens us.

However, just as we are to have fellowship with other Christians, we are also to have it with nonbelievers also. We are to associate with them in matters that are necessary. We are to be concerned about them, but we can't have that same intimate bond with them because they do not know Christ. We do hope that they can be brought to the point where they do accept Christ as Lord and Savior. We have to be careful that any fellowship with them does not lead us away from Christ.

FLATTERY (Complimenting)

Job 32:21-22; Ps 12:1-8; 36:2; 78:36; Prov 5:3; 7:5, 21; 20:19; 26:28; 28:23; 29:5; Lk 6:26; 20:20-26; 1 Th 2:1-20.

There is danger to the flatterer and to the one being flattered. It is a deception and an attempt to manipulate another person. Thus, if you believe the flattery, then you could be led into sin. You can feel yourself more important than you are. Flattery is a distortion of the truth and hides the person's real motives.

When we give compliments, and we should, let it be based on the truth and given in love, not as a means to gain favor with another person and to get them to do what you want them to do.

FOLLOW (BELIEF, COMMITMENT)

Mt 4:18-22; 8:31-38; 16:21-28.

Following Christ involves a conscious, total commitment. This is a decision that affects your whole life. It is very costly. Perhaps you may even be called upon to give your life, as martyrs in the past have or that some do today, in order to follow Him. But yes, in any sense of the word, you must give your life in order to follow Him. Jesus gave His life for each of us, and we must carry our cross in order to follow Him (Lk 14:27).

There are many different voices that are calling us to follow them. We must only follow Jesus. There are other leaders that we must follow: government officials, law officials, but the test is, can we still follow Jesus?

FORGET (Remembering)

Ex 2:11-25; Neh 9:1-38; Ps 9:17; 44:17-20; 50:22; 78:7-10; 103:2; 119:153; Jer 2:1-37; Heb 10:1-18; 12:5.

Have you ever forgotten God? You might say no at first, but most people, with their busy schedules, certainly often act as if they have forgotten Him in the sense that He does not matter. It seems strange that we could forget such a marvelous God, but we do. We get too busy to pray to Him, read His word, and spend some quiet time with Him. If that is your case, then correct that as soon as possible.

Sometimes it is because we want to follow our own plans and desires. This can be intentional or unintentional, but either way it is dangerous. The lures and pressures of evil also make us forget God. And, in addition to all of these, sometimes we simply take God for granted.

God does not forget His promises. He is faithful to them. God forgets our sins in that He does not hold them against us when we have been forgiven.

We also need to forget the wrongs that others commit against us. We have heard, and maybe even said, the expression, "I'll forgive him, but I won't forget what he did." This is not forgiveness. To continue to carry the wrong in your mind is harmful to you and the other person. Sometimes we cannot forget the wrongs because the consequences of that wrong are still with you even though you have forgiven the person. The death of someone and a physical injury are two examples, but even with the reminder still there, do not harbor resentment. When you forgive, desire the best for that person.

FORGIVENESS (MERCY, Pardon)

Gen 8:21; 45:1-28; Ex 34:6-7; Num 14:18-20; 1 Ch 16:34; 30:9; Ps 25:6-8; 30:5; 32:1-5; 51:1-19; 85:2-3, 10; 86:5, 13-15; 103:3, 8-17; 145:8-9;

Prov 24:17, 29; 25:21-22; 28:13; Mt 5:7, 39-46; 6:5-15; 18:21-35; Mk 11:25; Lk 1:50; 6:35-37; 17:3-4; Jn 13:31-38; 20:19-31; Rom 10:12-13; 12:1-21; Eph 2:4-7; 4:32; 1 Pet 3:9; Tit 3:5; Heb 4:16; 1Jn 1:1-10.

We experience God's forgiveness by confessing our sins and repenting (I Jn 1:9). Our sins have been forgiven by Jesus's death on the Cross. He paid the price of sin, for as Romans 6:23 says, the wages of sin is death.

Confession means to admit that you are a sinner, that you need a Savior, and that you want to turn away from sin and to Him. It is a reestablishing your relationship with God. Sin broke that relationship, but by confessing your sin and accepting God's forgiveness, which comes through Jesus Christ, your relationship with God is established anew.

Forgiveness is a conscious decision. If we want to receive forgiveness, then we must forgive others (Mt 6:14-15). Those verses point out that if we want to receive forgiveness from God, then we must also forgive others. In Matthew 18:23-34 is an example of this principle. In the story, the master takes pity on one of his servants and forgives him of a large debt; however, that same servant does not forgive a fellow servant who owes him and demands payment and has him thrown in jail when he cannot pay. When the master learns of this, he calls him wicked and that he should have shown mercy just as it was shown to him, and since he didn't, he was cast in prison and his debt was no longer forgiven.

God has forgiven a very large debt to each of us; therefore, we can do no less. But it must be a complete forgiveness. God cancels our debt. We must cancel the debt of those who have wronged us by forgetting that wrong, as was mentioned in a previous section.

FOUL LANGUAGE

Eph 5:1-20; Col 4:2-6; 1 Tim 4:16.

Our speech is a sign of the character within. Would people be attracted to you if you used foul language? What would they think if you claimed to be a Christian and used foul language? You would be a poor advertisement. You would be dishonoring God.

Using a lot of foul language is a very bad habit. Some people curse almost constantly, and when their attention is called to it, they say, "Did I say that?" Sometimes swearing is a form of rebellion. Sometimes it is an expression of frustration or anger. Foul language is like black sooty smoke from a chimney or off an engine. It pollutes the surroundings. It irritates. It breaks relationships.

We honor God with our words, our deeds, and our actions. Let our whole life reflect God's love for us. Swearing is unnecessary. The next time that you hit your thumb with a hammer, if you are tempted to swear, do not swear.

Instead you can simply say, "Ow, "Ouch," or "That really hurts," because it probably does.

FREEDOM (RESPONSIBILITY)

Jn 8:30-47; Rom 5:12-21; Gal 5:1-26.

Real freedom comes from knowing Jesus Christ. It is freedom from the greatest bondage of all—sin. As John 8:36 says, *"If the Son sets you free then you are free indeed."*

Our freedom is not an excuse for us to do as we please, but rather it frees us to serve and to obey. It frees us to reach our fullest potential, for that is what God wants for each of us. Our freedom in Christ is also not at the expense of others; otherwise it is an abuse of freedom. Freedom in Christ is a breaking-down of the barriers between man and God.

We have many freedoms, and they should be exercised and protected when necessary. But all freedoms must not infringe upon those of others.

FRIENDSHIP (RELATIONSHIP)

Ex 33:7-11; Ps 41:9; 55:12-14; 88:8, 18; Prov 11:13; 17:1-28; 22:24-25; 25:17-19; 27:6-19; Jn 15:1-17.

What makes a good friend? Are you a good friend? Who are your friends?

Good friends are honest with each other. They are loyal. They can be trusted and counted on and will not let you down. A good friend is not just a friend when it is easy to be a friend or when it is to that person's benefit to be your friend. A good friend will tell you things that you don't want to hear sometimes. A good friend helps you and supports you, but will also correct you in a brotherly manner.

Of course, the best friend that we can have is Jesus Christ (Jn 15:14-15). He is the only friend that will never let you down, for even our best friends will let us down sometimes. Jesus has called us to be His friends even though He is our Lord and Master.

Let us show our friendship toward Him by our love for Him. For as was said in John 15:14, we show that we are His friends by keeping His commands. Friends do not do things that would hurt the other or that the other would disapprove of. Likewise, if we love Jesus, then we follow Him. And we show our love for others by extending genuine love and friendship to them.

FRUSTRATION (ANGER, HOPELESSNESS)

Ex 2:1-10; Job 10:1-22; Eph 6:1-4.

All of us get frustrated from time to time. In these times, we must not give up or give in, but always be obedient and true to God. Being obedient and true to God is the key for overcoming frustration. By relying upon God, then we are laying hold upon the strength that we need. Often we are frustrated because we are trying to do something on our own strength and with our own resources, but they are insufficient.

We should not make decisions while we are frustrated. They will probably be the wrong ones. It is also important that we not be the cause of frustrating someone else.

The next time you are frustrated, stop for a moment. Why are you frustrated? Is the plan in God's will? And if so, have you sought God's help to carry out this action? Have you planned properly and counted the cost?

FUTURE

Deut 29:1-29; Mic 4:1-13; Mk 13:1-37; Jn 21:15-25.

Through the scriptures, God has revealed the future. There are many details that we do not know, but He has given us what we need to know.

The future is in God's control. Our task is to obey Him and follow Him in the present instead of worrying about future dates.

As long as we trust in God, there is no need to fear the future. In fact, trust in Him teaches that there is a glorious future coming.

Now, it is true that we should not ignore the future. As good stewards, we should make plans now. For example, we are polluting this earth; therefore, we need to take the steps now so that this pollution is lessened instead of letting it go on at an increased rate. Another example is that a person saves some money for living expenses for when he or she gets older. Persons building strong houses to protect themselves from the elements is still another preparation for the future.

GENEROSITY (GIVING, Sharing)

Ex 35:4-36:7; Lev 19:1-37; Act 11:19-30.

Generosity means a cheerful giving. We are not to give begrudgingly (see 2 Cor 9:7), but cheerfully. God has freely given to us, so we should give in the same manner. After all, we are simply stewards. We are not the owners. In addition to giving cheerfully, we give to honor God and not in an attempt to make ourselves seem important, or make a name for ourselves.

GIFTS (Offerings, Talents)

Deut 33:1-29; Jud 14:1-20; Ps 34:10; 68:18, 35; 84:11; Prov 2:6; Ecc 2:26; Ezek 1:19; Dan 2:21-23; Mt 2:1-12; 11:28; Lk 19:11-27; Jn 3:16; 4:10; 6:27; 16:23-24; Rom 6:23; 8:32; 1 Cor 7:7; 12:4-11; Eph 4:7-8; 1 Tim 6:17; Jas 1:17; 2 Pet 1:3.

We need to receive the gifts that God has given to us gratefully. We need to use them to glorify God and not ourselves. Let us use the talents and abilities that we have been given and not be jealous of the talents of someone else.

Because of who God is, we need to give Him our best, to give Him our all. God also expects us to make use of the gifts that we have been given. We will have to give an accounting of what we have done with our gifts.

In addition to talents and abilities, there are different spiritual gifts: teaching, hospitality, speaking in tongues, etc. With spiritual gifts, as with the other gifts that we have been given, we are to use them for God's honor and to serve Him. We must not look down on other spiritual gifts for they are all important. We should also not judge people. For example, in Paul's time, speaking in tongues was an important gift, which was, and is, true. However, some of the believers felt that if some persons couldn't speak in tongues, then they were not true believers and that is the way some feel today. Paul pointed out that this was wrong (1 Cor 14:4).

GIVING (HELP, Sharing)

Ex 35:1-35; Ezra 2:64-70; Mt 6:1-4; 1 Cor 16:2; 2 Cor 8:1-15; 9:6.

We are to give generously. Give personally. Your giving should reflect your talents and abilities.

We need to give on a regular basis. It should be sacrificial and not just what is convenient or the leftovers. What are we giving? We are giving our time, talent, abilities, money, and our very selves. We are giving service and honor to God. This is why giving is so costly. And this is why it is sacrificial. What are you willing to give? What are you giving? Giving a tithe (one-tenth)? Yes, that might be fine for money, but certainly that is only the beginning. God demands a total giving.

In any financial giving, we must keep commitments in mind. There are demands upon our income: food, utilitiy bills, rent or mortgage, educational and work expenses to mention a few. Each person has to make up in his own mind how much he will give. The Bible does give the principle of giving a tithe, and this is something to strive for and surpass. We need to give in proportion to God's blessings.

GIVING UP (ABANDON, Quit)

Ps 13:1-6; Mt 9:18-26; 2 Cor 4:1-18; Phil 4:13.

All of us feel like giving up from time to time. Everyone has given up at some time or the other. And sometimes we need to give up. The project may not be in God's will. It may be a bad time for it. It may be costing too much in time, energy, and expense. Perhaps it was something that should not have been started in the first place. We need to talk to God and to others. We need to be honest. Talking to God and others can help us get the strength that we need.

We need to encourage one another so that people will realize that they are not alone. Let Paul's words in Philippians 4:13 strengthen you, "I can do all things in him (Christ) who strengthens me." Thus, if this power is available to you, how can you give up? How can you be defeated (Rom 8:31)? And further on, Paul writes, "No, in all these things we are more than conquerors through him that loved us" (Rom 8:37). Act upon that faith. Live by that faith. You will give up temporarily, but start afresh in the strength that Christ gives to you.

GOALS (Aims, Objectives)

Ex 13:17-22; Num 14:1-9; Rom 8:18-39; Phil 3:1-21.

We need goals. They give us direction and purpose. What are your goals? How do you determine your goals?

We need to seek God's direction in all the matters of our life because His way is the best.

We need to seek Him because He can help us to attain our goals and surpass them. At the same time, we need to make sure that our goals are in keeping with God's purposes. His goals should be our goals. In Micah 6:8, it says, "He has showed you, O man, what is good. And what does the Lord require of you? To act justly and to love mercy and to walk humbly with your God." Our goals need to be ones in which we are serving God and helping other people. There is nothing wrong with the goal of becoming a millionaire, provided that God and other people are served on your way to becoming a millionaire and after you become a millionaire, and also that you don't hurt people as you strive to obtain that goal. It is unfortunate that some wealthy people do not know what to do with their wealth, and they spend it in frivolous ways instead of helping others. I thank God for those that are wealthy and do use it to help others.

Our most important goal is to get to know Christ better. Get to know Him more and more each day.

GOD (see concordance for complete references on God)

CREATOR

Gen 1:1-31; 5:1-2; Ex 20:11; Ps 8:3; 19:1-4; 24:1-2; 100:3; 104:2-6, 24, 30; 146:5-6; 148:5-6; Ecc 12:1; Jer 27:5; Act 17:24-26; Rom 1:20; 1 Cor 8:6; Heb 11:1-3, 10.

God is the Creator. People can debate that and have different ideas about how the universe came into being. Was it seven twenty-four-hour days, or a longer period of time, or chance? But for the Christian, there is no debate that God is the Creator of all life and the heavens and the earth (Gen 1:1).

When we consider the magnitude of the universe, the vastness of outer space, the infinitesimal minuteness of inner space (the world of the atom), all the species of life, the mystery of life itself, the complexity of the human mind, and countless other things, it is beyond our comprehension. We try to grasp it and understand it but we really don't. For example, we measure the distance of the stars in light-years. A light-year is the distance that light travels in a year (light travels 186,000 miles/sec.) that is over five trillion miles. We use these big numbers, but we really do not comprehend them either. A trillion (a one with twelve zeroes after it)—all we really grasp is that it is a very big number. We express our awe in the words of the hymn, "How Great Thou Art." It shows the mightiness of our God. To the people that do not believe in God, I would just say that as far as I am concerned, it takes a whole lot more faith not to believe in God than it takes to believe in God.

More important than this is the fact that God created out of love. He chose to create. He created us because God is love (1 Jn 4:8). Only God can create. We can take the material that is here and make things—all kinds of things—out of it. We forge iron and make it into steel to erect tall buildings, but there is nothing that we can create. Only God can do that.

HEAVENLY FATHER
Gen 3:1-24; 6:1-22; 18:1-33; Num 14:1-45; 2 Sam 7:14; Ps 68:5; 89:26; Is 9:6; 64:8; Mt 3:17; 5:45; 6:4-9; 7:11; 11:25-27; 18:10-19; Lk 10:21-22; 23:46; Jn 4:21-23; 8:19-49;2 Cor 6:18; Eph 4:6; 1 Jn 2:1, 13, 22.

God is our Heavenly Father. We can hurt Him by disobeying just as our children can hurt us by disobeying. Sometimes we do not understand His will for us, but we need to strive to understand His will and obey it. He is a loving, forgiving Father. We need to think of Him as a loving Father. He is not some cloudy Other as some religions would portray Him or that impersonal Ground of All Being that is described in philosophy. Think of the traits of a very loving and caring Father: He protects, provides, and loves. We fear Him because of His greatness, but we are also invited to come to Him.

SAVIOR (see JESUS CHRIST)

LORD

Ex 3:1-22; Ps 36:1-12; Mt 6:9-15; Jn 3:1-36.

In the light of God's majesty, He is Lord. He expects us to serve Him. We need to serve Him in a humble manner and not as a doormat or with complaining. We are to serve with joy. Our service is in response to His great love that He has bestowed upon us. The giving of His Son to us was done out of love. As the words in the song "Amazing Love" says, "Amazing love, how can it be that my King should die for me?" We cannot grasp the depth of that love, but we don't have to. All we need to do is accept it and live in it.

We as humans do not like to have a lord, and that is why man sinned in the first place. Man wanted to be ruler over himself. But we can't be the ruler just as a little child can't do what he or she pleases. That child needs guidance. God is a loving Lord. We owe everything to Him, even life itself. God rules and protects His creation. He is in control.

OTHER ATTRIBUTES

There are many other attributes of God: His love, justice, mercy, omnipotence, omniscience, faithfulness, grace, and goodness, just to mention a few.

(Also see God in the Topic Section at the end of this book.)

GOD'S WILL (GUIDANCE)

Num 9:15-23; Est 4:10-17; Mt 21:18-22; Phil 2:1-30.

What is God's will? This is a question we need to answer for ourselves time and again. We know what it is in general. Micah 6:8 and Matthew 5:22:37-38 are two definitions of it. We are to love God completely and to love our neighbor. We need to keep this general principle in mind when we make decisions. It is a little more difficult when we try to apply this in specific cases. We are asking what it means to love God in this situation.

God guides His people not in a robotic manner where they have no choice. Instead He guides us as a loving Father. We have the will to obey or not to obey. We need to seek Him out to find His direction. Go to Him in prayer.

It is His will that we accept Him. He has shown us in Jesus Christ what we should be like. Jesus showed us what it is like to be a human being who is obedient to God, but Jesus also shows us what the Father is like. In John 14:9, when the disciples ask Him to show them the Father, Jesus tells them that anyone who has seen Him has seen the Father. Therefore to know Jesus is to know the Father. Thus it is God's will for us to know and follow Jesus.

God's will can be summed up as we mentioned above in the statement *"To love the Lord your God with all your heart, mind, soul and strength and love your neighbor as yourself"* (see Mt 22:37-39).

GOODNESS (RIGHT)

Gen 50:1-26; Job 1:1-22; Ps 8:4; 33:5; 34:8; 36:7; 52:1, 9; 86:5; 100:5; Lam 3:25; Mt 7:11; Jn 11:1-16; Rom 8:1-39; 11:22; Jas 1:5.

Jesus said that only God is good. Because He is good, God wants good for us. Let us remember His great goodness when our circumstances are bad.

In spite of the evil around us and the evil that we see, God is working out His purposes. For example, the evil in men's hearts crucified Jesus, but God took this terrible evil and used it for the salvation of the world. Evil thought it had triumphed, but God showed that He can overcome even the worst evil.

GOSSIP (Deception, LYING)

Ex 23:1-9; Lev 19:16; Ps 50:20; Prov 11:13; 20:19; 25:18-28; Ezek 22:9;2 Th 3:6-15.

Gossip is a bad habit. It is destructive and breaks down relationships. Do you like a gossip as a friend? I don't think so. Do you listen to or engage in gossip? Gossip can cause damage that is more lasting than a physical scar. It breaks relationships (Prov 16:28). Gossips reveal confidences (Prov 11:13) and reputations can be ruined.

Before we talk about others, there are some questions that we need to ask ourselves: Is what you are saying true? Is it helpful? Does it need to be said? If the answer to one or more of these is no, then don't say it.

Don't be a gossip. You don't want someone gossiping about you so show them the same consideration.

GOVERNMENT (Leaders)

Deut 16:18-22; 17:1-20; 1 Sam 8:1-22; Rom 13:1-14; Tit 3:1-8.

Whether they believe it, or accept it, or not, all those in authority are responsible to God. They also only have any authority that has been granted to them.

We have a responsibility to choose good leaders. I am thankful that I live in a country where each of us can vote to try to place the best persons in places of leadership. Many countries do not have that freedom. We have a responsibility to God and we have a responsibility to the state.

Individually and collectively, we need to make our desires known. There are many other voices that are making their needs known. As Christians, we must not sit by and let our freedoms be taken away.

GRACE (FORGIVENESS, MERCY)

Ex 20:24; Lev 26:11-12; Josh 1:5, 9; 2 Ch 15:2; Neh 9:1-38; Ps 18:19, 25; 25:14; 37:18, 23; 115:12-113; Prov 10:6, 22-24; 11:20, 27; 16:7; Act 10:35; Rom 2:1-16; 1 Cor 1:9; 2 Cor 10:18; Gal 4:6; Eph 1:3-2:10; Heb 4:16; 10:19, 22; 1 Jn 4:17-18; Rev 1:5-6.

What is grace? Grace is the unmerited love and mercy that God shows toward us. We were only saved because of grace. There was nothing that we could have done to merit our salvation. All of us were under the death penalty because of our sin, as has been said before, for "the wages of sin is death" (Rom 6:23).

Because of that grace, we need to rejoice in His mercy and serve others with full abandon. We serve not because we have earned that right—we haven't—but because of the love that has been shown to us. We are to show kindness to others as a gift just as God has shown His grace to us as a gift. Thus, we have no right whatsoever to mistreat or not love someone whom God has already accepted and loved.

GREATNESS (Fame)

Mt 23:1-12; Mk 10:35-45; Jn 1:19-34.

Everyone wants to feel needed, to be important. What does it mean to be important? Different people use different yardsticks. The world has certain standards: power, money, worldly possessions. Jesus gives a much-different standard for those who would be great in the kingdom of God.

True greatness does not concern itself with recognition. Instead, Jesus says, if we would be great, then we must be servants to all (see Mk 9:35). If we would be great, then we must serve others, and serve in a humble, loving fashion. In Mark 10:45, He says that the Son of Man did not come to be served but to serve. And John 13:5 is the story of Jesus washing His disciples' feet. This is hard to imagine. Jesus, who is the Son of God, is washing the feet of His disciples.

GREED (Coveting, JEALOUSY)

Deut 6:1-25; Num 16:1-22; Jas 4:1-17.

Sometimes greed is in the back of ambition. Other times, it accompanies prosperity. Greed is dissatisfaction with what you have, and you want more.

There is no problem with wanting all that you can have, but how are you going about getting more? Is it a consuming passion so that you can never get enough? Are you hurting others to satisfy that desire?

Regardless of how greed comes, we need to go to God in humility, relying upon Him. Let us recognize that our talents, abilities, and possessions are a gift from Him. Let us receive them with gratitude and use them to serve God and others and not feel that this is what we accomplished or is what we deserve.

GUIDANCE (Counsel, DIRECTION)

Ex 11:1-10; 13:1-22; Num 9:15-23;2 Ch 18:1-34; Ruth 2:1-23; Act 8:26-40.

We need God's guidance and should seek it. If we know how He guided in the past, then that can help us in decisions for today.

He leads us through everyday events. Look for His hand at work. We need to be open to His leading, and we must not be surprised if His direction is different from our plan. Be submissive to His guidance and go in the direction that God is telling you to go. God may shut a door to where you want to go, but if He does, then He will open a different one. If you seek His will, then plan to follow it.

Prayer and scripture reading are two ways of finding His guidance. We can also find His guidance by the wise counsel of other Christians.

GUILT (FEAR, SHAME, SORROW)

Gen 3:1-24; Jon 1:1-17; Rom 2:17-29; 3:21-31; 8:1-17; 1 Jn 3:11-24.

Why do you feel guilty? Giving in to temptation is one source of guilt. Letting others or ourselves down is still another. What can be worse is when we involve others in the sin that we commit. Sin is another source of guilt. Guilt is failing to do what God expects us to do.

We are all guilty of sin. Guilt is like wearing dirty clothes. We feel uncomfortable and unclean. Jesus is the answer to our guilt. He takes away sin, and we are no longer guilty, when we accept Him as Lord and Savior.

If you are feeling guilty because you lied or did a wrong to someone, then go to that person and confess and seek reconciliation with that person. Don't continue to carry the guilt, but strive to resolve it and get it out of your life. Learn from your guilt also.

HABITS (Customs, Patterns)

Num 33:50-56; Deut 12:1-32; 14:22-29; Mt 6:5-15; Lk 4:14-30; 1 Jn 3:1-24.

Bad habits need to be replaced with good ones. What good and bad habits do you have? Are you aware of them? Often they can become so ingrained that a person is not even aware them.

Rely upon God's direction and power to help you overcome your bad habits. Since it is a habit, it will not be easy to change. Also, if you don't see a need to change, then you won't.

We use various excuses for not changing. One of the first things we should ask ourselves is, "Is it pleasing to God?" Also, we need to ask if this makes us attractive to others, and does it attract or repel others from God? Too many people have been repelled from God by the bad habits that they see in some believers.

There are many important good habits that we need to start and cultivate. Tithing is one. Decide on a portion and dedicate it to God. Regular worship of God is another. Just going now and then makes it easy to stop going at all. Prayer and daily devotions are still more good ones. All of these habits need to be done with joy, love, and expectation. They should not be done as a matter of duty or as an ordeal.

Another important thing to remember about habits is that if you get rid of bad ones, then be sure to replace them with good ones. If you do not, you will be like the man in Luke 11:24-26; an unclean spirit was cast out and left him and then returned with seven more evil spirits, so the last state was worse than the first. Thus, if good ones do not replace bad ones, then the same or worse habits will fill the void.

Did you ever think why we have habits, both good and bad? Our minds are constantly at work. Our minds have to have something to work on. Occupy your mind with good things and good habits, so bad habits will not creep in as mentioned in the story above. It also helps with your mental and physical health.

HANDICAPPED (BARRIERS, LIMITATIONS, Impaired)

Lev 21:1-24; Mk 10:46-52; Jn 9:1-12.

Do you have a handicap? Do you feel that you have one? How do you view others that have handicaps—for example, people in wheelchairs? Many people resent this term and say physically challenged or some other such term; so if this word offends you, I apologize, but I like it in the sense that it is not glossing over something. To me it expresses a reality. It says what it is. This is something that has to be and can be overcome. A handicap is no fun. I have a daughter who has cerebral palsy and cannot walk. She also has lupus. She has been in a wheelchair all her life. She is handicapped (and that is what she calls it), but she doesn't let that get her down. She strives to be a blessing to others.

The Bible regards these people as restricted in certain ways that they can serve, but the person is accepted, and some surpass amazing physical restrictions to do some amazing things. The person is not inferior or second class. You don't have legs and can't run as fast as me? So what? There are plenty of people that are much faster than I am. We must not look down on these people and do not let them look down on themselves. Encourage them. Help them to use the abilities that they do have.

Jesus showed His compassion as He healed people that were afflicted: the blind, the deaf, the lame. He treats all people as having worth. The handicap was also an opportunity to show God's power.

Sometimes a person may wonder why they were not healed when they prayed to be healed. Some faith healers say that is because the person lacked faith. That is not true. The apostle Paul prayed for his thorn in the flesh (see 2 Cor 12:7) to be removed but it wasn't. That man certainly had faith. His prayer was answered, for 2 Corinthians 12:10 says, *"For when I am weak, then I am strong."* God gave him the grace to bear his "thorn." Sometimes God uses the handicap to accomplish great things. Don't bemoan that you are handicapped, but let God work in and through your life. If you're healed, wonderful! Praise God! If not, then be a shining light that points others toward Him. Your example might be the very thing that is needed to turn someone's life around. As is pointed out in chapter one of the book of Job, it is easy to obey God and follow when you are richly blessed and protected. Why wouldn't you thank God? But Satan puts forth the challenge to God and says, "Take away your protection and Job will curse you." Hardship befalls Job, but he does not curse God. Thus, if a handicapped person or any Christian, for that matter, can give thanks to God when things are going against them, then it shows that that person really trusts in the Lord.

HAPPINESS (JOY, OBEDIENCE)
Job 5:17; Ps 37:35-37; 40:8; 63:5; Ecc 1:1-18; Is 12:2-3; Mt 5:1-12; Rom 5:2; Phil 4:7; 1 Tim 6:3-10; 1 Pet 3:14.

What is happiness? What makes you happy? Are you happy?

Many people seek happiness in many different ways, but there is only one way that will truly satisfy. If we would be happy, then we must have a close relationship with God. He has made us to be restless until we find that peace that comes when we know Him; for knowing Christ is the true happiness that lasts forever.

Happiness is more than just a feeling. Jesus teaches that blessing goes beyond circumstances.

Circumstances and other people can rob us of earthly happiness, but that happiness is only temporary; it is transitory.

HARDHEARTEDNESS (Stubbornness, PRIDE)

Ex 11:1-10; Mk 8:10-21; Heb 3:7-19.

Hardheartedness is the result of stubborn unbelief and is a rejection of God. It is a persistent resistance to God. This hardheartedness is often the result of pride. A person is too proud to change their mind. The person may know that he or she is wrong, but refuses to change their mind, refuses to change their action. Hardheartedness can be prompted by other people also. They may say, "What will people say or think of you if you change your mind?"

HATRED (ANGER, Dislike)

Lev 19:17; Est 5:1-14; Ps 139:1-24; Prov 10:12; 15:17; Ecc 3:1-8; Jon 1:1-17; Mt 5:43-44; 6:15; 10:22; Jn 15:18-19, 23; Eph 4:31; 1 Jn 2:9-11; 3:10-15; 4:20.

Hatred can be a consuming passion. If the hatred is not resolved, it eats away at a person. As has been said earlier, you are to resolve this anger so that it does not eat away at you; resolve it quickly (see Eph 4:26). We are to hate evil, and to hate sin, but we need to separate the sinner from the sin. We hate the act, but the person needs to be shown love and forgiveness. This is not easy but it has to be done. We want the person to be redeemed, to be restored to relationship with God.

HEALING (HEALTH, Miracles)

Ex 15:26; 23:25; Lev 14:1-57; Deut 7:15; 2 K 20:5; 1 Ch 16:12-13; 2 Ch 30:20; Ps 30:2; 67:2; 91:3; 147:3; Is 19:22; 57:18; 58:8; Jer 8:22; 17:14; 30:17; 33:6; Hos 6:1-2; Mal 4:2; Mt 4:23-25; 8:2-3, 7, 10; 9:1-8, 20-22, 35; 10:1, 8; 11:5; 14:22-36; 15:1-20; 19:2; 20:33-34; Mk 5:41-43; Lk 4:18; 14:2-4; 22:51; Jn 5:8; Act 9:40; 14:8; Jas 5:14.

Healing is an important ministry. Jesus ministered to physical and spiritual needs. He restored people to wholeness.

This is the ministry of every Christian. We are to help people get the wholeness that they desperately need. This wholeness comes from knowing Jesus Christ. Sometimes there is a miracle of physical healing and sometimes there is not.

If you are seeking a healing, first of all seek Jesus. All healing comes from God. We are healed in a variety of manners. Sometimes doctors can give us medicine or treatments that produce healing, but they didn't heal you. They simply provided the means for you to be healed, and this is all than they can do. A faith healer does not heal you, but the power of God flows through that person so you are healed.

Still another important source is alternative medicine. Some people scoff at this. It is true that some of it is rubbish. However, there is much that is beneficial. We need to remember that God created our bodies. He created the plants. Our bodies have wonderful mechanisms to fight disease and to heal themselves if they are provided with the right materials. Often just plain plants and herbs have important healing material that the body needs because God created those plants and herbs. Medicine is often just an extract of an herb, but sometimes the extract doesn't do the job that the herb does in its natural state.

Many have undergone natural means for treating heart problems that made transplants unnecessary. There are noninvasive treatments for cancer that do not have the side effects of chemotherapy.

HEALTH (see HEALING)

HEART (FEELINGS, EMOTIONS)
1 Sam 16:1-13; Ps 51:1-19; Rom 6:1-23; 1 Jn 3:11-24.

In the Bible, the heart is more than just the physical organ; it represents the core of a person. God is concerned with our hearts. He does not look upon the outward appearance as man does. Jesus saw what was in the hearts of men (see Lk 9:47). God looks at what is in a person's heart.

Because of our sin, we want to please ourselves and so we must be cleansed. We are told to serve God with all of our heart (Mk 12:30). This means with our total being. Our commitment must be complete and not halfhearted. We are to pray with our whole heart also.

Matthew 6:21 declares that where your treasure is, there is your heart. This points out that the things we treasure, that are valuable to us, that we seek, are an indication of who we are. What do you treasure? If we treasure the things of this earth, then we are going to be greatly disappointed. All of these things will pass away. If we treasure a relationship with Jesus, a walk with Him, then we will be rich indeed. Where is your heart? May you be like the man in Matthew 13:46-47. He found a pearl of great value and sold everything that he had in order to possess it. This pearl is the kingdom of heaven. May you give everything to possess it. Give yourself.

HEAVEN (ETERNAL LIFE)

Gen 1:1; Deut 26:15; 1 Ch 16:31; 2 Ch 2:6; 30:27; Ps 2:4; 11:4; 19:1; 20:6; 24:3, 7; 33:13; 102:19; 103:19; 113:4; 123:1; Ecc 5:2; Is 33:17; 66:1; Jer 51:15; Lam 3:41; Mt 5:3, 8, 20, 34, 45; 6:20; 8:11; 10:32-33; 16:17; 18:10; 19:21; 22:23-33; 25:34; Lk 10:20; 12:32; 23:43; Jn 10:20; 12:26; 13:36; 14:1-14; Act 7:55; 2 Cor 5:1; Col 3:1-17; 1 Th 2:12; Heb 8:1; 10:34; 11:10, 16; 13:14; 1Pet 1:4; 2 Pet 3:13; Rev 3:21; 4:1-5:14; 21:1-3.

In the Bible, there is the reference to the firmament or the sky as the heavens. A glorious starry night does declare God's glory, but heaven is more than just the sky.

Jesus instructed that it is more important to be concerned about relationship with God than trying to picture heaven in any human terms. All of these descriptions such as "streets of gold," "pearly gates" and things of this sort pale in comparison to the actual beauty of heaven. We cannot imagine it. Describing the beauty of heaven is like a person with sight, trying to explain a beautiful sunset to a blind person who has been blind all of his or her life. No words are adequate to convey to that person the sight, and no words are adequate to convey the beauty of heaven to us who have not seen heaven.

Jesus says that He is going there to prepare a place for His followers so that they can be with Him (Jn 14:2).

It is important to have the proper perspective. Just as a person can be no earthly good because he or she is so heavenly minded, so also a person can be no heavenly good because he or she is so earthly minded. Balance is essential. Jesus, the Son of God, pointed the way to heaven, but He was concerned about people's immediate needs too.

HELL (Eternal Punishment)

Ps 9:17; Prov 5:5; 9:13-18; 15:24; 23:13; Is 33:14; Mt 5:29; 7:13; 8:12; 10:28; 16:18; 18:8-9; 22:13; 25:41-46; Mk 9:43-44; Lk 16:23-26; Rom 1:18-32; 2 Pet 2:4; Jude 1:6; Rev 20:1-15; 21:8.

Is there a hell? And if so, what is it? Many people do not believe there is a hell, but the Bible indicates that there is.

The Bible speaks of eternal punishment. This is eternal just as life for those who accept Jesus is eternal.

It is a matter of choice. Those who go to hell are the ones that have decided to reject God for whatever reason. They go there because they have decided to go there. They cannot blame anyone but themselves. God does not want anyone to go to hell (2 Pet 3:9).

Jesus died for each one of us. He died and was raised so that our sin could be forgiven and we might receive eternal life. But there are many who refuse to accept Him as Lord and Savior.

HELP (Assistance)

Gen 18:1-15; Neh 2:1-10; Ps 46:1-11; Ezek 3:16-27; Mt 1:18-25; Mk 9:38-41; Gal 6:1-10.

We need to come to God for His help in every area of our life. He will help us to recognize our need for Him. He will also help us in times of trouble.

We, as Christians, are to help one another (I Th 5:11, Gal 6:2). We are to meet human needs (Mt 25:35-36). We show this mercy to all people, not just to other believers. We give whatever help is needed: support, comfort, compassion, words, and action.

HOLINESS (RIGHTEOUSNESS)

Gen 17:1; Ex 19:1-25; 22:31; 39:30; Lev 20:26; Deut 14:2; 18:13; 28:9; Job 5:24; 28:28; 36:21; Ps 4:4; 24:3-5; 32:2; 93:1-5; 97:10; 119:1-3; Prov 11:23; Is 4:1-6; Mt 5:6-8, 48; Jn 4:14; 5:14; 6:35; 15:19; 17:1-26; Act 24:16; Rom 8:1; 11:16; 12:1-2; 1 Cor 3:16-17; 6:12-13; 10:21, 31; 6:14-17; 2 Cor 7:1; 10:3, 5; Gal 5:22-24; Eph 1:4; 2:21-22; Phil 4:8; Col 1:22;1 Th 3:13; 4:3-7; 5:5, 22-23; 2 Tim 2:19-22; Heb 12:1, 14-15; 1 Pet 1:14-25; 1 Jn 1:6-7; 2:1, 5, 29; 5:4-5, 18-21; 3 Jn 1:11.

God is a holy God. He is not like any other of the gods that have been worshiped. He is not *a* god, but *the* God. He alone is God. He is a God of mercy and justice, who cares for His people.

We are called to be holy (set apart) (see Eph 1:4 and Col 3:12) just as God is holy. We are holy because He has chosen us, and we have been made righteous through Jesus Christ (Rom 5:9). Our righteousness is what Jesus gave to us. He placed His righteousness upon us. Therefore, we are to show mercy and justice. We are to have a high moral standard. Serving God is what makes us holy. This holiness comes from obedience to God.

HOLY SPIRIT

Gen 6:3; Jud 3:7-11; Job 32:8; Ps 51:11-12; 139:7; Is 40:13; 42:1; 44:3-4; 61:1; 63:10-14; Ezek 36:27; Joel 2:28-29; Zech 4:6; 12:10; Mt 1:18; 3:11, 16-17; 4:1; 10:16-42; 12:28; 18:15-20; 28:19; Mk 1:9-13; Lk 1:15, 35, 67; 2:25-27; 11:13; 12:12; 24:49; Jn 3:1-21; 4:1-26; 14:15-31; 15:26; Act 2:4, 33, 38; 5:5; 7:51; 8:15-19; 9:1; 11:15-16, 24; 13:2; 14:17; 19:2-6; Gal 4:6;

5:16-18, 25; Eph 4:30; 6:17; 2 Tim 1:7, 14; Tit 3:5-6; Heb 2:4; 3:7;2 Pet 1:21; 1 Jn 2:20; 3:24.

Who is the Holy Spirit? The Holy Spirit is the third person of the Trinity. He is God living in and amongst His believers.

The Holy Spirit empowers believers. At Pentecost, it was the Holy Spirit that empowered the disciples to proclaim the gospel boldly, and many people believed (see Acts 2). This same Spirit empowers us today. He also guides us into the truth. He is called the Spirit of truth in John 16:13. Jesus said, "Then you will know the truth, and the truth will set you free" (Jn 8:32). We find this truth in the Holy Spirit when we allow Him to work in and through us. We read scripture, pray, worship, listen to others, and then listen for the Spirit to speak to us through all of these means.

The Spirit is present in times of trouble. He is present to all believers. Don't let someone tell you that you don't have the Spirit. If you truly believe in Jesus Christ, then the Spirit dwells in you. There are times that the Spirit comes in an extraordinary manner to aid in special tasks.

The Holy Spirit aids in worship. He is a transforming power from within. He works in every area of life. The Holy Spirit gives us peace. He is called the *Paraclete* (one who is called alongside us). He is an Advocate, a Counselor. We should welcome the Spirit in the same manner that we welcome God the Father and God the Son.

HOME (FAMILY)

Deut 6:1-25;1 Sam 3:1-4:1; Act 5:17-42; Eph 6:1-4.

Home is a place where the word of God is to be taught (Deut 11:19). It is a place of nurture. Homes can be very hectic and a place of strife, but let that not be the character of your home. Let it be a blessed place. We must make sure that the teaching of children is not neglected no matter how busy a person may be. This teaching should be the Christian principles in action. Word and deed must not conflict. Sometimes Christian leaders are so devoted to serving their church that their family is neglected. This is wrong and must be corrected.

There should be mutual service, love, and respect in the home. Character is built in the home. The child who has a loving father will better understand God as a loving Father.

Small Bible groups can be in the home as a means of building relationships and reaching out to other people. Is your home a positive place? Does it have a positive atmosphere? Are people affirmed?

HOMOSEXUALITY

Rom 1:18-32; I Cor 6:1-11; I Tim 1:1-11.

The Bible condemns the homosexual lifestyle (1 Cor 6:9). For the Christian, it is not an option. Homosexuality is not natural. We are made to be heterosexual.

However, just as God condemns homosexuality (although some liberals would say that it is the writers of the Bible who condemned it and not God), He offers forgiveness. He will forgive you. Seek His forgiveness and let His grace act in your life. We must be careful of living in sin and not repenting and not having any remorse over that sin—then there is the question if the person really believes in Jesus Christ.

We can ask what is wrong with it. A person may claim that he or she has a homosexual desire instead of a heterosexual one and that is just the way that he or she is. One might say that perhaps there might not be anything wrong with the propensity; however acting on that propensity is sinful. In the same manner, the heterosexual person to have a lustful mind and to commit lustful acts is wrong. In Matthew 5:28 Jesus indicates that the very thought of lusting is commiting adultery in the mind. Thus promiscuous sex between heterosexuals is wrong and sodomy (same sex intercourse, usually between two males) is wromg.

There is the claim today that people are born with homosexual inclinations. There are no definitive studies that support that a person is homosexual because of a genetic nature.

Another thing that bothers this writer is that it seems to me that some homosexuals, at least, want to force their lifestyle on everyone else. They will even say, "I think that person is gay, but they don't want to admit it." I do not care how you try to defend it. Whether you say it is behavioral, in the genes, or whatever, this lifestyle is not what we are meant to be. We are made and meant to be heterosexual.

HONESTY (TRUTH)

Lev 19:35; Deut 16:20; 25:13; Ps 15:5; 24:4; Prov 11:1; 16:11; 20:10; Is 33:15-16; Ezek 45:10; Mic 7:1-20; Mk 10:19; Lk 6:31; Act 24:16; 2Cor 4:1-2; 7:2; 8:21; Phil 4:8; 1Th 2:1-20; 4:11-12; Heb 13:18; Jas 5:1-12; 1 Pet 2:12

Honesty is important in building relationships. Honesty is essential in order to build trust.

Honesty is important for the preservation of any society even though people may want to act selfishly and be dishonest. There has to be honesty so government, commerce, etc., can be conducted. Would you trade or do business with a dishonest person? Would you want a dishonest person to build your home? When we're doing business, we want to feel that we are not being cheated. We want good quality and legitimate merchandise and not cheap imitation stuff. We want the prices to be fair. If someone is doing work for us, then we want the work to be done properly and not with the use of shoddy materials as a shortcut.

There needs to be honesty in the home. The various members of the home need to feel that they are being treated in an honest and fair manner. Honesty is instilled in our children by the parents demonstrating honesty. Be honest in love and do not hurt. There is such a thing as being brutally honest. These people pride themselves on expressing honest feelings and do not care who they hurt. If you *have to* (because sometimes we do*)* express an honest opinion that would hurt someone, then do so as gently as possible and with love. This is possible, although sometimes it is difficult, because you separate the person from the act.

HONOR (REPUTATION)

Ex 20:1-26; Ezra 7:11-26; Rom 12:1-21.

What is honor? How do you get it?

As Christians, we must give honor to God. God, in His mercy, honors those who honor Him.

Honor is given for various reasons. Sometimes it is given to get something from the person being honored. For example, a worker may be honored in order to get more work out of him or her because now more is expected. Or a wealthy person may be honored so that he or she will contribute to a cause. There are honors that are given for heroic acts. There are scholastic and humanitarian honors.

God's way involves love. We need to love one another because we are created in God's image. Each Christian has an important part, an important contribution to God's church. Paul says, "Let us outdo one another in showing honor" (Rom 12:10).

We are asked to honor our parents. This means to follow their teaching and example of putting God first. Listen to them and obey them, unless obedience would be contrary to God's direction. We show honor to God by obeying Him, keeping His commandments, returning His love, and giving that love to others. In the song "Amazing Love," it says, "In all I do I will honor you." Therefore, let us think and act in a manner that is pleasing to God and then we will honor God.

HOPE (CONFIDENCE, TRUST, FAITH)

Lev 26:1-46; Ps 31:24; 33:18, 22; 38:15; 39:7; 43:5; 71:5, 14; 146:5; Prov 10:28; 13:12; 14:32; Jer 17:7; Lam 3:21-26; Mk 5:21-43; Act 23:6; 24:14-15; 26:7; Rom 5:1-11; 8:24-25; 12:12; 15:4, 13; 1Cor 13:13; 15:19; 1 Th 4:13-18; 2 Th 2:16; 1Tim 1:1; Tit 1:2; 2:13; 3:7; Heb 11:1; 1 Pet 1:3, 21; 3:15.

Our hope is based on God's faithfulness. It comes from trusting Christ. It comes from remembering all that God has done for us. It is based upon the resurrection. If your hope is built on anything else, then it is a false hope. That hope is like the house built on sand in Jesus's parable in Matthew 7:26. When the storms came, it fell. If your hope is built on Jesus, then it is a house built on rock and will withstand the strongest storm.

HOPELESSNESS (DISCOURAGEMENT)

Job 1:1-22; Ps 69:1-36; Is 22:1-5.

All of us feel hopeless sometimes from time to time, but we don't have to let that feeling remain and overcome us. We need to remember that we live in a sinful world, so there is evil and injustice all around us. God is in control. He rules. He reigns. Jesus reminds His disciples, in John 16:33, that the world will give them lots of trouble, but that He has overcome the world.

In our moments of hopelessness, let us turn these times into times in which we place our whole trust in God. We might pray a prayer, something like, "Lord, I'm really down right now. Everything seems to be going against me and I don't know where to turn. But I come and place myself in your hands and ask you to deliver me from this hopelessness. Refresh my spirit. Restore my soul." Trust God and He will deliver you. Turn to Him instead of away from Him. Trust in His promises.

In Dante's poem *Inferno,* above the portal of hell is written these words: "Abandon all hope ye who enter here." That is chilling, but true. Hell is hopelessness—eternal hopelessness.

HOSPITALITY (KINDNESS)

Gen 18:1-33; Ex 22:21; 23:9; Lev 19:10, 33-34; 24:22; Deut 10:18; 27:19; Mt 22:2-3, 8-10; 25:34-35; Lk 10:1-16, 38-42; 14:12-14; Rom 12:9-21; 16:1-2; 1 Tim 3:2; 5:10; Heb 13:2; 1 Pet 4:9.

Hospitality is one way to serve God. It is one of the spiritual gifts, and an important one at that. We should not be too proud to accept hospitality. It is one way that another can exercise their generosity. Hospitality should be given out of a wholehearted devotion to God. It is not done for show or reward but for love.

Let me give you an example of hospitality that was done for my wife and me. We have a multihandicapped daughter. She became very ill and was taken to the hospital. Later it was discovered that she had developed lupus and had fluid around her heart and lungs. She was very sick, and we almost lost her. We had just bought a house in Crystal Lake but had not completely moved in, so we were commuting from Chicago or Crystal Lake each day to St. Anthony's Hospital in Rockford, Illinois, so we could be with our daughter. This became too much, so we stayed in a motel for a week, but we couldn't afford that either. Then a lady, who lives close to Rockford and who knows my youngest son, opened her home to us when she learned of our problem, and we were able to stay there at night and visit our daughter during the day. That was truly a blessing. This was an answer to prayer.

HUMANNESS (Persons, IMAGE)

Gen 1:26-27; 2:7; Job 33:4; Ps 8:5-8; 139:14; Is 64:8; Mt 4:1-11; Rom 6:1-14; 2 Cor 4:1-18; Phil 2:5-11; Col 2:6-23.

Jesus became human in order to destroy the power of death. The resurrection gives us hope. He demonstrated that temptation can be resisted.

Jesus experienced all the limitations and temptations of being human, but He did not sin. Because of His humanity, He revealed God in a fuller way than He had ever been revealed. He was God in the flesh.

God has entrusted the news of salvation to humans. Through Jesus, we are given a new nature. And through Him we can have fellowship with God. We have been given the power to become children of God when we receive Him (Jn 1:12).

As humans, we are created beings created in God's image (see Image). We have sinned, and thus fallen short of our potential. However, there are no second-class humans. A person is not inferior because of race, color, or sex.

Jesus revealed to us what God is like. But He also revealed what it truly means to be a human being.

That leads us to the question of what it really means to be human. A human is more than an animal. We have animal instincts, that is true; and too often we act on this level, satisfying our basic desires. But as long as you are on that level, you are not really human, but an animal.

To be human, we have to live on a higher plane than this. We have to satisfy the basic instincts of life, that is true, but we have to move to our higher desires. That is what makes us human. God wants us to strive to develop ourselves as fully as we can. We do that by learning and growing because of our learning.

One basic need that we as humans have is the need for love. We have to have it as surely as we need food and drink. It has been demonstrated that babies that are deprived of love will die. Our love is conditional, so we need to develop it to a higher level. A conditional love has conditions: I love you because you make me feel good, you're fun to be around, etc. Our love is also very changeable because it is based on feelings that change from one moment to another. A love that is less conditional is that of a parent for his or her child. In Christ we see the kind of love that we are to strive for in our lives. God's love of us is unconditional. He gave His Son as a result of His love. We separated ourselves from God, but He took the steps to mend that separation (Jn 3:16). We are to accept that love and grow in it and show it to others. We are to follow Jesus's example. He has shown us how to live. Colossians 3:2 says, "Set your minds on things above, not on earthly things." Then in Philippians 4:8, it says to think on those things that are true, good, noble, right, pure, lovely, admirable, and praiseworthy. Scripture is calling us to excel. It is calling us to be like God, for we were created in His image, but not to take His place because we can't. We are to emulate Christ. That is what it means to be a human being.

HUMILIATION (Dishonor)

Ezek 7:1-27; Lk 15:11-32; Heb 13:11-16.

Humiliation can be a way that pride is overcome and be an opportunity for repentance. Humiliation shows you that you are not as great as you thought you were. It can be the result of serving Jesus. People will mock you as you try to serve God. Remember, they mocked our Savior and did humiliating things to Him, but He was *never humiliated*. To be humiliated, you have to accept what is said or what is done to you.

Learn from it. If you are humiliated, then turn from your pride and repent. If someone tries to humiliate you as a result of your serving God, then stand firm and rejoice that you are serving Him. Pray for those that would humiliate you. Do not humiliate someone else either.

HUMILITY (Modesty)

Josh 7:1-26; 2 K 5:1-19; Ps 8:1-9; Lk 14:1-14.

Humility or being humble doesn't mean being a doormat. It is the proper attitude toward God. It helps us to rely upon Him instead of our own strength.

It can be training for obedience. It challenges our pride. Humility is a sense of unworthiness, not of worthlessness. It is the proper motive for service. We do not serve for recognition but out of love.

Our model for humility is Jesus Christ, and Christ was a real man. He is really the only one truly entitled to be called a man's man. To be humble in the true sense is to be like Christ. In John 5:19, we see Christ's humility. He says the Son can only do those things that He sees the Father doing. What the Father does, the Son does.

HUSBANDS (MARRIAGE, FAMILY)

Eph 5:21-33; I Pet 3:1-7.

In Christ, all our relationships are transformed. They can't be based upon old standards. Christ is the standard. As a husband, you are to love and honor your wife and you are both to submit to one another. It is a tragedy how some husbands dominate their wives. This is not what the Bible teaches.

The husband should be the spiritual leader in the home. However, a spiritual leader is not a tyrant. Jesus gave us the model. Leadership is based upon service. Just as Jesus, who is Lord, demonstrated the service of a slave when He washed His disciples' feet in John 13:5, so the husband must be willing to show service to his wife.

The husband is to love his wife and family. Because of his love for his wife, the husband must share hopes, goals, and needs with his wife. This is a mutual sharing.

A husband does not regard his wife as property or a servant. She is not to work full-time outside the home and then full-time in the home. If it is necessary for the wife to work outside the home, then there should be a sharing of the responsibility.

HYPOCRISY (Deception, Fraud)

Job 15:31-34; 17:8; 20:4; 27:8-10; 31:33-34; Ps 101:7; Prov 14:8; 20:14; 23:6-7; 25:19; Is 9:17; 10:6; Jer 7:4-10; 9:4, 8; 17:9; Mt 5:21-26; 6:1-5, 16, 24; 7:5; 15:7-8; 23:1-39; 24:50; Mk 12:38-40; Lk 11:39; 18:11-12; 1 Cor 13:1; Gal 6:3; 2 Tim 3:5, 13; Tit 1:16; 1 Jn 1:6, 10; 2:4, 9; 4:20.

Hypocrisy is damaging to the church. There is nothing that turns people off and away from the Christian faith more than phoniness. This is true of individuals too, for just as there is nothing more attractive than a real Christian, so also there is nothing as ugly or unattractive as a phony or "plastic Christian." Hypocrisy can lead to self-deception so that a person feels that he or she is better than other people and he or she may even resent others. Pretending to follow Christ is hypocrisy. The statement "Church is just a bunch of hypocrites" is hypocrisy also, for the persons saying it are saying they are better than those people in the church.

What is hypocrisy? Hypocrisy is acting. It is doing, being, thinking, or acting other than what you truly believe. You are simply pretending. Giving for the wrong motives is hypocrisy. If a person gives in order to gain recognition instead of out of love and service, but claims to be giving out of love and service, that is hypocrisy. In Jesus's times, often there would be those who would pray out loud while standing in public places, just for the attention instead of humbly seeking God. Jesus called them hypocrites, and they have their reward. In Matthew 6, he mentions several examples of hypocrisy.

Hypocrisy is following a set of rules instead of the heart of faith. It is outward conformity without the inner reality. It is acting. It is imitation. Jesus, in Matthew 23, has some very harsh remarks about some of the religious leaders of His day and calls them hypocrites. Jesus tells the people to obey what they say, but do not do what they are doing, for they do not practice what they preach. In Matthew 23:37, He says that they are like *"whitewashed tombs pleasing on the outside but inside is rotting flesh and dead bones."* He made these strong remarks because with all of their man-made rules, they were leading people away from God.

IDLENESS (see LAZINESS)

IDOLATRY

Gen 35:1-15; Ex 20:3-6; Ex 23:13; 32:1-35; Lev 19:4; Deut 27:15; Ps 97:7; 115:4-5, 8; Is 42:17; Jer 10:11, 15; Act 17:16; 1 Cor 8:4; 10:14; Rom 1:18-32; 1 Jn 5:21; Rev 21:8.

There are many different forms of idolatry, and a person can be engaged in them and not even know it. What is important to you? What do you spend your time and energy pursuing? For some, it is money. Some people will do anything for money, and they can never get enough of it. For others, it is power and seeking pleasure, and still for others, it is material possessions. These things are not bad in themselves; however, when they take the place of God in our life, then they become bad. Idolatry is worshipping, pursuing, or serving anything in the place of the Living God. If money or anything else becomes more important to you than God, then that thing has become your idol.

God Himself becomes an idol when you try to use Him for your own purposes and try to manipulate Him. You are worshipping a false god; you are not worshipping the Living God. God cannot be manipulated. He will not allow you to use Him for your purposes.

IGNORANCE (KNOWLEDGE)

Job 28:12-13, 20; 38:1-41:34; Ps 139:6; Prov 7:6-10; 20:24; 22:3; 27:1; Ecc 7:23-24; 8:6-7, 17; Jer 10:23; Mal 2:1-9; Mt 27:11-26; Lk 23:34; Jn 13:7; Act 1:7; 3:14-17; 17:23;1 Cor 2:7-8; 3:19; 13:9, 12; Jas 1:5-6.

Our knowledge of God is very limited and incomplete because of the very nature of God. We are finite creatures and He is the Almighty, the All-Powerful, and the All-Knowing God of the universe. Language to describe Him or to try to comprehend Him is inadequate. Our ignorance or what we don't know about God should simply be a basis for trusting Him. Let us begin with what we do know about Him and go as far as we can with that knowledge and then trust Him. There is one thing that we do know about Him, and that is that we can trust Him. He is always faithful (Deut 7:9).

We need to read His word so we can learn more about Him. In scripture God speaks to us. As we trust and walk with Him, we learn more about Him. Ignorance must not be used as an excuse but as a challenge to gain more information. This is true of any subject. Learn more about God and learn more about anything else in which you are ignorant. There is no excuse for ignorance. Learn. Study. Inquire.

IMAGE (CREATION, HUMANNESS)

Gen 1:1-31; 9:1-7; Mk 12:13-17.

We are made in God's image. There may be disagreement about how God created us, but God did create us. He breathed into us the breath of life (Gen 1:26, 27; 2:7). It is important to have this point in your theory of creation, whatever that theory may be, for this indicates an important relationship between God and Man. We are different from all of His other creations. It signifies a special act in the creation process. The fact that we are created in His image means that we share certain characteristics with our Creator: love, reason, creativity, a self. God is spirit (Jn 4:24) but He does have a spiritual body. The Hebrew word for image is *tselem*. This word is used over and over in the Old Testament to refer to a likeness. For example, it says in Genesis 5:3 that Adam had a son born after his own image *(tselem)*. This image is not questioned to mean a physical likeness. The use of this word in this sense seems to imply that it also has to apply to God. God has a form. Jesus is speaking in John 5:37 and says that they have not heard the voice of God or seen His form. Thus, God does have an audible voice and a form that can be seen. Matthew 22:20, Jesus answers some Jews who were trying to trap Him. He asks whose image is on the coin. They say Caesar. He says give to

Caesar what is Caesar's and to God what is God's. This idea of image gives the sense of ownership. The fact that we are made in God's image means that we belong to Him.

In the New Testament, the Greek word for image is *icon*. *Icon* not only means image or likeness, but it also means drawn from the original and serving as a prototype. As we have said, God is Spirit, and at present He is not seen by us but 1 Corinthians 13:12 says, "Now we see but a poor reflection as in a mirror; then we shall see face to face. Now I know in part; then I shall know fully, even as I am fully known."

The fact that God created us gives us a sense of self-worth. Male and female were created in His image. Thus, each person is important. One sex is not inferior to another.

This idea of the image affects our relationships. All people are made in His image. We need to show respect for one another. All of us belong to God.

IMMORALITY (SIN)

Gen 5:24; Jud 3:10-11; Ps 16:10-11; 21:4; 22:26; 23:6; 31:5; 37:18; 86:12; 133:3; Ecc 12:7; Mt 10:28; 16:26; 19:16; 25:46; Mk 10:30; Jn 6:39; 10:28; 11:25-26; 14:19; Rom 6:22-23; 1 Cor 6:1-20; 1 Th 4:13-18; 1 Tim 4:8; 2 Tim 1:9-10; Tit 1:2; Heb 11:5; 1 Pet 1:3-5; Rev 9:13-21; 22:5.

Immorality can begin with a small compromise. That compromise can make immorality spread in wider and wider circles in your life. This is just like the ripples on a pond.

After we accept Jesus, we should not continue in the immoral practices that we committed before we knew Him. If we accept Him there should be a change in our life. Do not let immorality take root in your life.

IMPATIENCE (see PATIENCE)

IMPORTANT (VALUE)

Ps 62:1-12; Mal 2:1-9.

What is important to you? We need to look at God's standard. The things that God considers as important are important. When we are determining what is important, we need to keep His will and purpose in mind. Are the things that we consider important the same as God's?

The Bible is a record of what is important to God. He is speaking, working, and guiding people in the direction that they should be going.

We show what is important to us by what we say and think and do. How you use your time is another indication. Matthew 6:21 indicates that where your treasure is, that is where your heart is. Our "treasure" is that which is really important to us.

IMPULSIVENESS (Rash)

Gen 25:19-34; Jud 14:1-20; Mt 14:22-33.

Impulsiveness does not take the consequences of an action into account; the impulsive person simply runs right ahead. It can stem from self-centeredness, "This is what I want, and I want it right now." The rash person is harmful to himself and to others because the act and the results of the action can have far-reaching consequences.

Let us think before we act or say something. Is the act selfish? Is the word harmful? Are we doing it to satisfy some selfish desire? Or are we reacting out of anger? Is our action and speech in keeping with God's will? Have we weighed the consequences? Seek God's guidance.

INADEQUACY (Inability)

Gen 50:22-26; Ex 3:1-22; Mt 14:13-21; Phil 4:13.

We all feel inadequate sometimes. This should not be used as an excuse to refuse to do God's will. Moses tried to do this when he was called to free the Israelites from Egypt, but God didn't accept the excuse. God is able to take our weaknesses and work through them to accomplish His purposes. God prefers it when we feel inadequate because then the task is being done in God's strength instead of the person's strength. In 2 Corinthians 12:10, Paul asserts that when he is weak, that is when he is strong. With God's strength we are more than able to accomplish the task we are given. Rom 8:37 says that "we are more than conquerors". Again, Philippians 4:13 says, "I can do all things in Him (Jesus Christ) who strengthens me."

Don't feel inadequate. Trust in God's power. If He has called you to do something, then He will enable you to do it.

INCARNATION (see JESUS CHRIST)

INCONSISTENCY (CONSISTENCY, Wavering)

Mt 7:3-5; 23:3-4; Rom 2:1, 21-33

Consistency is an important trait. Jesus condemned the Pharisees for their inconsistencies—*straining out a gnat and swallowing a camel* (see Mt 23:24). Make sure your deeds and actions go together and do not conflict with each other. Inconsistency ruins a person's testimony. They say one thing and do something else. There is the old saying that goes, "Your actions speak so loudly that I can't hear what you are saying."

INDECISION (see DECISION)

INDEPENDENCE (FREEDOM)
Jud 17:1-13; Lk 2:41-52; Eph 4:11-16.
Independence is important, but it does have its limits. One important limit is God's commands. We must exercise our independence within His commands. We are not free to do as we like.

Another important limitation is the rights of other people. Our independence must not be at the expense of someone else's rights. Unfortunately, this is not always practiced. Some people don't care if they are hurting or infringing upon other people. Smoking is one example. I have the right to breathe fresh air, but a smoker thinks he has the right to pollute the air. Smoking is a habit that you can't keep to yourself unless you are in a room by yourself. Drinking is another example. "I'm of legal age. I can drink as much as I want to." Then that same person gets in a car and kills or injures someone because of their drunkenness.

As our children grow to maturity, they must be given independence to become mature adults who can learn and develop their interests and abilities. They must not be allowed to do anything that they please because they will be going into a world that does have restrictions. Give them the needed guidelines so that they grow into mature responsible adults (Prov 22:6).

INDIFFERENCE (DESPAIR, Insensitivity)
Mk 15:21-32; Rom 13:1-14; Rev 3:14-22.
Often people are indifferent to other people. "I don't want to get involved. It's none of my business." Have you ever been indifferent? Why?

There are certain things that we cannot be indifferent to. Whether or not you like it, you cannot be indifferent to Christ's sacrifice for us. Christ died for our sins. This is the supreme example of love. As long as you are indifferent to this sacrifice, to this great love, then you are dead in your sins. Can you afford to be indifferent?

As Christians, we are called to be involved in the needs of others. Just as Jesus was concerned about us, we need to be concerned about others. The parable of the Good Samaritan in Luke 10:25-36 illustrates that we are to help others. In the story, we see some were indifferent to the man's need and passed by on the other side. But the Samaritan stopped and gave the man aid and saw that he received further aid until he was healed.

We cannot be indifferent to our faith in Jesus Christ. In the Book of Revelation, there is a scathing denunciation of the Church in Laodicea. The problem of this church is it is lukewarm, neither hot nor cold. This type of faith turns others away. We must have a firm faith. You cannot pretend. You cannot be a hypocrite.

INDUSTRY (see WORK)

INFIDELITY

Ex 5:2; 14:11; 17:7; 2 Ch 36:16; Job 15:25-26; 21:14-15; 35:3; Ps 1:1; 10:11-13; 12:3-4; 14:1, 6; 42:3; 50:21; 59:7; 64:5; Prov 1:22; Dan 3:15; Zeph 1:12; Mal 1:7; Mt 12:24; 27:39-44; Lk 19:14, 27; Act 23:8; Rom 9:20-21; Heb 10:29; 2 Pet 3:3-4.

There are different kinds of unfaithfulness. It begins with doubt. When you doubt God, let it be the beginning of a search for truth. God is truth, so any legitimate search for truth will bring you closer to God instead of leading you away from Him. But if doubt is simply an excuse to forsake Him, then it is evil. Be true to God. He demonstrates His faithfulness.

Be faithful to your spouse and your friends. Trust is built and grows when there is faithfulness and loyalty.

Unfortunately too many times a small problem causes a man and his wife to start to drift apart, and one or both look to someone else to fill the void that they are experiencing. Do not drift apart. As soon as you start to move in that direction, seek God. Talk to one another and mend the relationship.

INFLUENCE (POWER)

2 K 15:1-12; Prov 22:24; 29:12; Hos 4:9; Mt 5:14-16; Mk 4:21-22; Lk 11:33; 12:1; Rom 1:18-32; 1 Cor 5:6-7; Heb 12:15; 1 Pet 2:11-12.

Who and what influences your life? Whom do you influence? What kind of an influence are you?

Christ is the model that we must follow. We are to let His words and life be our example. We are to be influenced by Him. We are to have "the mind of Christ" 1 Cor 2:16).

We are called to be the best examples that we can be. We are to show good works; we are to be a light (Mt 5:16). Let us pray that when people look at us, they will see Christ at work in and through us and be drawn to Him. We need to study the scriptures to get the principles that we need to live by.

There are many bad influences in the world. That is why it is important as Christians, as parents, and as citizens that we set good examples.

INJUSTICE (DISHONESTY)
Deut 16:18-20; Hab 1:1-17; Mt 5:38-48.

God is a just God. If we follow Him, then we must practice justice. When we see injustice, we must not feel that God does not care or that He has forgotten His commandments. God does care, and He has not forgotten His commandments. God is a patient God and is granting time for repentance. We must take action to speak out against injustice, but we do not attack injustice with hate. We attack it with God's redeeming love.

More than one nation has experienced the consequences of forsaking justice. Injustice may reign temporarily but it will be defeated.

In the Book of Acts is a significant account. The disciples were ordered to stop preaching Jesus, but as soon as they got out of jail, they continued to preach about Jesus. When the Jewish leaders asked why they had defied them, Peter and the other apostles said, "We must obey God rather than men" (Acts 5:29). The Pharisees were furious with them, but a Jewish teacher of the Law, Gamaliel, gives some wise counsel. He cites some earlier examples of men arising and having followers. These men were killed and nothing came of their movement. He states in Acts 5:38-39, "If their purpose or activity is of human origin, it will fail. But if it is from God, you will not be able to stop these men; you will only find yourselves fighting against God."

INSECURITY (see SECURITY)

INSENSITIVITY (Unfeeling)
Ps 5:1-12; Mt 15:21-28; 23:37-39.

Are you sensitive to the needs of others? Are you concerned about other people? Are you sensitive to God's direction for your life? Are you so sensitive that you get your feelings hurt?

We are called to be sensitive to sin, to needs, to God's presence and action. Insensitivity can cut us off from all of this. Insensitivity is hardheartedness, indifference, and complacency.

INSULTS (Slander)
Jud 1:1-7; Prov 12:1-28; Jn 2:13-23.

Insults make us angry. But do not respond to evil with evil. Don't return insult for insult. This simply makes the matter worse. We are called to return good for evil. Jesus, when He was led away to be crucified and as He hung on the Cross, was cursed, mocked, jeered at, and insulted, but He did not open His mouth (Act 8:32).

When you are insulted, answer in a quiet, calm, controlled manner. Give a gentle (kind) response. Do not raise your voice. Respond in a positive manner. If there is a grain of truth in the insult, acknowledge it and try to do something about it.

INTEGRITY (HONESTY)

Gen 18:19; Ex 18:21; Josh 14:1-15; Job 13:15; 27:4-6; Ps 24:3-4; 25:1-22; 26:1-3; Prov 2:2, 5; 3:3-4; 11:3, 5; 12:22; 19:1; 20:7; 21:3; Mal 2:6; Lk 16:1-5, 10; Act 24:16; 2 Cor 4:2; 7:2; 8:21; Heb 13:18; 1 Pet 12:12.

Are you a person of integrity? (Integrity is being upright, honest). Can you be relied upon? Are you true to your word? Do your actions agree with your words? Are you for real?

There are many temptations that would try to lure a person away from being a person of integrity. Resist them.

Seek God to have the strength, courage, faith, and love that it takes to be a person of integrity.

INTENTIONS (MOTIVES)

Num 14:36-45; Mt 5:27-30; 14:22-33; 21:28-32.

Intentions are important. We must always weigh our intentions. We must weigh the intentions that others have toward us also. What are your intentions? Are they in keeping with God's will?

We can hide our real intentions from others (and sometimes even ourselves), but not from God. He can see into our heart.

Jesus extended the idea of bad intentions. The Old Testament said certain things were wrong, such as adultery. But Jesus said that the very desire to do them is sinful (see Mt 5:27-30). In this example we should clarify something. Jesus says that whoever looks at a woman and lusts after her has committed adultery with her in his heart already. The key here is lusting after the woman. I, as any other man, will look at a pretty woman and appreciate her beauty. This is all right and is natural. However, if I lust after her and have relations with her in my mind, then I have sinned and have committed adultery. This is one of the things about pornography. The person looking at the pictures is committing adultery or some other immorality.

In order for us to accomplish our good intentions, we need to look to God for His help.

INTIMIDATION (Bullying, Threatening)

Ezra 5:1-5; 2 Tim 1:1-18.

When we are faced with intimidation, let us look to God for His strength. Rely upon Him. We need to make sure that what we are trying to accomplish is in accordance with God's will. If it is, then we should proceed with confidence, for God's will cannot be frustrated.

There are different kinds of situations in which intimidation occurs. One place is in the marriage. A spouse may intimidate or bully the other with various threats; children bully one another. Gangsters bully people in the so-called protection rackets.

If you cannot defend yourself, don't just accept it, but go to a source that can stop it.

INVESTMENT (Ownership, RESOURCES, VALUE)

Ps 49:1-20; Mt 25:14-30; 2 Cor 9:6-15.

What kind of investments should we make? What kind do you make? Investment plans for the future is good stewardship, provided it is done with the right motives and from the right perspective. A person should plan ahead for retirement, for family needs. However, we need to remember that we will not be taking any of this wealth out of this world with us. Mark 10:17-31 is the story of the rich young ruler. It is sad that he invested in the world instead of in Jesus.

The best investments must be in other areas. We are to invest our time, talents, and abilities. These should be done for God's work, for helping others. God expects us to invest our gifts in Him and to use them wisely.

Where is your wealth? Where your wealth is, there your heart will be also (Lk 12:34).

INVITATION (ETERNAL LIFE)

Lk 14:1-24.

God calls us to accept Him. In Revelation 3:20, He states, *"I stand at the door and knock."* Jesus wants us to invite Him in. He waits patiently. Have you made that decision and invited Him into your life? We can find all kinds of excuses not to respond to His invitation, but respond to Him before it is too late. You do not know what is going to happen tomorrow. There is a time coming when it will be too late.

We must not only accept the invitation, but we must accept it with our whole heart. A halfhearted acceptance is unacceptable to God. We should respond with joy. Just imagine what you are being invited to. Stop and think about the rich blessings that God is offering. How can a person not respond with joy to the offer of our loving and gracious Heavenly Father? If you have not accepted this invitation, then respond to Him right now without any further delay.

INVOLVEMENT (Participation)

Mt 5:31-46; Jn 12:12-19; 17:13-19.

We must be involved. We cannot be indifferent. Jesus tells us that by doing acts of mercy to those in need (hungry, naked, in prison), we are doing those acts to Him (see Mt 25:35-40). Our involvement with those in need is an imitation of Jesus, for He was concerned with needs when He walked this earth, and He still is concerned about needs.

Wherever we go and with whomever we are, we are to be involved. We are not just involved when it is easy or convenient. We are demonstrating God's love and mercy. We are doing it out of love and not for show or recognition.

ISOLATION (ABANDON, Alone, SOLITUDE)

Ps 130:1-8; Is 1:1-31; Eph 3:14-21.

There are various causes for a person to feel isolated. One cause is despair. If we concentrate on it, then we will go into deeper despair and feel more isolated. Turn to God. Tell Him why you feel so hopeless, down, and alone. Ask for His help.

Sin is another cause of isolation. "See what I have done? How can you love me?" Sin makes a person feel that they are unlovable and thus are alone. The person engages in self-pity. You must repent and ask for forgiveness for your sin. In this way your relationship with God can be restored. He is reaching out to you even while you feel unlovable. God loves you.

It is also important not to isolate yourself from other believers. We are part of God's family. By being separate from other members, then you lose much of God's power. He blesses you through other people.

Isolation can be beneficial also. Just as a person with a disease is isolated so as not to contaminate other people and for that person's treatment, so also it can be beneficial for spiritual health. A person is away from distractions and can sort out things, pray, listen to music, and read the Bible. You can have some quiet time with the Lord.

JEALOUSY (Covetousness, ENVY)

Gen 26:12-35; I Sam 18:1-16; Nah 1:1-15; Rom 13:1-14.

Jealousy is normally treated as bad. In most cases, it is. However, God says that He is a jealous God, and He has a right to be (Deut 5:9). In Exodus 20:3,

God commands that the people shall have no other gods, and Deuteronomy 4:39 says, "Acknowledge and take to heart this day that the Lord is God in heaven above and on the earth below. There is no other." It could not be said any plainer. God is God alone. Thus, God has a right to demand our complete allegiance to Him. He has a right to demand that we treat Him as God and no other since He alone is God.

Thus, God's jealousy is good because it is legitimate. Another type is connected to faithfulness. A husband or wife should expect their spouse to treat them as their spouse so that they should be jealous *of that relationship* and only of that relationship, and not of one another. In other words, that relationship is precious and should be treasured. This is what I mean here by being jealous of your relationship. Do not be jealous of your spouse, but regard your relationship as precious. Spouses should have a mutual respect for one another but not a possessiveness that prevents the person from having any contact with those of the opposite sex. There also needs to be room for each person to grow as a couple and as individuals.

Jealousy in most instances is destructive. In fact, it can even repel the person of whom you are jealous. For example, a man says he loves a woman. He is jealous if she shows any attention to other people (especially men). This can become so obsessive that the woman is stifled and has to break off the relationship. The man is not showing trust to the woman. Hence, true love cannot grow in that situation. Another problem is that jealousy can lead to violence when the person feels that the other person is not true to him or her.

Another form of jealousy is a person feels someone is more popular, smarter, richer, prettier, etc., than him or her. This can lead into sin. A person might have bad thoughts about that person and then put those bad thoughts into action. Harm or even murder can be a result.

Pray for God's strength if you feel jealous of that person. Strive to outdo that person in Christian love (Rom 12:10). If you have love for that person, then there is no room for jealousy. There is nothing more powerful than for God to be at work in your life.

If you are the person of whom someone is jealous, try to make friends with that person. Pray for that person. Show him or her genuine love (the love that is concerned for their good but not necessarily romantic love). Be genuine.

JESUS CHRIST
Ps 18:30; 19:14; 27:1; 33:18-19; 37:39-40; 98:2-3; Is 53:1-12; Ezek 37:23; Mt 1:18-25; 4:1-25; 5:1-20; 16:13-20; 27:57-66; Mk 1:19-13, 21-28;

3:7-19; 10:13-16; 16:1-8; Lk 8:40-56; 9:18-36; 11:29-32; 24:1-12; Jn 1:1-18; 3:16-17; 6:39; 14:1-14; 20:1-9; Rom 1:16; 6:23; 8:30-32; 1 Cor 1:18; Gal 2:1-21; Phil 2:1-11; 2 Th 2:16-17; 1 Tim 2:3-4; 2 Tim 1:9; 1 Jn 5:11; Rev 19:1. (See concordance for complete references.)

Jesus is the second Person of the Trinity. He is the Son of God. He is God Incarnate, for in Jesus Christ God came in human form. He is all man and all God. That is something we can't understand, but it is something we just have to accept. Even today there would be people that would claim that Jesus never did live. However, there have been numerous studies. In fact, a few years ago, it was very popular to search for the historical Jesus. These studies, references from nonbiblical sources of those times, and the testimony in the lives of people down through the ages, prove that indeed Jesus of Nazareth lived, but more than that, He also lives today.

Jesus is the Savior. Salvation for all humanity comes through Jesus. In Acts 4:12, it says salvation is in Jesus alone, "for there is no other name under heaven by which we would be saved." Jesus died on the Cross and rose again so that we might have forgiveness of our sins. The Old Testament looked forward to a Messiah. Jesus is that Messiah.

He is the Great Physician. He healed physical ailments (such as blindness, lameness, lepers, and even death), but more important, He healed the brokenness and the sin that separated man from man and man from God that He saw all around Him. If you need healing, go to Jesus.

Jesus's resurrection demonstrated His power over death. And because He is raised, we also will be raised from the dead (2 Cor 4:14). The resurrection is a confirmation of all of His promises and teachings and way of life.

Jesus called his people to repent of their sins and to give complete commitment to Him. He stated that He is the only way to God, for *"He is the way the truth and the life"* (Jn 14:6). We are to follow Him and be a light to the world (Mt 5:14).

Jesus is crucial because, as has been said before, the concept of God is beyond our understanding. Who is God? What is He like? We cannot picture God although He does have form and is not some amorphous blob. We are made in God's image, and we are not blobs. But Jesus is in the form of a human being. That we understand. If we want to know the Father, then look at Jesus. Jesus does the things of the Father. In John 14:9, He says, *"Anyone who has seen me has seen the Father."* Jesus makes God known.

An additional word needs to be added. Down through the ages, Jesus's Divinity has been challenged. Some have claimed that at first the people did not believe that He was God and this claim came later at a church council, but that is not true. Jesus enemies did not say He didn't claim to be God. They claimed that He did say it and thus called Him a blasphemer. None of these claims that Jesus is not divine can stand up under the facts. Let's examine a few lies:

There is no resurrection. Jesus did not rise from the dead. His body was stolen by His disciples. These same disciples preached that He had been raised and underwent persecution and death. Can you imagine anyone giving up his or her life for something that they knew to be untrue? I know I wouldn't. Also, there were plenty of nonbelievers that would have stated that this is not true. Jesus appeared to a large number of people after His death as proof that He had indeed risen.

The Christians believed that Jesus was God. John chapter 1 points this out very strongly. Jesus is God, not *a* god.

Probably the greatest verification of the whole Christian faith is the apostle Paul. Paul was a devout Jew. He felt that the Christians were enemies of God and that they were leading people away from God; therefore, he got letters that gave him the authority to have Christians arrested. On the road to Damascus, Saul (Paul) had a revelation from God (see Act 9:3-8). He saw a bright light and a voice from heaven said, *"Saul, Saul, why do you persecute me?"* "Who are you Lord?" he said. *"I am Jesus, whom you are persecuting,"* the voice replied. This was a big shock to Him. He found out that he had been the enemy of God. He had been persecuting God. With that, he made a complete about-face and served Jesus. Paul knew that the Christian faith was real. He knew that Jesus is Lord. Countless others have known that too.

Until the end of time, people will try to discredit Jesus for many reasons. The main reason is that they do not want a Jesus that makes a demand upon them. *They want to be Lord.* Any honest search will prove that **He is Lord**. Search honestly. Test anything that says that He is not God. God is truth and is not afraid of any search. Don't accept something just because you are told that it is true. Look at the evidence. What is the source of the evidence? Is it reliable? Jesus asks His disciples two questions in Mark 8:27-29. First, He asks them, *"Who do people say that I am."* The people are giving different answers. Then He asks them, *"But who do you say that I am?"* Peter makes the confession that He is the Christ. This is the question that Jesus asks each of us, and each of us must give an answer. It is the most important question and answer that you will ever make. ***Who do you* say that He is?** I pray that you accept Him as Lord and Savior, follow, and serve Him. He will never let you down. You cannot accept Him as Savior only. You must accept Him as Lord and Savior. However, He is a loving Lord.

Who do you say that He is?

Some people try to say that Jesus was a prophet, a teacher, someone who went about doing good, but that He is not God. As C. S. Lewis has stated very well, there are only three positions that you can take concerning Him. Either he is a liar, a lunatic, or He is who He said He is. If he lied and is not God, then He cannot be regarded as a good anything (teacher, prophet, etc.), but instead He is a devil. In addition, it is hard to imagine a liar undergoing the beating and crucifixion that He endured when a confession would have avoided that. If He is crazy and believed that He is God but is not, then again He cannot be regarded as a good teacher or anything. We know that if He is just a man making this claim, then that claim will not stand. It will fail. When you look at His composure and His teachings, these are not the ravings of a lunatic. The advice of Gamaliel, a Jewish teacher of the Law, is appropriate here (see Act 5:38).

However, when we look at His life, we see that He lived His teachings. The bold statement in John 14:9, where He says that if you have seen Him, you have seen the Father, cannot be tolerated unless it is true. He showed that the statement is true. There is no contradiction. His teachings testify for Him instead of against Him. The miracles and works that He did are still further testimony to Him. The changed lives of people, then and now, whom He touched proclaim that He is the Son of God. He always pointed to God the Father. In John 5:19, He says, *I tell you the truth, the Son can do nothing by himself; he can do only what he sees his Father doing, because whatever the Father does the Son also does.* When we look at the three positions, the only logical conclusion is that Jesus is who He said He is. He is God.

JOBS (WORK)

2 Th 3:1-15.

How do you view your job? God wants us to be faithful in our jobs, even the simplest and most menial. The attitude that we show on our job and toward our job speaks to those with whom we come in contact with. It is done as a service to God. Think of God as your boss, instead of your earthly one.

Let us honor God by how we do our jobs and what we do on our jobs. A lot of people hate their jobs and regard them as drudgery. Yes, some jobs are monotonous and boring. Why do you hate your job? Take the steps necessary to remove the reason that you hate it, or get a different job. Be joyful on your job. Be honest and helpful to all those that you come in contact with. Your job is going to occupy a large block of your life, so it is important that you have the right attitude on it. Worship God through your work.

JOY (CONTENTMENT, HAPPINESS)

Lev 23:1-44; Deut 12:18; I Ch 16:27; Neh 12:43; Job 8:21; 33:26; Ps 5:11; 9:2; 13:5; 16:1-11; 19:8; 20:5; 21:1, 5; 28:7; 30:5, 11; 32:11; 40:16; 68:3; 71:23; 100:1-2; 104:34; 105:3, 43; 126:5-6; Is 44:23; 51:11; Mt 25:21; Lk 1:47; 2:10; 6:22-23; 15:6; 24:52; Jn 15:11; Act 13:52; 16:25; Rom 15:13; 2 Cor 1:12, 24; Gal 5:16-26; Phil 4:1-23; Col 1:11; 1 Pet 4:13; 1 Jn 1:4.

Joy is a happiness that surpasses circumstances. The world might say, "How can there be joy in that situation? Real joy comes from fellowshipping with the Living God. To have Him, in the form of the Holy Spirit, reside within you is true joy.

If we are doing God's will, then no matter what kind of circumstances that we find ourselves in, we can rejoice because there is nothing that can separate us from the love of God (see Rom 8:38-39). And Jesus as He approached the Cross discarded its shame, for He saw the joy that was set before Him (see Heb 12:2). He saw joy because He was obeying the Father.

Thus concentrate upon God's goodness, upon all the blessings that are ours for knowing Him. Yes, we will pass many difficult times, but we can rejoice, knowing that in Christ we are more than conquerors (see Rom 8:37).

JUDGING (Criticism)

Is 11:1-16; Mt 7:1-6; 1 Cor 5:1-13.

We must be fair in our judgment of others, for there are times that we have to judge each other. For example, there is the judgment of a person's qualifications for a job, a person's motivations for doing something, and the evaluation of a person's work, just to mention a few. However, our judging must be done in a loving manner that is not destructive or hypocritical. Be constructive in your criticism with an aim of helping the person.

JUDGMENT (GOD'S) (GRACE, HELL, JUSTICE)

Deut 7:1-26; 1 K 22:29-40; Ps 9:7, 16, 20; 96:13; Ecc 3:17; 11:9; 12:14; Is 59:18; Ob 1:1-21; Mt 3:12; 7:22-23; 10:14-15; 11:22; 12:36-37; 16:21-28; 22:13; 23:14; 25:31-46; Mk 13:32; Lk 12:2-3; Jn 5:22; 9:41; 12:48; 15:22; Act 10:42; 17:31; 24:25; Rom 2:1-16; 20:11-15; 1 Cor 3:13; 5:10; Gal 6:5-7; 2 Tim 4:1, 8; Heb 2:2-3; 9:27; 10:26; 2 Pet 2:4; 1 Jn 4:17; Rev 20:11-15; 22:12.

As we read through the Old Testament, we see God's judgment falling upon sin. It comes in His timing and it is a just judgment.

One of the attributes of God is justice. God is a just God. He is not capricious like the gods of Greek and Roman mythology. God is patient but there is coming a final judgment. For all those that have not repented of their sins and accepted God's forgiveness, there will be eternal punishment.

Christians will be judged too. Their eternal destiny is secure because of Christ's sacrifice for them. But their use of the gifts that God gave to them will also be judged.

At the final judgment, death, all evil, Satan, and those who did not accept Jesus Christ will be cast into the lake of fire (this is the second death) (Rev 20:14-15).

JUSTICE (FAIRNESS, TRUTH)

Gen 18:20-33; Lev 19:13-15; Ezra 7:26; Ps 72:1-2; 82:2-4; Prov 17:15, 26; 18:5, 17; Ecc 5:8; Is 1:17; 3:1-26; 56:1; Zech 8:16; Mt 5:23-24; 7:24, 51; 12:7; Col 3:1-17,

God is a just God, but He is also a merciful one. The Cross demonstrates His justice and His mercy. Because of God's justice, sin had to be punished. The rightful punishment of sin is death because the wages of sin is death (Rom 6:23). But God's mercy caused Him to send His Son to die in our place, so that through Him we might have eternal life (Jn 3:16).

We also must be just and promote justice. In promoting justice, we do not take the law into our own hands. We do not seek vengeance.

JUSTIFICATION

Gen 15:6; Ps 32:2; Is 42:21; 45:25; 53:11; 56:1; 61:10; Zech 3:4; Jn 5:24; Act 13:39; Rom 1:16-17; 2:13; 4:5; 5:1, 9-11, 21; 6:22; 8:1, 30; Gal 2:16; 3:8; 5:4-6; Eph 6:14; Tit 3:7; Heb 11:4-7; Jas 2:20.

What is justification? Justification is being made right before God (Rom 4:25). Through faith in Jesus Christ, we have been counted righteous (Rom 5:1). His righteousness is counted toward our credit. It is not the result of anything that we did or could ever do. It is because of Jesus that we are no longer condemned.

KINDNESS (Gentleness)

Lev 19:34; Ps 112:5; Prov 14:21; 19:22; 31:26; Mt 5:7, 42; 25:34-36; Lk 6:27-36; Act 20:35; Rom 12:9-21; 15:1, 1 Cor 13:4-7; Gal 6:1-2, 10; Eph 4:32; Col 3:1-17; 1 Pet 4:8; 2 Pet 1:7; 1Jn 3:17-18.

We are to be kind in order to imitate Jesus. In many cases this is easy, but in other cases it is not easy. We are told to love our enemies (Mt 5:44). Do good to them that persecute you. This doesn't mean that you like what is being done to you—far from it. What you are to do is to act with goodwill toward these people. You are to have a genuine concern for the person. You hate what they are doing, but you pray for that person and pray that your concern will take root in their heart so that they change their ways.

We are kind as a response to God's love to us. This is to be a daily characteristic in your life.

KINGDOM OF GOD (or HEAVEN) (Authority, Rule)
Mt 6:5-15; 13:1-58; Mk 10:35-45; Lk 12:22-34.

The kingdom of God and the kingdom of heaven are two synonymous terms that Jesus used frequently. They do not refer to an earthly kingdom. He said that His kingdom was not of this world (see Jn 18:36). The kingdom of God is present among us right now. It has not been brought to full completion, but it is here. The kingdom of God is God's rule in our heart.

That kingdom is precious. As Jesus says, it is the pearl of great price (see Mt 13:16). There is nothing that compares to it. We need to give our all for it, and that means to give you very life for it (see Mt 10:39). It is more valuable than everything else. We strive for many other things, and we even mock His rule. But His rule in our hearts is what we are hungry for. It is what each one of us is searching for.

KNOWLEDGE (TRUTH)
Gen 2:9, 17; Prov 1:7, 22, 29; 2:10; 8:10; 12:1; 15:14; 18:15; 24:5; Jer 9:1-26; Hos 4:6; Mk 3:7-12; Jn 3:1-21; 1 Cor 12:8; 13:9-12; Phil 3:8.

Knowledge of Jesus is not enough. It is easy to know facts about Him, but what we are called upon is to have a commitment to Him. It must begin with knowledge, but you must accept that knowledge and give yourself to Him. Thus, saving faith is whom you know and not what you know.

In a similar manner, a person can have a lot of Bible knowledge, but what are they doing with it? Are you obeying the messages that the Bible reveals? We are to know intellectually, but also on a deep, personal level. This is the kind of knowledge that God wants us to have.

The Christian faith is not a body of secret teachings, of secret knowledge. It does contain some teachings of Jesus, but His teachings are amplifications and clarifications of the Old Testament. He gets at the heart of matters. He reveals the inner meaning. He identifies Himself with God. Repeatedly, He uses the phrase, "I am." In the Old Testament, God revealed Himself to Moses as the I AM (see Ex 3:14). In using this term, He identifies Himself with God. Jesus and the disciples emphasize a relationship with God as important, rather than just knowledge of God. Love the Lord, your God. A relationship with Jesus Christ is the heart of the Christian faith.

LABOR (see WORK)

LASCIVIOUSNESS (see LUST)

LAZINESS (Idleness, WORK)
2 Th 3:1-18; 2 Pet 3:1-18.
Sometimes people say that because Christ is returning we do not have to plan for the future or work. But just the opposite is true. Since we do not know when He is returning, we are to be faithful in carrying out His work (see Lk 12:38-40). We are to be active in serving and helping other people, instead of waiting on a mountaintop. We are a servant people. There is a big difference between rest and laziness.

LEADERSHIP (OBEDIENCE, SERVING)
Ex 6:1-12; 39:32-43; Deut 1:9-18; Neh 3:1-32; Lk 22:7-38; 1 Cor 12:12-31; Heb 2:1-18.
An effective leader does not let tough going get him down. An effective leader knows how to delegate authority. One person cannot do all the work. This develops other leaders and it lets people make use of the skills that they have.

A good leader recognizes and appreciates other people's contributions and encourages and is willing to listen to the advice of others. He or she is not a one-man show or a person that has to have things go their way.

The Christian leader has a servant attitude and strives to imitate Christ; whereas the worldly leaders are often arrogant, selfish, and even rude, and use any means that they can to get ahead.

Each person has an important role, and a good leader helps people to see their role and to develop the skills that he or she has for the accomplishment of the goal.

LEGALISM (FREEDOM, SELF-RIGHTEOUS)
Mt 12:1-14; Gal 4:8-20; Col 2:6-23.
Legalism is a system in which rules are more important than God. Jesus repeatedly had strong arguments with the religious leaders of His day over this. Jesus called them hypocrites. *"You strain out a gnat and swallow a camel"* (see Mt 23:24). In another instance, Jesus healed on the Sabbath, and He answered His critics by saying, *"The Sabbath was made for man and not man for the Sabbath"* (see Mk 2:27). Another example was mentioned in the section on Adultery. In John 8:3-7, a woman was caught in the act of adultery. Legalism

said that she should be stoned. However, Jesus in love knew that the woman needed forgiveness, not death.

In legalism, rules are followed instead of meeting human needs. The inner spirit of the law is violated. The Christian faith is not a legalistic faith although some would try to make it so. Paul had to fight this in the early days. There were teachers called the Judaizers that were trying to convince people that they had to become Jews and do the Jewish requirements in addition to accepting Christ. Paul makes it clear that salvation is by faith in Christ alone and not Christ plus something else. Too often people feel that they must add works to salvation. Works are a result of salvation and not a way to salvation. Ephesians 2:9 tells us that salvation is because of God's grace and not because of anything else.

LIFE
Gen 9:1-17; Deut 8:1-20; Ps 39:1-13; 90:1-17; Mk 8:31-38; Lk 9:18-27; Jn 1:1-18; 4:1-26; Rom 6:1-14.

What is life? I defy any scientist to define it. They can say that a living thing needs certain things and does certain things, but this is all that they can say. Is it an accident? Some people would try to say so, but when you look at the variety and complexity of an organism, you know it can't be an accident. It is interesting that the people who think that life is an accident, with all of its complexity, would think that you were crazy to believe that a machine (even a simple one) could come together by accident. And of course you would be crazy. To be polite, I will say that those who believe that life is a result of chance are very mistaken.

Does it have any meaning? We really do not know what life is. I simply know that I am alive. How can you describe it? Somehow chemicals and energy are combined by God so that there is life. Life is not an accident. God created it. In the story in Genesis of the creation, it says that God breathed life into man and he became a living being. Life is a gift from God.

Life is precious since we are made in the image of God. Since it is precious, we need to make the most of it. Do not waste it with bickering. Build relationships, do good, love people, love God. Make the most of your life.

We have been created to love God. We want to develop ourselves to the fullest, and the way to do that is by letting God into our life.

It is a shame that some people let the problems of life get them down so much that they want to take their life. They commit suicide. In Jesus Christ, we have the answer to those problems. Seek Him.

In a previous section, eternal life was described. This is a life that begins right now. What kind of life are you living? Let it be one that is filled with joy and love because you know the Lord.

LIFE-STYLE (EXAMPLE. Habit)

Ex 23: 20-33; Mt 5:1-12; 1Cor 9:1-27; 2 Tim 2:14-26.

There are many different lifestyles. What kind do you have? Is it pleasing to God?

Our lifestyle reflects our beliefs; it reflects what is important to us. If material possessions are important to you, then you will have a lifestyle that pursues this interest. If pleasure is important, then you will pursue pleasure. If your lifestyle is not pleasing to God, then it will fail and come crashing down. You will be bankrupt. Maybe not in this life, but certainly in the next if you have not laid up treasure in heaven.

If we are Christians, then that style should be consistent with God's word. It should be imitating Jesus. Just as we could look at Jesus and see the Father, then we must reflect Jesus by the life that we live.

LIGHT (TRUTH)

Ps 27:1; 119:05; Prov 6:23; Is 8:20; 49:6; Mt 4:16; 5:13-16; Mk 4:21-25; Lk 2:32; 11:34; 16:8; Jn 1:1-18; 5:35; 8:12; 9:5; 12:35; Phil 2:15; 1 Th 5:5; 1 Tim 6:16; Jas 1:17; 1 Jn 1:5-7; Rev 21:23.

Light represents many things in the Bible. It represents truth, knowledge, and influence upon others.

As Christians, we are called upon to be the light of the world (Mt 5:14) just as the Jewish nation was called to be a light to the Gentiles (Is 60:3). In that sense, we are showing God's redeeming love to a world that needs light. It is a world that needs a direction toward which to go, a way out of the darkness, which is evil. Our actions and words are to point people to God through Jesus Christ.

In John 8:12, Jesus says that He is the light of the world. He reveals life and people as they really are. Evil is overcome by the light. It is exposed by the light.

LIMITATIONS (BARRIERS)

Jud 6:1-40; 1 Cor 15:35-38.

Each of us has various limitations. However, these should not frustrate us, but instead we should work within these limitations. Do not accept a limitation because someone says so. Try it yourself, and you may surprise yourself. It is also possible to overcome various limitations.

Go as far as you can go in any situation, and then turn it over to God to be completed. God can take our weakness and accomplish great things. We are limited, but God has no limitations. (Mt 19:26). Trust Him.

LISTENING (Attention, Concentration)

Deut 5:1-33; 1 K 19:1-18; Mt 4:1-20; Jas 1:19-27.

Listening is an important skill. We must listen to each other, and we must listen to God. We cannot obey God if we do not listen to Him. God speaks so we must listen to Him. In order to help others, we must listen to them so that we know what their needs are.

When you are in a conversation, listen. Too often, people are not listening to the other person but trying to think what they will say as an objection. Hear the person. We want to be listened to, so pay that same respect to someone else.

To listen means that you must be open with your heart and mind and not just with your ears.

LONELINESS (Alone, Isolation)

1 K 19:1-18; Ps 4:8, 27, 91; Is 54:10; Mk 4:30-34; Jn 14:18; 16:1-16; 3 Jn 1:1-14.

What do you do when you feel lonely? Too often, a person engages in self-pity.

Remember that you are not alone, for God is with you. Seek out other Christians. We are to minister to one another. If someone appears alone, give them encouragement. Seek out God. Jesus has said, *"I am with you always"* (Mt 28:20). God never forsakes us. This is especially important when you feel lonely because of the loss of a loved one. The loss of a spouse hurts very much, especially on a birthday or on special occasion or at night when you are by yourself. Lean strongly on God. Make this loss an occasion of drawing closer to Him and not one of pulling away from God.

LORD'S SUPPER (Communion)

Mt 26:17-30; Mk 14:22-24; Lk 22:19; Jn 13:1-4; Act 2:42-47; 20:7; 1 Cor 10:16; 11:17-34.

There are different names for the Lord's Supper. Holy Communion, Communion, and the Eucharist are a few. The different names emphasize different aspects of the Lord's Supper. It is thanksgiving and also remembrance.

The Lord's Supper is a recollection of the last meal that Jesus had with His disciples. It is a time of remembrance. We remember that meal, but we remember much more than that. We remember all of His teachings, His body that was broken for us, and His blood that was shed on the Cross for the forgiveness of our sins. We also remember His promises to us and the mystical bond that unites us to Him, and we are assured of His continued presence with us. In addition to remembering, it is also a time of reflection and thanksgiving. We reflect upon what He has done for us and how we are to serve Him. It is a time for seeking forgiveness. We thank Him for His sacrifice.

The bread represents His body, which was broken for us. As Isaiah 53:5 says, *"With his stripes we are healed."* The cup represents His blood. He says that it is the covenant which is poured out for the remission of sins (Mk 14:24). Some say that the bread and wine turn into the actual body and blood of Christ. But Jesus was sitting right there with His disciples when He instituted this Holy meal. These symbolize His body and blood.

The Lord's Supper is not a ritual and should not be entered into in that manner. In addition to the remembrance and thanksgiving that has just been mentioned, it is also a communion with His spirit. By participation we are symbolically uniting with Christ. This is why it is important not to enter in an unworthy manner. An unworthy manner can mean a lack of reverence or understanding of the love that these symbols represent. These symbols represent Christ's love of giving Himself for us. Partaking in an unworthy manner can also mean partaking while we are angry or have bad feelings, or anything of this sort because we are causing a discord or disunion in the body of Christ. Pray or do whatever it takes to get rid of these feelings and attitude before you join in. If you can't get rid of them at the time, then don't participate.

Different churches have different policies on how often Communion is observed. Some do it at every service. Others do it every three months. Still other churches, when they think it is appropriate. I myself prefer observing it once a month. This is not too often to make it a routine, yet often enough for it to have meaning. I don't think it has that much meaning if it is just done now and then. I think to myself, "Don't they believe in the Lord's Supper?" Of course I know that they do, but I feel it is being neglected.

LOST (SIN)
Is 53:1-12; Lk 15:1-32.

The term *lost* is not always clear to everyone. If some people are told that they are "lost," they would wonder what you mean. Lost is a term that means a person has not accepted Jesus Christ. Everyone who has not accepted the salvation that comes from knowing Jesus as Lord and Savior is lost. You are spiritually lost because you have strayed from following God. Psalm 119:176 reads, "I have strayed like a lost sheep." God sent Jesus to seek and to save the lost (see Lk 19:10). God is patient in His mercy. He does not want anyone to be lost (see 2 Pet 3:9). Seek the Savior while there is time.

LOVE
Ex 20:6; Lev 19:18; Deut 6:5; 7:9; 10:12; 13:3; Josh 23:11; Ps 18:1; 31:23; 37:4; 73:25; 91:14; 97:10; 116:1; 133:1; 136:1-26; 145:20; Prov 8:17; 10:12; 15:17; 23:26; Mt 5:38-48; 10:37, 41-42; 19:19; 25:34-36; Mk 9:41; 12:28-34; Lk 2:29-32; 7:47; 10:36-37; 11:42; 15:1-7; Jn 3:1-21; 15:9, 12-13; 16:27; 17:26; 21:15-25; Rom 5:5; 8:28-39; 12:9-10; 13:8; 1 Cor 8:3; 13:1-13; 2 Cor 5:8, 14-15; Gal 5:6, 22; Eph 4:15; 5:2; Phil 1:9; 3:7-8; 1 Th 3:12; 4:9; 2 Th 3:5; 2 Tim 1:5, 7; Heb 6:10; 13:1-3; Jas 1:27; 1 Pet 1:8; 1 Jn 2:1-11; 4:12, 16-21; 5:1-3.

There are many different kinds of love. The Greeks used different words for different types, but we only have one word, and we use it for many different kinds of love. I love chocolate ice cream or I love that dress. I love America or (a city), etc. There is brotherly love, familial love, and sexual love. Without God's help our love is conditional. We attach conditions to it. I love you because you're good to be with, or you're fun to have around, etc.

The highest love is God's love. God is love (1 Jn 4:8). This is one of His attributes, His very nature. His love is an eternal and forgiving love. It is an *unconditional* love. God does not place conditions on us. He does not tell us to clean up our act and then He will love us. On the contrary, while we were still enemies, He showed His love by having His Son die for us so we could be reconciled with Him (Rom 5:10 and Jn 3:16). There is the strong assertion in Romans 8:35-39 that nothing can separate us from the love of God, which is in Christ Jesus.

In 1 Chronicles 13, some of the characteristics of Christian love are mentioned. One characteristic is that this type of love is a genuine concern for the other person as opposed to an emotional feeling. To have this love, we must ask for God's strength to forgive even those who harm us. It is this type that is meant when Jesus says to love your enemies (Mt 5:44). This love is a concern for that person.

Loving God means to exercise this love, for John 4:20 points out that if a person says that he loves God, but hates his brother, then that person is a liar. We demonstrate our love for God and people by serving others.

LOYALTY (Allegiance, COMMITMENT)

Ex 22:28; Ezra 7:26; Prov 17:1-28; Ecc 8:2; Mt 6:19-24; Lk 12:49-53; Rom 13:1; Tit 3:1.

Loyalty is an important trait. Part of friendship is loyalty. We want friends that we can depend upon. We do not want or want to be the type of friend that is there when it is convenient for them. In other words, we do not want "fair weather" friends, and we should not be one either.

The most important loyalty is to God and His truth. We are to be committed to following Him. Sometimes this will not be easy, for Jesus said we must be willing to bear our cross, but we must still be true to Him. When we do fall short and temporarily fall away, then let us quickly repent of this and make a fresh start.

LUST (DESIRES, Passion)

Gen 3:6; Ex 20:17; Num 11:4-25; Jud 16:1-22; Mt 5:27-30; 1 Tim 6:9; 2 Tim 2:22; 4:3-4; Tit 2:12; Jas 1:14-15; 1 Pet 2:11; 4:3; 2 Pet 2:18; 3:3; Jude 1:16-18.

What is lust? It is more than a sexual craving. It is any strong unnatural craving. There is the lust for power, money, and sex. It is an excessive craving. A sexual desire or desire for possessions or knowledge is all right unless it becomes excessive. The object lusted after takes dominance in the mind.

The difference between love and lust is seen in 1 Corinthians 13. Love is patient, but lust demands satisfaction now. Lust demands its own way. Pornography is one means of feeding lust. Rape is another. Ruthless power, in which people are hurt to satisfy the person's goal, is still another example of lust. Lust is sin and often leads to other sins.

LYING (Falsehood)

Lev 19:11-16; 1 Sam 15:1-35; 2 Ch 18:1-27; Job 27:4; Ps 5:6, 9; 10:7; 31:18; 34:13; 36:3; 50:19; 62:4; 63:11; 101:5, 7; 109:2; 116:11; 120:2-4; 144:8, 11; Prov 3:3; 6:12-19; 10:9-10, 18, 31; 12:17, 19-22; 17:4, 7; 19:5, 22, 28; Hos 4:1-2; Mic 6:12; Mt 26:69-74; Jn 8:44-45; Act 5:1-9; Eph 4:17-32; 1 Tim 4:2; 1 Pet 3:16; Rev 21:8.

Lying is harmful in many ways. It breaks relationships, and even fools the liar when he starts to believe his own lies. It is harmful to integrity. A person of integrity is true to their word; they do not lie.

It leads to injustice when people become false witnesses. Thus, a person could be sent to jail or even killed because of a lie. One lie leads to another as the person tries to cover up their lies. A person's reputation can be ruined because of lies done to them. Still another strong reason not to lie is found in John 8:44. This verse calls the devil the father of lies. Thus, if you lie then you are following Satan.

As Christians, we must be honest with one another. Tell the truth, but try not to hurt others by telling the truth.

MAN (see HUMANNESS)

MANAGEMENT (LEADERSHIP)
Ex 18:1-27; 39:32-43; Rom 12:1-8.

Good management involves sharing of responsibility as well as supervision and encouragement. A good leader lets those who are working underneath him or her know when they have done well.

Management is a gift of God and should be used for God's service.

MARRIAGE
Gen 2:1-25; 24:58-60; 34:8-9; Ex 21:8-9; Num 36:8; Deut 7:3-4; 24:1-5; Ezra 9:1-15; Song 1-8; Jer 29:6; 33:10-11; Mal 2:14-15; Mt 5:31-32; 19:3-12; 24:38; Mk 10:11-12; 12:25; Lk 16:18; Rom 7:1-3; 1 Cor 7:1-40; 11:11-12; Eph 5:21-33; 1 Tim 3:2; 5:14; Heb 13:4.

What is marriage? The Bible tells us that God instituted it. It is the joining of one man and one woman together, and they become as one flesh (Gen 2:24). It is not to be taken lightly. Some people go into marriage with the idea that if it doesn't work, then they will simply get a divorce. But marriage is supposed to be a lifelong commitment.

Marriage is to be entered with a sense of commitment to one another. It is permanent. There is romance, but there has to be very much more than that in order to have a lasting marriage. The principles of love are involved and not just feelings.

Marriage is a partnership between a man and a woman. There is a oneness that is the goal: oneness of body, mind, and sprit. It is a submission of each partner to the other. However, it should be remembered that each individual does not give up his or her identity. Too often this is what happens. Usually it is the wife, so she feels subordinate to the husband and his goals. She is fulfilling his needs and gets lost in the marriage. She has become less than what she was before. The reverse should be true. You should become more than what you were before. This is only possible if each goes into the marriage with this expectation, knows the interests and goals of one another, and makes sure that all of this is compatible. If one person is a non-traveler and the other is a traveler, then this will not work unless the traveler becomes a person that is perfectly content to stay home or travel less, or the stay-at-home person learns to enjoy traveling. Any compromise should be by mutual consent and result in mutual satisfaction so there is not resentment. "I gave this up for you." Can you each grow in this relationship? Each should stimulate the growth of the other person and not stunt it. In this way they can better serve the Lord. A domineering, overbearing spouse has no place in a Christian marriage. The reason is that a domineering spouse is not living the Christian life. He or she is not exercising the love that God shows to us.

Marriage is the best environment for raising children. Not that a single parent can't do it, but a single parent has to do the job of the mother and the father. The home was meant to have two parents.

Paul uses marriage as the symbol to represent the relationship between Christ and the Church.

There are many problems in marriage because we are human, but a lot of the problems are made as a result of going into the marriage for the wrong reasons. A person may get married for wealth, for sexual gratification, for protection, for the romance. Thus, as a result, the person may not know that much about the person they are marrying. That person may change considerably after the marriage and become a domineering, jealous, overprotective person. He or she may become abusive, a drunkard, faithless.

Because of the nature of marriage, it must be spiritual as well as physical and emotional. And because it is meant to be permanent, you should be sure of the other person before you get married. Have a thorough knowledge of one another and of each other's expectations of the marriage. If a guy has this attitude: "My wife is my property. I'm the boss. We have sex when I want it. And she cooks my meals and has them on the table in time . . ." then women run from this type of man as fast as you can. He is not only not ready for marriage, but he is not even a man. I will let you give him an appropriate name, How many children do you want, if any? What happens if you cannot have children? Do you want to adopt?

What values do each of you have and what are they based upon? If you are Christian, then you should marry another believer. Look at all the details and plan your life together. Do this ahead of time. If you can't resolve them ahead of time, then don't get married. Look for a resolution of the problems that will arise, because they will, rather than a way out of the marriage.

Not everyone should get married for some of the above reasons. However, celibacy is not easy either. A person should only select celibacy if they are suited for it.

Jesus said that marital unfaithfulness (an unrepented sexual immorality) is the only ground for divorce.

Whether abuse is a ground for a divorce or not can be disputed, but the relationship is to be severed. There is to be no abuse in marriage. Marriage was for the purpose of love.

I have been married for over thirty-nine years. My wife and I have had disagreements just as any couple does. We have had the stress of raising a multiple-handicapped child in addition to two younger boys, who are married now and have families of their own. Rebecca was born with cerebral palsy and now has lupus also. It is sad that some families are split when a handicapped child is born. I have tried to be a good father, but the children certainly had a good mother. Karin has had to put up with a lot, but she does it because of her strong faith. I know I do not share some of the burdens with her that I should share. I try to settle them on my own, and consequently I am shutting her out. Do not do that to your spouse. Part of the wedding vow says, "In good times and bad."

MATERIALISM (Possessiveness, Worldliness)

Deut 7:1-26; Col 1:15-29; Heb 6:1-20; 13:1-25.

Materialism is love for things. We need things, but when they become a too-important part of our life then they are wrong. The desire for things can make us slaves. We want more and more. Materialism becomes our god.

The values that God teaches are contrary to materialism (Mt 6:20-21). The material things will pass away, but God's values never will pass away.

You can seek material things provided that God is still God, and that your goal is to use these material possessions to help other people. There are many human needs that have to be met. By meeting those needs, you are serving God. Be sure that they point to God and He is given the praise instead of giving the honor to yourself.

MEDIATOR (Advocate)

Rom 1:1-17; Heb 7:11-28; 1 Tim 2:1-15.

There is only one mediator between God and man and that is Jesus Christ. We, as His servants, will be called upon to act as mediators in certain situations. In the Sermon on the Mount in Matthew 5:9, Jesus says, "Blessed are the peacemakers for they shall be called the sons of God." Thus, we need to be agents of reconciliation by word and deed. Let us put out the fires of prejudice, anger, and hatred.

MEEKNESS (Gentle)

Ps 22:26; 25:9; 37:11; 76:8-9; 147:6; Prov 16:32; Ecc 7:8; 10:4; Is 11:4; 29:19; 53:7; Lam 3:28-30; Amos 3:3; Zeph 2:3; Mt 5:5; 11:29; 26:47-50; 27:13-14; Rom 12:14; 14:19; 1 Cor 6:7; 13:4-5;2 Cor 10:1; Gal 5:22; 6:1; Phil 2:14-15; 1 Tim 6:11-12; 2 Tim 2:24-25; Tit 2:29; 3:2; Heb 10:36; 12:14; Jas 1:4, 19, 21.

What is meekness? This word, like being humble, is often misunderstood. Some think of it as having no backbone, but this is far from the biblical meaning, and it is not being a doormat either. Jesus was meek, and He was certainly no doormat and He certainly had backbone. He stood strong for what He believed, and expects us to stand strong. It is a strong gentleness. A patience that is slow to anger. Meekness does not demand to have its own way, but will stand up against wrong.

MERCY (FORGIVENESS, GRACE)

Gen 20:1-18; 2 Sam 22:26; Ps 6:1-10; 37:25; 85:10; Prov 3:3; 11:17; 12:10; 14:21-22; 21:21; Hos 12:6; Mic 6:8; Zech 3:1-10; Lk 6:36; 18:9-14; Rom 12:8; Jas 2:13.

We are to express mercy because God has shed His mercy upon us. It was His mercy that sent Jesus to die on the Cross for our sins. Our rightful penalty for our sin is death because the wages of sin is death (Rom 6:23). However, God in His mercy sent His Son to die on the Cross in our place for our sins. God is merciful even at times when we are not aware of it.

Thus, in return for that mercy, let us show mercy and forgiveness to others.

MESSIAH (JESUS CHRIST)

Is 53:1-12; Lk 2:21-40. (For complete references on this topic see a concordance)

Jesus is the Messiah that the Jews were looking for. Messiah is the Hebrew term that means "Anointed One." The Messiah is a deliverer. In Greek, Christ means "Anointed One." He is the suffering servant that is described by Isaiah in chapter 53. He fulfilled the sacrificial system by bearing our sins.

Jesus did all the deeds that were prophesied about the Messiah: healing the blind, deaf, lame, and raising the dead. Jesus, however, was a different Messiah than what the people of His time were expecting. They were expecting a political figure to rise up and throw off the hated rule of the Romans; since He did not do this, many turned against Him. Instead of a political deliverance, Jesus brought deliverance from sin.

MIND (Reason, THINKING)

Rom 12:1-8; 1Cor 2:6-16; Phil 2:1-11; 4:1-9.

Christianity is not opposed to mental activity. In fact, it is a God-given gift and should be exercised. Jesus even encourages it. In John 8:32, He says to seek the truth and the truth will set you free. And in John 14:6 He says that He is *"the way, the truth and the life."* Thus, Jesus is saying, "If you seek the truth, then you will find me."

What we think, and how we think, influences our character. Our relationship to God should influence how we think and what we think. Is your mind on good, uplifting things or on that which debases? Philippians 4:8 says we need to think of good things.

We are called to have the mind of Christ. That mind has the traits and character of Christ (1 Cor 2:16).

There is much more that could be said about the mind that is not in the scope of this book, but let me say a few words. The mind is an amazing, complex computer. There is a conscious and subconscious structure or element to it. By changing one's thoughts, some very amazing things can be done. An ordinary computer can be reprogrammed and upgraded. Our minds can be reprogrammed and upgraded also. Each of us can do a lot more than we think we can.

MINISTRY (Minister)

Lev 21:6; 1 Ch 23:13; Is 6:8-9; Jer 3:15; Mal 2:6; Lk 10:1-8; Act 13:2; 1 Cor 9:1-27; 10:1-17; Gal 2:1-10; Eph 4:11-12; 1 Tim 2:7; 2 Tim 1:6-7; 2:1-3, 14-16; 3:14-17; Tit 2:1, 7; 3:1-2.

We are all called to be ministers (I Pet 2:9). Yes, there are some that are called to the pastoral ministry and other forms, but we are all called to ministry. Second Letter to the Corinthians 5:18 says that we have the ministry of reconciliation. We are to use the gifts and talents that God has given to us to carry out His purposes. God's message is more important than the way it is preached. Ministry is the meeting of needs.

God has given you rich blessings, use them. Use His word. Live a life that shows the message.

MISTAKES (Errors, SIN)

Gen 4:1-26; Neh 9:1-38; Eph 4:1-16.

All of us make mistakes, but do you learn from your mistakes? As we make mistakes, we need to let these help us in our decisions so that we do not repeatedly make errors.

We must not be afraid of making mistakes because this can freeze us into inaction. It can also prevent our spiritual and emotional growth. We must also not beat ourselves up about the mistake. Do not brood over it and make silly assessments, such as, "I am stupid." You may have done something foolish, but that does not make you foolish. Recently, I made an error that only my wife could correct because it is a matter of replacing some items that she can replace but I cannot. Thus, that meant a lot of work for her, and I felt very bad about that. It made her angry. However, I knew that I could not dwell on the consequences of the mistake, for that would be no help to anyone. I would feel miserable and those around me would feel miserable. As I said above, we must learn from mistakes.

Why do we make mistakes? Because we are human is one reason. But too often it is because we don't have all of the facts and act on partial knowledge. A lack of skill and experience can cause mistakes.

Whenever we do make mistakes let us take steps to correct them. Let us learn from them, and pray for God's guidance to avoid them.

MONEY
Ecc 10:1-20; Mt 19:16-30; Mk 10:17-31; Lk 16:1-15.

Money is necessary and can accomplish much good or evil, depending upon how it is used. A common saying is that money is the root of all evil. But the actual saying is found in 1 Timothy 6:10, where it says, *"The love of money is the root of many kinds of evil."* It is the *pursuit*, not the money itself. Sometimes money becomes a substitute for love. Some children need the love of a parent but are given money and presents instead. There is no substitute for giving of yourself.

Money can even become our god. It is what is important to us. It is what we pursue. It is this love of money that is evil because it has replaced the living God.

Money is not a measurement of our standing with God, but how we use it shows what we value. Let us make the best use of our money. Let us do great things for God. Let us help others. But let us begin where we are right now and give our portion to God. Let's not say, "When I become a millionaire I'm going to give large sums to the church." I hope that you do give large amounts when you become a millionaire, but start your giving right now. Give what you can now. Also, do not let your integrity be compromised by money.

Sometimes even the church shows preferential treatment to the wealthy in the hope that they will donate some money to it. This is wrong. James 2:3 points that out. We must not discriminate between the rich and the poor.

MOTIVES (Goal, PURPOSE)

Gen 27:1-46; Jer 17:1-18; Jas 4:1-12.

How we react in a situation often reveals our motives. It is only God who knows our real motives.

Many times, we do things with the wrong motives. We may be doing something for self-importance instead of doing it for service to God. What are your motives? Are you helping someone to do good or in the hope of gaining a favor?

Prayer and worship needs to be done with the proper attitude and motives also. Prayer is a communication with God. We should praise God in prayer. We should seek guidance and strength. But we should never try to get His stamp of approval upon our work, but rather go to Him and find out what He wants us to do and then do His will.

Prayer and worship are not an attempt to act holy, or a ritual that we do, but rather they are responses to His holiness. We have to have this motive for our prayer life and worship time to be effective.

MOURNING (Grief, SORROW)

Gen 50:1-26; 2 Sam 1:1-16; Jn 11:7-44.

Mourning is an important part of life. It takes time. Some require more than others, but there are stages that have to be dealt with in the grieving process in order for the person to be restored to wholeness. When this process is stifled, then problems occur.

We mourn because we have lost someone who is dear to us. It is good to mourn. We rejoice that they are with God, but there is some mourning also.

Jesus showed His compassion. John 11:35 is the shortest verse in the Bible it says, "Jesus wept." This was an example of Jesus showing His compassion.

MOVING (CHANGE)

Num 10:11-36; Est 2:1-18; Mt 2:1-18.

Moves can be upsetting, especially for children as they leave friends and change schools. I moved many times when I was in my school-age years and I did not like it. But one certainty in life is change. I used to live in Chicago, and there was the saying, "If you don't like the weather just wait a while and it'll change."

One consolation is that in spite of all the change around us, God never changes. Hebrews 13:8 says that *"Jesus is the same yesterday, today, and forever."*

There are different kinds of moves and different reasons for moves: safety, career, educational, vocational.

As we make moves, it is also helpful to realize that God is in control, and He has a purpose. Let us trust in Him. One example of a move is with Joseph. His brothers threw him in a pit and had considered killing him, but instead sold him to a caravan that took him to Egypt. After some more moves there, including a time in prison, Joseph rose to a high position and saved not only Egypt from a famine but his own household (Gen 39-46). This is a marvelous example of God at work. Thus, we must always rely upon Him.

MURDER (Kill)

Gen 4:1-26; Deut 5:1-33; Jas 5:1-6.

Murder is a terrible sin. It is destroying someone who is made in the image of God. Thus, it is a crime against God as well as against other people.

Murder begins with lesser sins. It can start with hatred. You hate or get angry, and this can progress to the point of murder. Or if it does not progress that far, then you have committed murder in your mind. Lust can lead to murder. The story of David and Bathsheba illustrates that. David committed adultery with Bathsheba, and then in an attempt to try to hide it he had her husband come home from the battle. He was hoping that Uriah would sleep with his wife and that would cover up the adultery. But Uriah did not sleep with her. Finally David had Uriah put at the front of the battle and the others drew back and he was killed. Thus, David had him murdered to cover up his lust (2 Sam 11:1-17).

I wonder about another kind. Isn't a rejection of Christ's sacrifice for you actually a murder of Him? You are killing, or trying to kill, what He has done. You can't kill what He has done, but you have killed its effect upon you unless you repent of that sin.

NATURE (CREATION, WORLD)

Ps 19:1-14; Mt 8:23-27; Rom 1:18-32.

We learn many things about God just by looking at nature. We see the magnitude of the universe, and we must be amazed at His greatness, His power. How awesome He is. We see His glory in the beauty everywhere: in birds, flowers, autumn leaves, the blue sky, a sunset, and starry night. We see orderliness in His nature, for it is not capricious, but rather there are natural laws at work.

We can learn humility and wonder from nature. What are we compared to such splendor? His wisdom is seen from the intricate details that we see at work in nature. Nature involves the magnitude of the planets and solar system to the infinitesimal world of the atom.

There are things that nature does not teach us, and for that we must read the scriptures. In them, we learn of His grace, love, and salvation.

Since this is my Father's world, we need to care for it. Unfortunately we exploit it. The oil is being used for energy, and is being depleted. Coal was an earlier source that we used. We pollute the air. We need to be faithful stewards of this planet to prevent it from becoming a garbage dump.

NEEDS (DESIRES, SERVING)

Ex 20:1-21; 2 K 6:1-7; Ruth 2:1-23; Ps 104:1-35; Mt 23:1-39; 25:31-46; Mk 8:1-13.

God made us and knows our needs. We should not be anxious about them. As Christians, we are called to help the needs of other people. This is one of our services. We are to look to Him for the strength in meeting our needs and the needs of others. The deepest need that we have is a need for fellowship and for a genuine relationship with the living God. This is the hunger that we all have. Unfortunately, some try to fill that hunger by drugs, alcohol, and various other types of things. Let God into your life. That is the only thing that will satisfy your soul. That is the food that it needs.

NEIGHBOR

Ex 20:16; Lev 19:13, 16-18; Prov 3:28-29; Jer 22:13; Mt 7:12; 25:34-35; Lk 10:25-37; Rom 13:8-14; 15:2; Jas 2:8-9.

We are expected to show love to one another. We are to have a healthy love for ourselves so that we can love other people. Matthew 22:38-39 tells us to love God with all our heart, mind, and soul, and to love our neighbor as ourselves. Matthew 25:34-35 says that by meeting the needs of others, we are doing it unto the Lord. Luke 10:25-37 tells the story of the Good Samaritan. He helped the man in need and thus acted as a neighbor. He indeed was a neighbor. Our neighbor is anyone in need.

NEW COVENANT

Jer 31:1-40; Lk 22:1-38; Heb 7:11-28.

Since the Old Covenant had been broken, God replaced it with the New Covenant. At the Last Supper, Jesus institutes the New Covenant (see Lk 22:20.) In Jeremiah 31:33, God says that He will put the law in their minds and write it upon their hearts. Ezekiel 11:19 says that a heart of stone will be removed from them and be replaced with a heart of flesh.

The New Covenant centers on Christ and is not only for the Jews but for all nations. A special relationship with God is offered. This relationship comes from knowing God through His Son, Jesus Christ. It is not a ritual or a law but a relationship. It is a daily walk with God.

The New Covenant is established through the death of Jesus on the Cross. He died for our sins. Our sins were atoned for once and for all. His death covers all sins past, present and future. Through Him, we can go directly to God. We do not need someone to pray for us. We can pray directly to God.

OBEDIENCE (Cooperation, Submission)

Gen 3:1-24; Ex 5:4-9; 15:22-27; 19:5; 20:6; Deut 30:11-19; Josh 9:1-6; 22:2; I K 3:14; 1 Ch 15:11-29; 2 Ch 14:1-15; Ps 1:2; 25:10; 111:10; 112:1; 143:10; Prov 28:7; Mt 5:17-20; Mk 3:35; Lk 8:21; 11:2, 28; 12:37-38; Jn 9:4; 15:10, 14, 16; Act 5:29; Phil 2:12; 1 Jn 2:3-6, 17; 3:22-24; 2 Jn 1:6, 9; Rev 22:7, 14.

It is important to obey God, for He has our best interests in mind. This is in the same manner as a young child should obey his or her parents, because the parents want to protect the child and help the child to grow up to be a responsible young man or woman. God wants good for us because He loves us. We please Him when we obey Him and return the love that He has shown to us.

Obeying God can bring peace of mind, for we can rest assured that this is the most beneficial for us; that this way will succeed but all other ways will fail. It brings us a peace of spirit because we are doing the Father's will.

Sometimes obedience is very difficult. It was not easy for Jesus to obey and die on the Cross. But regardless of the difficult situation or circumstances that you find yourself in, or if you don't understand what is in store, we must still obey—obey in love. We each have to carry our own cross (Lk 14:27).

OBLIGATION (Debt, DUTY)

Deut 5:1-33; 1 Sam 25:1-44; Rom 8:13-14.

Religion, for some, is an obligation. We don't like it but it has to be done. We have many obligations, but our religion should not be one of them. We are not to serve God as an obligation, but out of love.

In the light of all that He has done for us, how can we not love Him? How can we not love and forgive those for whom Christ died? But it must be in a response of love, not out of duty.

We need to carry out all of our obligations in an honest and loving manner. Do not regard them as burdens but as a means to serve God.

OCCULT (EVIL, Satanic)

Deut 18:9-13; 1 Sam 28:1-25; Is 8:19; 47:12-14.

Today, as has been through the ages, people are seduced by the occult. The occult pertains to various secret practices. It is a satanic lie. It professes to show truth, but it is Satan's way of luring people away from the saving knowledge of Jesus Christ. The occult professes a secret knowledge. Follow this way and you can have all of the riches of the world. Does that sound familiar? It is one of the temptations that Satan offered to Jesus (see Mt 4:9) when he told Jesus to bow down and worship him.

Some of the occult involves animal or even human sacrifice, and the worship of demons. It is a worship of something or someone other than God. It is an attempt to gain power.

Do not let things as numerology, tarot cards, palm reading, astrology, and things like that take root in your life. Know the word of God. This is the strongest weapon against the occult. Occult leads to destruction. Take the way of life and not destruction.

OFFENSE (ANGER, Hurt)

Mk 6:1-6; Act 17:21-26; 1 Cor 8:1-13.

All of us get angry and are hurt and hurt people from time to time because we are human. This makes it all the more important to forgive one another and to seek forgiveness. We also need to remember that any time that you speak the truth, no matter how loving and sensitive you are in speaking it, someone will probably be offended.

You have to compromise on unimportant things so the really important things can be received without offense. Like Paul, we need to limit our freedom so as not to be a stumbling block to anyone (1 Cor 8:9).

OPENNESS (HONESTY)

Josh 17:1-18; Mt 2:1-23; Mk 4:1-20.

Openness is an important characteristic for a Christian. Are you open-minded? We need to be open to change, to God's leading. As others share with you, listen with a receptive mind and a loving heart. It is this type of relationship that is needed.

Openness does not mean that you accept everything that you hear. But you listen to it and weigh it. When we are wrong then we change our mind. We do not adopt the maxim, "We've always done it this way."

OPPORTUNITIES (FREEDOM)

Num 14:1-45; Prov 1:24-26; Jer 8:20; Ezek 3:19; Hos 5:6; Mt 10:14-15; 11:20; 25:1-10, 36-37, 41-43; Mk 6:30-44; Lk 12:47; Eph 3:1-13; Phil 12:1-30.

How do you look at opportunities? Some of them are felt to be too good to be true, and many times they are. Let us look for God's will in a given situation. How can God be served and honored? In Matthew 25:1-10 is the parable of the wise and foolish virgins. The wise were prepared for the opportunity, but the foolish were not, and so they missed out on the opportunity. In verses 36 and 37 of that same chapter, we have an example of an opportunity for service and it is taken advantage of and the person is blessed for doing that service.

We have opportunities to share the good news of Jesus Christ. We need to take advantage of these and do it in word and in deed. An opportunity can even arise out of hardship.

If a situation seems difficult, then do your part, but also pray for God to receive your effort and magnify and bless it for the accomplishment of His goals.

OPPOSITION (Difficulties)

Ezra 4:1-24; Lk 10:1-24; Jn 3:1-21.

If we obey God, we will meet opposition because we live in a sinful world in which Satan is at work. Jesus tells that to His disciples in John 16:33, but in that same verse, He states, "I have overcome the world."

The opposition takes many forms. Sometimes it is resistance to change, and sometimes it is ignorance. It can even be religious opposition, for Jesus's strongest opposition was from the religious leaders. Whatever the reason, let us use it as an opportunity to get stronger.

We should not react to opposition in anger or hatred, but go ahead in confidence and do God's will.

OPPRESSION

Ex 22:16-31; Deut 24:14-15; Ps 9:9; 10:17-18; 12:5; 74:21; 119:134; Prov 3:31; 14:31; 22:22; 28:3; Ecc 4:1; 5:8; 7:7; Is 1:17; 58:6; Zech 7:10; Mt 23:2; 1 Tim 5:1-25.

We need to be aware of the needs of all people—both our friends and strangers. Are some of these people being oppressed?

There are different kinds of oppression. This can be political, financial, sexual, racial, etc.

We are to meet the needs of the oppressed and not be indifferent to them.

PAIN (Hurt)

I Sam 5:1-12; Mt 8:14-17; 16:21-28; Mk 14:36; 2 Cor 4:17; 12:7-10; Heb 12:1-13.

We don't like pain, but sometimes it is necessary. Physical pain can be a warning that something is wrong with the body. Physical pain teaches also. A little child touches something hot and learns that he or she better not touch that again. A parent can warn a child about something and say, "That will hurt." There are emotional pains also. The loss of a friend or a loved one causes pain.

Pain can be a test of our commitment. Are we willing to be uncomfortable, endure pain, even death for our faith? Jesus endured the brutal scourging and agonizing death on the Cross for our sakes. In Luke 14:47, Jesus tells us that we must be willing to bear our cross also if we would be His disciples.

We need to pray to God for His strength to face the pain that sometimes comes as a result of serving Him. We also need to pray and do what we can to ease the pain of others.

PARENTS (FAMILY, HOME)

Ex 10:2; 12:26-27; 20:5; 21:17; Lev 20:9; Num 30:1-16; Deut 4:9-10; 6:1-25; 11:18-19; Ps 103:13; Prov 1:1-9; 3:12; 13:22-24; 19:18; 22:6, 15; 27:11; 31:28; Is 38:19; Joel 1:3; Mal 10:37; Mt 20:20-28; Lk 11:11-13; Eph 6:4; Col 3:21; 1 Tim 3:4; 5:8; Tit 1:6; 2:4; Heb 12:7.

Parents must be good role models for their children. A child cannot understand what it means for God to be a loving Father if the father that he or she has is a cruel, abusive person. The children are to learn about God and His laws about moral decisions from their parents' examples. It means that by word and deed, parents help them to learn the truths of the scriptures and apply those truths to daily living.

Being a good parent is not easy. It is a big and important responsibility, but it is well worth the effort when you see your children grow up to become responsible young men and young women who love the Lord. Thus, parents should seek God's help in this important task.

PASTORS (Ministers)

Lev 21:6; Deut 18:1-8; I Sam 2:35; 2 Ch 6:41; Prov 11:30; Jer 3:15; Mal 2:6-7; Mic 3:1-12; Mt 5:19; 7:15, 22-23; 10:16; 20:25-27; 28:19; Lk 10:7-8; 12:11-12; 24:49; Jn 3:27; 4:36; 10:2-5, 11-15; 15:20-21; Act 1:8; 10:42; 20:17-38; Rom 12:6-7; 1 Cor 4:1-13; 15:10; 2 Cor 3:6; 4:1; 5:14, 18, 20; Phil 3:17; 1 Tim 2:1; 3:1-15; 5:1-2, 17; 6:11-14; Tit 1:5-9.

To be a pastor is an awesome and high calling with a huge responsibility. A pastor is like a shepherd. He is to guide His congregation. There are many expectations of a pastor, and very often they are not realistic. What then is a pastor?

A pastor is a human that has been called by God to serve by leading a church. (Some will debate whether it is proper for a woman to be a pastor. I am ignoring that debate here and using the masculine pronoun throughout simply to avoid the awkwardness of having to use him or her.) This involves a lot of skills. No pastor has all of the skills needed. Some pastors have more of these skills than others; therefore, it is important to help the pastor instead of looking at the pastor's shortcomings.

The pastor should model personal obedience to God. He should be concerned first and foremost in serving God and not in seeking the favor of men. It is unfortunate that sometimes a small clique controls the church in its decisions, etc. This is wrong. The pastor must also not forget his family. Sometimes in the name of dedication the pastor neglects his family. This is wrong. He needs to show to the congregation and to his family that the family is important. This will serve as a warning to those that would neglect their families because of work. If that pastor is a parent, then the pastor has the same responsibilities as any other parent.

Pastors serve people. They teach, preach, visit, counsel, conduct administrative duties of the church, and seek the lost, to mention a few of their duties.

He constantly seeks to lead others to God by his word and deed. He prays to God for the strength to carry out his work. He opposes evil.

The pastor is not perfect just as none of us is perfect. To the best of his ability, he has dedicated his life to use the gifts that God has given to him to lead the church. A pastor is a shepherd. A pastor should also be an enabler. He uplifts his flock and those with whom he comes in contact with, and he reaches out. He must love his people, and his people need to love him. Pray for your pastor. I am a former pastor, and I know that they need much prayer, for this is an awesome undertaking and a big responsibility that has been entrusted to them.

PATIENCE (Calmness)

Gen 6:1-22; Ex 5:1-23; Josh 23:1-16; Neh 9:1-38; Est 6:1-14; Lk 15:11-32; 2 Th 1:1-12.

God has great patience. He shows us patience so that we may turn from our sin, repent, and be saved (2 Pet 3:9). It should not be taken for granted. There is a time of judgment coming in which unforgiven sin will be punished.

Often we grow impatient. We are too quick to act. We need to stop and think before we act or speak. Is this deed, act, or word beneficial?

We must learn to wait. God will act in His time. Trust Him and believe in His great love. Look for Him at work in every situation. Even hard times can be opportunities to develop our patience.

PEACE (Rest, SECURITY)

Gen 21:1-7; 45:24; 2 Ch 14:1-15; Ps 3:1-8; 34:14; 37:4, 11, 37; 119:165; 120:6-7; 122:1-9; 133:1; Prov 15:17; 16:7; 17:1, 14; 20:3; Is 26:3, 12; 32:2, 17-18; 53:5; Hos 2:18; Mt 5:9; Lk 2:14; 21:1-38; Jn 14:1-31; 16:33; Act 7:26-29; Rom 5:1-11; 12:18; 1 Cor 14:33; 2 Cor 13:11; Gal 5:22; Phil 4:7-9; 1 Th 5:13; 1 Tim 2:2; 2 Tim 2:22; Heb 12:14; 1 Pet 3:10-11. (see concordance for complete references on this topic)

What is peace? There are many different kinds, and it is sought in different ways. Are you at peace? What are you doing to seek it?

Peace is more than an absence of hostility although that is one form of peace. We all hunger for peace, but too often it is sought in the wrong way, and thus it is not found.

Peace comes from knowing God not just with the mind, but with your whole being. In this way we become whole; for apart from God, we are broken. We must find our rest in Him. He has made us for Himself.

Peace is resting in Him. John 14:27 Jesus says that He gives us His peace. He is stronger than any worries that we might have. The cares of the world press in upon us, but do not let them rob you. Rest firmly in Jesus Christ for that calmness of spirit, heart, and mind that we need.

PEER PRESSURE (Conformity)

Mt 14:1-12; Lk 23:13-25; 2Cor 6:3-13.

Peer pressure is not just confined to teenagers. We do not want to be considered as odd or different, so we conform. However, this type of thinking can lead to bad decisions and sin. Keeping up with the Joneses can be devastating financially and morally. You might have to do some immoral things to get the funds, or it may cause you to engage in an immoral lifestyle.

We must have a strong faith to stand up for what we believe and act on those beliefs. Let our joy be in serving God and not in pleasing the crowd. The only word of caution here is that we need to be sensible in the exercise of our faith so that it is attractive (without any compromise of principle) instead of repulsive. People were drawn to Jesus. True faith is attractive also. But we also need to remember that it was that same crowd that turned on Jesus and shouted, "Crucify Him."

PERSECUTION (Intimidation, Opposition)

Ps 11:2; 42:3, 10; 69:7-9, 20; 109:25; 119:51, 61; Is 53:3-7; Mt 5:1-16; 10:16-17; 12:14; 24:1-51; Mk 3:6; Lk 11:53-54; 20:20; 21:12; 22:2; Jn 5:16; 7:1; 10:20; 15:18-19; 17:14; 18:22-23; Act 5:29; 7:52; Rom 8:17, 35-37; 2 Cor 4:8-9; 11:24-25; 1 Th 1:6; 2:2, 14-15; 2 Tim 1:8, 12; Heb 11:25-26; 12:2-3; 1 Pet 1:1-12; 3:14-17; 4:1, 12-19; 1 Jn 3:1, 13.

We do not want to be persecuted, but we are, to a greater or lesser extent. You must not let persecution cause you to stray from your faith. Perhaps this persecution will not cost you your life but it has in the past and even today sometimes does.

We must let any persecution that we face be an opportunity to develop our character, our faith. Let people see that we are ready to be faithful even when it hurts and even when it is unpopular.

Rely upon God's strength to see you through these times. Persecution is a method that God has used to spread the gospel. The Christians in the New Testament times were persecuted in Jerusalem, so they left the city and the gospel was spread in wider and wider circles (see Acts 8).

PERSEVERANCE (ENDURANCE)

Neh 4:1-23; Ps 37:24, 28; Prov 4:18; Hos 12:6; Mk 13:1-23; Lk 22:31-32; Jn 8:31-32; Act 14:21-22; Rom 8:38-39; 1 Cor 15:58; 16:13; Gal 6:9; Phil 3:16; Col 1:10, 22-23; 1 Th 3:8, 13; 5:21; 2 Th 3:13; Tit 1:9; Heb 2:1; 3:1-19; 4:14; 6:1, 11-12; 10:23, 35-36; 12:1; 2 Pet 1:10-11; Rev 21:7; 22:11.

Perseverance or endurance shows a genuine commitment to God because that means that you continue to be faithful even when it is not easy. It shows that you take your faith seriously. You are for real. Let us daily trust in God to help develop this endurance. Let us rely upon Him in confidence. And may we affirm, like Paul in Romans 8:38-39: **THERE IS ABSOLUTELY NOTHING, NO NOTHING THAT CAN SEPARATE US FROM THE LOVE OF GOD WHICH IS IN CHRIST JESUS.**

PERSISTENCE (ENDURANCE, HOPE)

Gen 8:1-22; 32:22-32; Mt 7:7-12; Heb 1:1-14.

Because God has such great patience, He is also persistent. He is constantly seeking us so that we may return to Him. It is a love that knows no limits and is pursuing us.

Persistence, if it is merely stubbornness, is a bad habit in us. But we should be persistent in seeking Him, in helping others find Him, in developing our talents for Him. We must respond to His persistence. We must be steadfast in our love for Him.

PLANS (Goals)

Gen 41:1-40; Josh 1:1-18; Prov 13:1-25; Mt 6:25-34; Eph 1:1-14; Jas 4:13-17.

Plans are important. To accomplish a task, we must know what we want to accomplish and how we intend to accomplish it.

Planning can save time, money, and mistakes. If we don't plan, then we find that we only have money or material for part of the task (see Lk 14:28). We may run into tasks that we can't do. There may not be enough, or even any, workers. There may not even be a need for your task. These and many more problems are solved by planning ahead of time.

There are many things that we need to plan for. It is good to plan a day's activity so that it is a fruitful day and not just wasted. You can even plan a day of relaxation too. Encourage your children to plan for the future. What do they want to be? Planning is good, but don't become so organized that there is no room for spontaneity. "We can't do that. It's not in the schedule." You may have to say that some of the time, but not all of the time. And of course, one of the biggest things in your plan is to make sure that we are doing God's will and going in the direction that He wants us to go, and that we are taking time for Him to be in our schedule. God should not be an afterthought or something that is tagged on.

God from the beginning of time had our salvation in mind. First Letter of Peter 1:20 says that Jesus was the Lamb chosen before the foundation of the world. His plans have our best interests in mind. We must read the scriptures and have the Spirit fill us with His purpose. Let us seek first His kingdom in our planning and all of the other things that we are seeking will be added to this. Too often we seek the other things first, and this is just the reverse of what we should be doing (Mt 6:33).

PLEASURE (enjoyment)

Gen 1:1-2:1; 25:19-34; Prov 21:17; Ecc 2:1; Is 5:11-12; 47:8-9; 1 Tim 4:1-16; 5:6; 2 Tim 3:4; Tit 3:3; Heb 11:25-26.

What gives you pleasure? Is it wrong to have pleasure as a Christian? Is being a Christian boring?

God was pleased with His work, so we know that pleasure is not wrong, but good. What is wrong is the way in which some people try to find pleasure and what they find pleasure in. For example, good, healthy, sexual pleasure between married couples is good, but wanton sexual lust is evil. Drinking yourself into a stupor is another wrong pleasure. Are the things in which you take pleasure in pleasing to God?

The pleasure in using money for great things for God is a great joy, but the accumulation of money and lust for it for selfish things is wrong.

Let us appreciate the great gifts that God has given to us. Let us appreciate them but not abuse them. Enjoy good food, but don't be a glutton. Love but do not lust. Enjoy life to its fullest, but do not take it.

The only true pleasure comes from serving God. Being a Christian is occasion for great joy. It is not boring. *Show this to others.* Too often we give the impression that God takes all of the fun out of life. The reverse is true. Any pleasure that comes from Satan is really a poisonous apple. It may appear attractive but it is deadly.

POPULARITY (Fame, Glory)

Mt 9:9-13; Lk 6:17-26; Jn 2:12-25; 1Jn 4:1-6.

We want to be popular, to be liked, but what are we willing to pay in order to be popular?

Sometimes, if you would be popular, you must put others down in order to build yourself up. Sometimes the truth has to be compromised. Popularity can be costly.

We need to seek God's way and let His truth dwell in us. Let us be great in His kingdom by following His example of serving others. In John 13:5, Jesus did the act of a slave and washed His disciples' feet. And in Mark 10:42-45, He says that whoever would be great must be the servant of all, and that He came not to be served but to serve. Thus, have a servant attitude. Instead of regarding it as demeaning and lowly, think of it as following our Lord, of obeying Him, and let us rejoice in our service. As a pastor visiting some people in the hospital, sometimes I felt that I received a greater blessing than those to whom I ministered.

Popularity is fleeting and fickle. On Palm Sunday, when Jesus came into Jerusalem, He was popular, but before the week was over that same crowd was shouting for Him to be crucified.

POSSESSION*S* (MONEY, Property)
Lev 25:1-55; Mt 6:19-34; Phil 4:10-20.

Too often people try to find happiness in possessions, but these are only temporary. No one will take his or her possessions with them after they die, so then who will get them? In Luke 12:16-21, Jesus tells the parable of the rich farmer who has a large crop and decides to build new barns to store his large harvest. Jesus calls him a fool, for that very night his soul is going to be demanded of him, so these possessions will belong to someone else.

Possessions can get in the way of our serving God. The rich young man Matthew 19:17-21 illustrates this. He came to Jesus wanting to have eternal life. Jesus told him to obey the commandments, and when he had said that he had done this, Jesus said, *"Sell what you have and give it to the poor and follow me."* The young man was sad because he was rich and went away. He loved his possessions too much to follow Jesus. He lost everything in that decision. Jesus does not demand poverty from all of His followers, but it was needed in this case. He needed to pursue God and be willing to abandon his possessions. In Matthew 6:19-21, Jesus says to lay up treasures in heaven, for these treasures cannot be stolen or corrupted. He says, in Matthew 16:26, *"What will it profit you to gain the whole world but lose your soul?"* The true contentment comes from knowing God. This is what fills the yearning, the longing that is in our hearts and souls.

Possessions can be and should be used for God's work, but they must not come to the point that they possess you. Possess your possessions but do not let them possess you.

POWER (Control, INFLUENCE)
Ex 4:1-17; Est 10:1-3; Nah 3:1-19; Mt 4:1-11; Mk 4:35-41; 5:21-43; Act 1:1-11.

There are different kinds of power. Many people seek it so much that that becomes their god. God's power is all around us. It is evident in the running of the universe. The natural laws operate at His command. He also works in less-evident ways. He works through people. He uses their skills, their gifts to accomplish His purposes.

To experience His power, we must trust Him so that He can work in and through us. The greatest demonstration of His power is through His Son,

Jesus Christ. Here we see His power over sin, evil, and death. The power of the Holy Spirit at work down through the ages is another demonstration of God's great power.

Human power is subject to God, and it is temporary. Human power can be corrupt and is a temptation. One of Satan's lies to man is, "I will give you this power and you will be like God."

If we are in a position of power, let us seek God to use our human power for His purposes, for good rather than in a selfish manner.

PRAISE (Adoration)

Gen 14:20; Deut 10:21; Jud 5:3; 1 Ch 23:30; Ps 7:17; 9:1-20; 28:6-7; 30:4; 35:18, 28; 41:13; 48:1; 66:1-4, 8; 67:3-4; 81:1; 89:5, 52; 103:1-22; 117:1-2; 146:1-10; 150:1-6; Lk 1:46-50; 2:20; Act 16:35; Eph 2:1-10; 3:20-21; 5:19; Phil 4:40; 1 Tim 1:17; Heb 13:1-25; Rev 14:7.

What is praise? God desires our worship, our praise. Praise is giving thanks to God. It is recognition of who He is. He alone is worthy of praise (Ps 145:3). In Revelation 5:12, Jesus as the Lamb of God is praised, *"Worthy is the Lamb."* It is a rejoicing of His mighty acts, His goodness, and His greatness. We give Him praise for His love, for our salvation through His redeeming love, and just for all that He is. We also should give praise to God for all those that He sends and uses to carry out His mighty purposes.

We should be thankful to God and to others for their kind deeds. Let them know that their efforts are appreciated and that you think that they did well.

PRAYER (Communicating)

Gen 18:16-33; 25:19-34; Ex 17:1-7; 22:23, 27; Josh 7:1-26; Jud 16:23-31; 2 Ch 6:1-42; Ezra 8:1-36; Neh 2:1-10; 4:9; Ps 4:1-8; 37:4; 145:18; Prov 3:6; 15:8; Is 55:6; Mt 6:5-15; 7:7; 18:19-20; Mk 9:28; Lk 18:1; 23:42-43; Jn 14:13-14; 17:1-26; Rom 8:26; 2 Cor 12:8; Phil 4:6; Col 1:1-14; 1 Th 5:17; 1 Tim 2:8; Heb 4:14-16; Jas 5:16; 1 Jn 5:14-15.

What is prayer? How do you pray? What should you pray for? Some people have mistaken ideas about prayer. For some, prayer is a desperate last-minute, last-effort plea. It is resorted to when everything else has failed. Then for others, prayer is a magical method to get God to do what you want Him to do.

Of course, true prayer is none of this. Prayer is a genuine communication with God, not some ritual. We communicate petitions, thanksgiving, and adoration; we seek guidance and numerous other requests. We need to remember that prayer to be communication involves listening. We must listen for God's response.

Through prayer we can find God's strength and will for us. Thus, prayer should be the first step in making a decision or when we are facing a problem and not the last. When we consider the nature of prayer, that it is communicating with the living God, then we realize that it is an awesome privilege that we have been given. Just think that the Creator of the heavens and earth is listening to you. He has allowed us to have this means of approach to Him.

Prayer shows our dependence upon God. We need Him. Some people think that they don't need Him and will say He doesn't exist. But God created you and sustains you, regardless of whether you believe it or not. Prayer is a means of restoring or maintaining the proper relationship with God.

Prayer should be done in a humble, respectful attitude. God does answer prayer. Sometimes the answer is *no*, and sometimes it is *wait*. And sometimes it is answered differently than we expect. Don't worry about flowery language, but just speak honestly from your heart to a loving Father. Make prayer a part of your daily life. Use this gift and count it precious. Have specific times, but also go about your life in a prayerful mood. That means with thanksgiving, confidence, and joy. Joy doesn't mean going around with a silly grin on your face, but an inner peace because we know that in Christ we are more than conquerors (Rom 8:37); nothing can defeat us. When you blunder, seek forgiveness.

PREJUDICE (Discrimination)
Est 3:1-15; Mk 6:1-13; Lk 10:25-37.

When a person has prejudice, they really do not have a healthy self-love. If we have hatred toward our fellow man, we cannot love God (see 1 Jn 4:20). In a similar manner, if we do not love ourselves, then we cannot love others.

There is a difference between healthy self-love and self-centered pride. A healthy self-love recognizes your shortcomings and sees the worth that is in you. Pride is to the point of putting yourself and your goals first.

Prejudice works on presuppositions instead of the truth. If we are prejudiced toward someone, we need to ask for God's forgiveness and guidance to overcome that attitude so that a proper attitude can be restored toward that person. We have absolutely no right to be prejudiced toward anyone.

There have been terrible things that have been done and are still being done because of prejudice. People have even lost their lives because of the hatred that prejudice promoted. Even more terrible is that some of the people have claimed to be Christians.

PRESSURE (INFLUENCE)

Gen 25:19-34; 39:1-23; Mt 14:1-12; Mk 14:32-42.

We experience pressure daily and from a variety of sources. There are good pressures and there are bad ones. Often we need a certain amount of pressure to keep us going. Then, too, some people work better under pressure than others. If you do not work well under pressure, then try to take steps ahead of time to try to prevent or lessen the pressure. In the case of bad pressure, do not let those pressures cause you to do wrong things. One type of bad pressure is that someone holds something over your head that you do not want revealed. Do not let them control you. Admit the wrong. Take the power away from them.

There are the pressures from your job. The job expects you to accomplish certain things within a certain time frame and in an acceptable manner. Sometimes the job may try to get you to compromise your beliefs. "If you don't do this, then you can kiss your job good-bye." Do not compromise your beliefs. Challenge the person that is causing this pressure. He or she may not be acting with the company's blessing. Do not let the job's demands on your time rob you of your family.

There is the pressure of debt, of paying bills, and completing other obligations. Time itself is a pressure as you try to accomplish several things in a short amount of time. Often parents exert pressure on their children in expecting them to make good grades, in the choice of their friends, and in their career choice. Parents, you should expect good grades, but do not be overcritical and recognize the child's limitations. One child may be an A student and another may not. Another might be athletic or artistic and another is not. Encourage them and help them to do their best and be pleased with that. You should also encourage them to develop their strengths and talents and abilities.

There are political and moral pressures trying to force you in a certain direction and to make a certain decision. We even exert pressure on ourselves, and that is good, provided you are not too hard on yourself.

Let us seek God's help in meeting our pressures. Do not let them overcome you. Sometimes we need to escape from the pressures, but sometimes we need to endure them.

When faced with pressure, we need to look at it honestly and use good reasons in the decisions we make on how to deal with the pressure. Do not rationalize. We need to consider the long-term effects of this pressure or temptation. Is it harmful? Seek God's guidance. Pray about your decision.

PRIDE (Arrogance, CONCEIT)

Deut 8:11-14; 1 K 20:11; Job 11:12; Ps 9:20; 10:1-18; 18:27; 31:23; 75:4; 101:5; 138:6; Prov 15:5, 10-12, 25, 32; 26:5, 12, 16; 27:2; Zeph 3:11; Mal 4:1; Mt 23:6-7; Mk 6:1-12; Lk 18:9-14; 20:46; 1 Cor 3:18; 8:1-2; 10:12; 2 Cor 12:7; Eph 2:11-22; Jas 4:6; 1 Jn 2:16.

Pride separates us from God and others because we let our self-importance get in the way. We do not seek God for a need for Him, but to show how good we are.

For God to rule in us and be able to use us, we must be humble enough to recognize our need for Him. We must depend upon Him.

Have respect for yourself, for after all, a human being is one of God's wondrous works. But have a great love for God and for others. Have a great dependence upon Him.

Let your pride be in the greatness of God, of His mercy, of His majesty, of His saving grace in Jesus Christ. As Paul writes in 1 Corinthians 1:31, "Let him who boasts boast in the Lord."

PRIORITIES (Objectives)

Prov 3:1-35; Mt 6:25-34.

What are your priorities? Many people's priorities begin with themselves. *I am number one. It is all about me.* Our first priority should be to God. We must seek Him first. Jesus, in Matthew 10:39, says that whoever loses his life for Christ's sake will find his life. Again, in Matthew 6:33, Jesus says for us to seek the Kingdom of God and His righteousness first and then all these things will be added to us. Thus, if I pursue myself first, then I will lose everything, but if I pursue God then I will gain everything.

Your family, friends, your country, and other basic needs have their priorities, but the first priority must be God, not religion, but God. Be obedient to God and He will show us the proper order of our priorities.

PRIVILEGES (OPPORTUNITIES)

Rom 1:1-7; Eph 3:1-13; Heb 10:19-39.

Here in America we have many precious privileges. We should take advantage of those privileges and use them for good. Let us appreciate them and not take them for granted. It is tragic that here in our country some people try to take away the privileges of others just so theirs can be exercised. The freedom of religion means that we are not to be forced to participate in a particular religion. In other words, there is no state church, but it does not mean that those who want to participate in that religion cannot.

There are also precious privileges that God offers to us. Like our privileges in America, we need to take them, use them, appreciate them, and not take them for granted. What are these privileges? He offers us forgiveness of our sins, of coming to Him in prayer, and a new life in Christ. He gives His great love, the love of a Heavenly Father.

It is awesome to imagine the intimate fellowship with the Almighty God that is offered because through Jesus Christ, we have been made children of God (Jn 1:12).

We are also given the gift of eternal life, which begins right now.

Take advantage of these privileges. Give God thanks for them. Enjoy them and help others to know them. Share this feast with all who will come.

PROBLEMS (Adversity)

Gen 12:10-20; 16:1-16; Job 2:1-10; Jn 6:1-15; Rom 8:28-39; Phil 1:12-30; 2 Th 1:1-12; Jas 1:1-18.

Life is full of problems. How do you meet them? Do you run from them? What strength or resources do you use?

Sometimes we meet problems because we bring them upon ourselves. We have all heard the saying, "He (or she) is asking for trouble." That person usually finds it. Sometimes we meet problems because we are obeying God in a sinful world. Let these times be an opportunity to serve Him and others. Let us show how strong our faith is. Not how strong we are, but how strong the One that resides in us is.

Then sometimes we have problems because we are impatient. We do not wait for God. We do not think God is acting fast enough, or we think that God somehow needs some help. One example of this impatience that has resulted in a problem that still exists today is with Abraham and his wife Sarah. God promised him a son that would be his heir, and nations would be blessed through him. But when the promised son was long delayed and Sarah was barren, they decided to take matters into their own hands. Therefore, Sarah had Abraham lie with Hagar, Sarah's handmaiden, and Hagar became pregnant and bore him a son named Ishmael (see Gen 6). But Ishmael was not the intended son of promise. Ishmael hence became a rival to the real son of promise, who is Isaac, that Sarah bore. If they had been patient, a lot of the turmoil that we have today would not be there. We need to wait on the Lord!

When we experience problems, we should not be surprised or bemoan our fate. Let us use it as an opportunity to grow. Pray for His strength in facing the problem. Trust in Him to accomplish His purposes and to see you through the situation.

PROCRASTINATION (Delay)

Josh 18:1-10; Prov 10:1-32; 26:1-28.

Do you procrastinate? Why? This is a bad habit. We delay doing something, and often the problem is more difficult because the delay has created other problems. Another surprise is that when we concentrate and do the task, often it is not as difficult as we imagined it to be. Procrastination causes worries because there is an undone task looming over our heads.

Procrastination burns up energy. There are imagined problems that are used for not doing something.

Procrastination can be very serious in many ways. You cannot be counted upon do a task. But worse of all is that if you put off accepting Jesus Christ as Lord and Savior, then it is possible to put it off so long that it is too late.

Let us be good stewards of time. Do not be lazy. Do it now. And if you have not accepted Jesus as Lord and Savior, do it right now.

PROMISES (COMMITMENT)

Gen 47:28-31; 50:22-26; Ex 2:11-25; 1 Sam 1:21-28; Mk 1:1-8; Phil 4:10-20.

The scriptures tell us of the precious promises of God. Because of His promises, we can face the future because He is faithful. A hymn entitled "Because He Lives," says, "Because He lives I can face the future, because He lives all fear is gone, because I know who holds the future, and life is worth the living just because He lives." Let that be your faith. Let that song sing in your heart.

If we would be faithful to Him, then our promises should be kept. God's promises were costly, for His Son died on the Cross in order that God could keep His promise of salvation. Thus, we must keep our promises even when it is difficult. We should not make promises lightly or ones that we have no intention of keeping. To break a promise has an effect upon your reliability, upon your word. Often parents make promises to children but break them.

Occasionally a promise has to be broken because of something unseen happening that keeps you from keeping that promise. This should happen as little as possible, and the other person needs to be told why the promise was broken.

So be careful what you promise. We should be regarded as dependable people. Our promises should not conflict with God's will.

PROPHECY (Prediction)

Deut 18:15-22; Mk 13:1-37; Rev 1:1-8.

Prophecy is a message from God to His people. It was to encourage obedience and trust in God. However, it also involved admonition. The prophets of the Old Testament gave many warnings to Israel when they wandered away from following God. The prophets stated that certain things would happen if the nation did not repent of its sin. The prophets called for repentance. As we look back upon fulfilled prophecy, we see it as confirmation that God is at work.

In Isaiah 53, we see many prophecies of the coming Messiah. These were fulfilled in Jesus Christ.

PROTECTION (Safety)

Ps 18:1-50; 31:20; 91:11; 121:7-8; Lk 21:5-24; Rom 8:38-39.

God protects His people. This does not mean that they will not experience physical harm or even death because they have, and they do, but His protection is from eternal loss In John 10:28-29, Jesus calls His followers sheep. He says that they know Him, *"I give them eternal life, and they shall never perish; no one can snatch them out of my hand. My Father, who has given them to me, is greater than all; no one can snatch them out of my Father's hand."* This is a tremendous promise. We are secure in God's hand. When you are secure in God, there is nothing that can touch your soul, and nothing can separate you from God (see Rom 8:38-39). Nothing can pluck you out of God's hand as we have just said. Therefore, no matter how dark things may appear, we are safe if we have committed our life to God.

We have the police for protection and there are laws for our protection. But we, as Christians, need to offer protection also. We are to help those who are being prejudiced against and taken advantage of. We can help protect them by standing up for beliefs and speaking out against evils.

PURITY (GOODNESS)

Josh 6:1-27; Ps 24:3-5; Prov 30:12; Is 1:18, 25; Dan 12:10; Mt 5:8; 23:1-39; Jn 15:2; 17:1-26; Phil 4:8; 1 Tim 1:5; 3:9; 5:22; Tit 1:15; Jas 4:8; 1 Pet 1:22; 1Jn 3:3.

True purity must come from a changed heart. It comes from within. This inward change comes from God. If we would be pure, then we must follow the example of Christ. We must confess our sin and follow Him. This involves a radical commitment of our whole being. Turn yourself over to Him to make that commitment. It is not easy, but dare to do it. Then allow Him to work in you so that indeed you do become pure. It is a process. It is growth.

PURPOSE (Meaning)

Num 9:15-23; Prov 3:1-35; 2Th 1:1-12.

Does life have any meaning? The Bible says yes. Everyone wants to feel that their life means something, that their life counts and that they are not just a "waste of good space." We find meaning and purpose by seeking God. God's love for us is proof that we are worth something. God gives life meaning. Many people look in other areas for meaning and purpose, but these will all fail. Trust in God for the meaning that you are searching for. Obey Him and find His will for your life. Follow Jesus.

If life seems senseless, then go to God to find direction. We are created by God, and therefore, if we would find our purpose, then we must find it from the Creator. The maker of something determines the thing's purpose, not the reverse. God determines our purpose. As a Christian, help others to find that meaning and purpose that comes from knowing Jesus as Lord and Savior. This is a knowing, which involves a personal walk with Him.

QUARRELS (ARGUMENTS)

Prov 13:1-25; Jas 4:1-12; Tit 3:1-11.

There are many reasons for quarrels. Evil desires are one of the reasons. They are a hunger for more, and this brings us in conflict with others. Sometimes quarrels are the result of petty details or misunderstandings. Pride is still another reason. A person does not want to admit that they are wrong. Sometimes quarrels continue long after anyone knows what started the argument. All they know is that the other person is wrong.

We need to seek God's guidance to help end the quarrel and end it quickly. We need to seek to try to heal the broken relationships, not cause divisions. Rely upon God. Jesus said, "Blessed are the peacemakers." If you are in an argument, don't demand to be right even if you are.

Even on a strong point of faith, don't demand agreement. You can assert that this is what you believe and if the two of you can discuss it in a calm manner, fine, but if not, then you will simply have to say in a calm manner, "We disagree on that."

Also remember that to receive forgiveness, you must give forgiveness. Therefore, you cannot maintain an unsettled quarrel with someone. You must forgive one another and end the quarrel. If the other person is not willing, then they have to face the Lord with that.

QUESTIONS (Curiosity)

Job 38:1-41; 42:1-17; Lk 17:18-35.

We have many questions, and we should have, because that is the way that we learn things. Not all of our questions are answered. Some of them are answered in unexpected ways. Let us be open to those answers.

We should encourage questions. Some feel it is wrong to question their faith. But Jesus is **the Way, the Truth, and the Life**, and He fears no honest question. Truth sought earnestly will lead you to Him. It is only when basic truths are ignored because they don't fit your theory that you can be led astray. Questions can help us grow. It can make our faith stronger.

Many skeptics have approached the Bible in an attempt to disprove it, but instead have been convinced by the truth that they find there.

QUITTING (see GIVING UP)

RACISM (see PREJUDICE)

REBELLION (DISOBEDIENCE)
Deut 31:1-29; Josh 24:1-33; Jude 1:1-25.

By nature we are rebellious. Genesis 3 tells of man's sin. It was disobedience to God. Sin is rebellion against God. We try to take God's place. Rebellion is a conscious decision and it leads to judgment. God punishes rebellion against Him.

Why do we try to take God's place? We don't want someone to tell us what to do. We want to be boss. Yet it is silly. What can we control—nothing. We can't control anything because we have to use the laws that God has created. We can't change those laws. We can't create anything. We can manipulate the material that is already here to build something, but we can't create. Part of what is back of our rebellion is a belief in one of Satan's lies. And that is that God can't be trusted (see Gen 3:5). We have to look out for ourselves. If God can't be trusted, then life would truly be terrible, for we would be in the hands of a cruel person who can do as He pleases with us. But praise God that He is a Person that can be trusted, and trusted more than anyone else. That Person loves us with a mighty love. It is a love so great that He gave His Son for us (Jn 3:16).

Let us stop being foolish. Let us stop rebelling against the very one who wants to save us. God is the answer to what we are looking for. Through God we can become what we are striving for, but through Satan we will lose everything.

RECONCILIATION (FORGIVENESS)
Mt 18:15-20; Rom 5:1, 10; 11:15; 2 Cor 5:11-21; Eph 2:15-18; Phm 1:1-25; Heb 2:17.

Reconciliation is the work that Christ did on the Cross. He reconciled man to God and man to man. He restored the broken relationship between God and man, and man and man. This is the message of the gospel.

We too are to be ministers of reconciliation (2 Cor 5:18). We proclaim the good news that Jesus provides the way back to God. By word and deed, we perform reconciling acts. We are to heal brokenness. Let us show His love at work in us as we restore brokenness.

REDEMPTION (see Salvation)

REJECTION (ABANDON, Disapproval, LONELINESS)
1 Sam 10:1-27; Job 13:1-28; Ps 14:1-7; Mt 21:33-46; Mk 6:1-13.

Have you ever felt rejected by God or by others? When that happens, ask yourself why. God does not reject sinners, but sin. While we were still sinners, He provided a way to Him (see Rom 5:8). That way is Jesus Christ. He died so that we might receive forgiveness of our sins.

Others will reject you. It may be because of misunderstandings, some bad habits, or it can even be because you believe in God. When others reject you, get the support of other Christians, for we are to support one another (I Th 5:11). If you are rejected because of some sin in your life, then seek God's forgiveness of that sin and turn from it.

We sometimes reject God. Peter the disciple rejected His Lord but this was only temporary, and He asked for forgiveness. We can reject God by relying upon ourselves, our own judgment and will instead of God. We can reject Him by failing to trust Him and trusting others more than God. The most serious rejection of all is the rejection of His salvation.

Do not reject God. In Him only are the words of eternal life (see Jn 6:66).

RELATIONSHIPS (FELLOWSHIP)
Ex 33:7-11; Jn 16:16-33; 2 Cor 6:14-18; Eph 2:11-22.

Each of us has many different relationships. A relationship is simply a connection in some manner. There are relationships with family and relatives, with friends, with enemies, doctors, bankers, and many other professional people; grocers, mechanics, neighbors, people at church, coworkers, and any number of others. Some of these connections are temporary and superficial, and sometimes you are only a number or statistic while others are quite personal and deep. In fact, life is relationship.

A good relationship with another person is based on trust and mutual interest and respect. You enjoy being with that person. When a relationship develops beyond just a speaking acquaintance, then the persons become friends, or if the development goes in the opposite direction, then they become enemies. For the Christian, we still strive to love that person even if they regard us as an enemy and try to do us harm. We stand up for the rights of people, but we must always separate the act of a person from the person.

The highest and most important relationship that we can have is with God. Through Jesus this relationship is a very intimate one. We can approach God directly. Through Him we are called children of God (Jn 1:12). **The heart of the Christian faith is relationship**. There is lifestyle, philosophy, belief, and actions, but these all must flow from the heart. They are the signs and result of a changed heart. But the heart of the Christian faith is a **personal relationship** with the Living Lord, with Jesus Christ.

This relationship affects all of our other relationships. Instead of using people, manipulating for your ends, and taking advantage of them, you now are concerned in helping people, in serving others. If they do not know Jesus, then in a loving, nonjudgmental way, point them to Christ by your love, concern, word, deed, your whole life. Treat them with respect because Jesus did. He ministered to them and loved them. We can do no less.

With your Christian friends, you have an even closer relationship since you each know the Lord. Support and encourage each other. Bear each other's burdens (Gal 6:2). Since our fellow believers are children of God, just as we are, then they should be treated in that manner. They are our brothers and sisters. Treat them that way. But finally we need to remember that as we minister to people, we must not compromise our faith.

RELIABILITY (CONSISTENCY)
1 Ch 19:17-34; Ruth 3:1-18; Ps 33:1-22.

Are you reliable? Can you be counted upon? This is a very important trait. We like to have friends that are reliable and we need to be reliable. If you are reliable, then that means that your word is good. If you say you will do something, then you will do it. You are a responsible person. God is faithful. Therefore, we must be faithful also. We must be reliable people. Sometimes it is difficult, but we still need to carry out our commitments.

REPENTANCE (Regret, Remorse)
2 Sam 24:10, 17; Ps 22:27; 31:10; 34:14; 51:1-4, 17; 95:7; Prov 28:1, 13; Is 6:5; 55:6-7; 57:20-21; Jer 25:5; Lam 1:20; Ezek 14:6; Zech 1:3; Mt 3:1-12; 4:17; Mk 1:4; 2:17; Lk 3:1-18; 5:32; 13:28; 15:17-20; Jn 12:1-11; Act 2:37-40; 3:19; 5:31; Jas 4:8-10; 1Jn 1:9; 3:20.

Repentance is critical in our relationship with God. It is a turning away from sin and turning to God. It is an inward change, but will have outward results. Genuine repentance (as opposed to lip repentance) is demonstrated by action. It is an action that stems from the heart. In James 2:17-18, he points out that faith without works is death. He is not saying that we are saved by works. Faith is the only means for salvation. What he is saying is that if you have genuine faith, then that faith will show itself in works.

Confess your sins and show that this is true by the way that you live your life. God knows our heart. He knows when you are really repenting and when it is merely words.

REPUTATION (Fame, Name)
Deut 4:1-14; Ruth 2:1-23.

What kind of reputation do you have? There are many things that go into making that reputation. How you conduct yourself is part of your reputation. Are you a busybody, liar, cheat? Those are reputations, and not good ones. We don't want friends that have these reputations, and we shouldn't want to have such a reputation. Are you honest, reliable, and loving? Those are some more reputations, and they're good ones. We would like to have these reputations and would like for our friends to have these also.

Who you hang out with has an effect upon your reputation. If you are in a rowdy bunch, then people will assume you are rowdy too. It is guilt by association. The reverse of that is true. If you are in a well-mannered group, then they will assume that you are too, unless you demonstrate differently.

If you have a bad reputation, determine to change it. First, don't believe the label that is put on you. Yes, you may be telling a lot of lies and are performing like the label says you are, but the label only defines your actions. It does not define you. Don't let your actions define who you are. You don't have to continue telling lies. You can change your actions. Do so, and quickly. Also watch your associations. Associate with people of a good reputation. However, to a certain extent, the Christian needs to associate with those of ill repute. Jesus was criticized for associating with the prostitutes and disreputable people of His society. He associated with them to present God's love and give them a chance to change. Jesus said, *"The Son of Man came to seek and save what was lost."* This is why He associated with them—in order to redeem them. He did not engage in wrongful acts. He extended to them love and forgiveness and a chance to be restored to wholeness.

The next step in changing a bad reputation is to rely upon God's word and keep it in your heart. God's word changes people. With God's word in your heart, if you live it, then you will have the best reputation that counts and that is God's. You will also be demonstrating love and service to others. Do not be argumentative or overbearing. Be humble and imitate Christ.

RESENTMENT (ANGER)

Ex 20:1-26; Jud 8:1-3; Jas 1:1-27.

Do not let resentment rule your life. All of us get angry sometimes. Let that anger pass quickly; otherwise, your resentment can lead you into sinful actions and wrong and hurtful accusations of others. Also, anger can eat away at you like a cancerous growth. Do not let resentment prevent you from growing. You cannot love God and have anger in your heart (see 1 Jn 4:20).

RESPECT (HONOR)

Ex 3:1-22; I Sam 24:1-22; Act 5:12-42.

We are to respect God more than anyone else. Thus, we should come to Him in a humble, reverent manner.

We show those in authority respect, except where it would interfere with God's laws. Religious leaders should be given respect. Respect one another. We do this by listening to them and treating them as we would like to be treated ourselves. We need to treat all people with respect because of God's love for them.

RESPONSIBILITY (OBEDIENCE)

1 Ch 21:1-46; Mt 11:20, 22; 25:14-46; Lk 21:1-4; Jn 3:18; 12:48; 15:22-24; Act 6:1-7; 17:30; Eph 4:7.

God expects us to be responsible. We are to take what has been given to us and use it for His service. This also means working within our limitations.

Responsibility means admitting mistakes when they are made, making plans to accomplish short-, intermediate-, and long-range goals, and sharing workloads.

We have many responsibilities. In our jobs, our work carries certain responsibilities, depending upon your job and kind of job. One responsibility is just to get there on time. Another is to use your time and talents for whatever the task demands—clerical, managerial, teaching, construction, or whatever. On that job you should be doing your best.

There are responsibilities in the home. There is cooking, cleaning, paying bills, buying the groceries for the home, and disciplining the children if you are a parent with children. There are responsibilities at school. Life has many, many responsibilities. We must live as responsible people.

The Christian has the big responsibility of serving God and other people. We are to tell other people about God's salvation in Jesus Christ.

REST (Relaxation)

Gen 2:2-25; Ex 20:1-26; Heb 4:1-13.

Rest is part of God's plan. Life is more than all work. It is needed in order to maintain our well-being. Otherwise we can break down physically, emotionally, and spiritually. We rest to give God glory, to worship Him.

Enjoy the Sabbath. Use it for a time of refreshment of your body, mind, and soul. In Jesus's day, many restrictions were laid on the people because certain things were considered as work. Jesus stated in Mark 2:27 that the Sabbath was made for man, not man for the Sabbath. In other words, it was made for our benefit, to help us. It was not meant to be a hindrance.

RESTITUTION (Payment)

Ex 22:1-17; Lev 6:1-7; Num 5:5-10.

Restitution is essential for justice, righteousness, and forgiveness. It is the righting of wrongs. If you have harmed someone in some way, make the necessary amends that you need to do by repayment or whatever. If you have been wronged, then take steps to restore that relationship. Don't try to seek vengeance. The Old Testament did advocate punishment (Ex 24:20 for example). But the purpose was to limit the punishment. An eye for an eye meant that I could take the other person's eye, but I could not kill him. In the New Testament, Jesus tells us to not even take this limited approach (in Mt 5:38) He tells us not to resist someone who does us evil. The aim of course is to try to restore a broken relationship. God will punish sin.

RESTORATION (HEALING)

Ps 126:1-6; Mt 8:1-4; Eph 4:1-16.

God restores relationships. He heals. We, as the body of Christ, are to minister to one another. We are to help restore one another.

We carry out this ministry of restoration by showing love to each other, by carrying out acts of love. Jesus on the Cross provided the means by which we can be restored to a proper relationship with God and with each other.

RESULTS (ACHIEVEMENTS)

Ex 6:1-12; Jud 13:1-25; Lk 10:17-24; 17:1-10.

We expect instant results, but God's results are on His timetable. Thus, although we are obedient to God, we may not see the results right away. If we are faithful, then true results will come.

God said that He would deliver the Israelite people from the Egyptians and He did. He said that He would send a Messiah and He has. God always delivers on His promises.

RESURRECTION

Ps 16:9-10; 17:15; Hos 13:14; Mt 24:31; 27:52-53; 28:1-10; Jn 5:21, 25-28, 40, 44, 54; 11:23-25; Act 17:32; 1 Cor 6:14; 15:12-28, 35-58; 2 Cor 4:14; 5:1; 1 Th 4:14-16; 2 Tim 1:10; 2:18; Rev 1:18.

The resurrection is the crucial point of the Christian faith. It verifies all that Jesus said and did. Because He is raised, death has been conquered, and our sins are forgiven. Because He has been raised, we too shall be raised and have eternal life (Eph 2:6).

In the section on Jesus Christ, we mentioned some of the proofs of the Resurrection. First, the tomb is empty. There is no question about that. His enemies confirmed that. If the tomb were not empty, then they would have shown the body. Second, Jesus appeared to His disciples and many others after His resurrection. Third, His disciples were killed. They would be foolish to die for something that they knew was a lie when a confession would have saved their lives. Then, there is the testimony of changed lives down through the ages that testify that Jesus is alive.

Our resurrection body will be a body and soul that is eternal, without our present limitations (1 Cor 15:35-44). (My daughter, who can't walk, but is confined to a wheelchair, says, "When I get to heaven, I'm going to run all over heaven.") The resurrection body will be different in some ways but the same in other ways.

REVENGE (Retaliation)

Ex 21:23; Lev 24:17-22; 1 K 1:28-53; Ps 10:2; 24:29; Mt 5:38-48; 7:1-2; Rom 12:9-21; 1 Th 5:15; 1 Pet 3:9.

We are to forgive rather than seek revenge. Jesus told us to love our enemies (Mt 5:43-44). We are to do good things to those who persecute us. This is a love that seeks the best for a person. Forgiveness heals wounds. Hopefully by loving your enemies they may become your friends. All revenge should be left to God. He will punish evil.

REWARD (Payment)

Lev 25:18-19; 26:3; Deut 4:40; 25:15; 2 Ch 15:1-19; Mt 6:1-34; 10:32; 16:24-27; 19:16-30; 25:34-39; Mk 13:13; LK 6:22-23; 1 Cor 3:8; Heb 12:1-2, 28; Rev 7:14-17; 22:12.

God gives abundant gifts to those who love and serve Him, but we should serve out of love, and not with the idea of *what's in it for me,* because if you don't serve out of love then you will benefit nothing (see I Cor 13:1-3). The praise that men will heap on you is all the reward that you will get (see Mt 6:5). Love must be genuine. Do your acts with no thought of reward other than the pleasure of doing good deeds. Let doing good to others become a habit, a vital part of your life. Enrich your own life by enriching others.

RICHES (see WEALTH)

RIGHT (Honest)

Josh 7:1-26; Jud 17:1-13; Is 5:1-30; Rom 2:1-16.

What is right and what is wrong? Different people have different ideas about that, and some of those ideas can be very much distorted. Then again, there are many people that do not believe there are any absolute truths. It is all relative, so what is right for you may not be what is right for me. This is not true.

We must look to God for the correct answer to what is right and what is wrong. He has provided His standard. It has been true for centuries, it is true today, and will always be true. His will tells us to do what is right. We must strive to do it all of the time, and not just when it is easy, comfortable, or convenient. Thus, we have to search the scriptures to find God's standards of right and wrong. If we follow Christ's example, then we will always do what is right.

RIGHTEOUSNESS (GOODNESS, Morality)

Ps 1:1-3; 15:1-2; 24:3-5; 37:3-5, 9; 51:1-19; 58:11; 112:1-3; 121:3-8; Prov 3:1-10, 25-26; 26:3; 33:15-16; 64:1-12; Mt 5:20; 7:7; 12:35; 25:21, 33-34, 46; Mk 13:13, 27; Jn 3:15-18; 5:24, 29; 14:1-3, 12, 21-23; Rom 6:22-23; 8:4-6; 10:9; 14:17-18; 2 Cor 5:11-21; Gal 6:8-9; Phil 1:11; 4:7, 19; 2 Tim 1:1; Heb 4:9, 15-16; I Pet 5:4-10; 1 Jn 1:7-9; 5:1-4.

Our natural inclination is to please ourselves. We must seek God to cleanse us, to put a new heart within us. Our righteousness does not come from doing good deeds. Compared to God, all of our good deeds are nothing. We can only become righteous when we receive Jesus Christ (see Rom 5:8-9,19). Christ's righteousness is counted as our own. This is what He accomplished on the Cross.

RULES (Standards)

Mt 5:17-20; Rom 7:1-6.

God gives us rules that are meant to benefit us. Society has rules by which we need to live by, and loving parents need to give their children rules so they can grow up to be responsible adults. If they don't, then that child is going to run into problems because they're going to have to obey rules outside the home.

Sometimes rules need to be broken so that a higher rule can be obeyed. In each case, always obey the spirit of the rule if you can't obey the letter of the rule. In following Christ, we follow His spirit rather than some legalism. Salvation is not in rules but in following Jesus Christ.

SALVATION

Ex 15:2; Ps 3:8; 86:13; 107:9; Is 1:18; 55:1-2; Mt 7:7-14;18:1-25; 18:3, 14; Mk 2:17; 16:15-16; Lk 2:10, 31; 13:22-30; 14:15-24; 19:10; 24:47; Jn 3:1-21; 5:24; 6:35-37, 60-71; 12:32; 17:1-5; Act 2:14-41; 3:19; 4:12; 15:7-11; 28:28; Rom 1:5, 14-17; 5:1-2; 10:1-15; 1 Cor 1:18-31; 2 Cor 5:17, 20; Gal 2:16; Phil 3:7-10; 1 Th 5:8-10; Heb 2:3, 10; 5:9; 1 Pet 1:5, 9-10; 1 Jn 2:25; Jude 1:3; Rev 22:17. (See concordance for complete references on this topic.)

Salvation could not be accomplished on our own so God provided the means for us, and it is the only means. That salvation is through Jesus Christ.

Salvation has three elements: it is a past event (we are saved), it is a present event (we are being saved), and it is future (we will be saved).

The past event is Jesus's death on the Cross. Our sins were nailed to the Cross; He bore our sins and died in our place. God is a righteous God and sin is serious to Him (not light like we sometimes treat it). It had to be punished, and that punishment is death (Rom 6:23). With His death, our sins are forgiven and His righteousness was counted to our credit that we might become the children of God (Lk 20:36, Jn 1:12) when we receive Him (Rom 5:8-9).

Salvation is also a present and continuous act. This is the work of the Holy Spirit in and through us. This is the daily walk of following Christ. It is making His values our values.

Salvation is future. There is a day coming in which we will be in God's presence. We will dwell with Him forever. We will have a resurrected body.

Of course there are some that do not believe in God and in salvation. "I don't need it. What do you mean I'm lost?" For these I can only pray that God will work in their heart to change their thinking. I can also add that when you are deciding if something is true or not, then you look at the evidence, any witnesses, and the validity of the resources. I will simply say that I feel Jesus's testimony outweighs anything else. I believe Him.

Salvation is an important, life-changing commitment. It is a joy beyond words. It is the profession of Jesus as Lord, confession of your sins, and repenting of those sins by turning to Jesus with your whole being (heart, mind, soul, and strength). Baptism is not part of salvation. We are baptized after we are saved, not in order to be saved. Do not put this great salvation off. You may not have another chance.

SANCTIFICATION

Jn 17:17; Act 26:18; Rom 6:1-8:39; 1 Cor 1:2, 30; 6:11; 2 Cor 1:21-22; Gal 2:20; 6:14; Eph 1:3-4; 3:19; 4:7, 12-13; 1 Th 4:3-4; Heb 2:11; 10:10, 14; 1 Jn 1:9; Rev 7:14.

What is sanctification? This is a process (and it is a process, not an act) of making us holy. It is the effect of God's spirit upon a person and is seen in the exercise of faith, love, and humility toward God and man. We are set aside for a holy purpose. We are made holy by confessing our sins and receiving His forgiveness and cleansing from unrighteousness. We are made righteous through Jesus Christ.

It is the change that has been made in our lives as we grow in the Christian faith. The three elements of sanctification are: First, we are freed from our sin. Next, we strive to follow Jesus as we struggle with sin. Then, finally, we have victory over sin.

SATAN (Devil)

Gen 3:1-24; Mt 3:22-26; 4:1-11; 25:41; Jn 8:38, 41; 12:31; 13:2, 27; 14:30; 16:11; Act 5:3; 13:10; 2 Cor 12:7; Eph 6:10-20; 1 Th 2:18; 3:5; Heb 2:14; Jas 4:1-10; 1 Pet 5:8-9; 1 Jn 2:13; 3:8; 5:18; Rev 20:1-10.

Satan is the great deceiver. In John 8:44, Jesus calls him the father of lies. Some feel that there is no Satan or Devil, but Jesus treated him as real. Satan tries to lead us away from serving God. He uses our weaknesses. Often he tries to make his appeals look attractive and even good. He uses whatever will attract you.

He tempted Jesus (see Mt 4), but Jesus used the word of God to resist his temptations. This is the weapon that we need to use also. But we must know it to use it. The devil tries to use the word also, but he twists it and misuses it.

Satan is at work against God's church. If you try to serve God, then you can expect him to try to give you trouble. He will try to use problems to lead you away from God. He has power, but it is only temporary, and God is stronger than Satan. Satan is a defeated enemy.

Do not yield to temptation. Constantly go to God for the strength that you need. Satan says, *"All this I will give to you, if you will bow down and worship me* (even the world)" (Mt 4:9). He said that to Jesus and he says it to us. *"But what good is it to gain the whole world and lose your own soul?"* (Mk 8:36). All that follow the Devil will be destroyed (Rev 20:15), but those who follow God will receive eternal life.

SATISFACTION (CONTENTMENT)

Gen 25:27-34; Ps 63:1-11; Ecc 2:11-26; Jn 6:22-40.

Are you satisfied? What are you looking for? What does it take to satisfy you? All of us are looking for satisfaction, but is the kind for which we are searching worth the price?

People are searching in many different ways to find satisfaction. Some look for it in work. And yes, that is important: to do good work and to be pleased with what you do. Some find satisfaction in material things, in sexual gratification, in eating, in various pleasures, and any number of other ways. We should get our satisfaction in a number of good things, but we must not settle for the immediate pleasure at the expense of eternal pleasure.

We have a deep hunger in our souls that cannot be satisfied apart from God. You may try to fill it with other things, but they will not satisfy that hunger. In John 6:35, Jesus says that He is the bread of life and those that come to Him will never hunger. This is because Jesus can fill that void that we are feeling. True satisfaction is knowing Jesus Christ.

SAVIOR (JESUS CHRIST)

SECOND COMING

Mt 24:1-51; Jn 12:37-50; 14:1-7; 1 Cor 1:4-9; 1 Th 4:13-18; 2 Th 3:6-15.

The second coming of Jesus Christ is a known fact, but what is not known is when. How is it known? Jesus said that He is coming again. There will be signs, but these can be and have been misread. Many times we have heard someone give a date for the end of the world. But the scriptures say that only the Father knows the date.

We are to be ready for His coming again. Jesus gives the parable of the wise and foolish virgins in Matthew 25:1-13. He tells us that we must be ready. We must be faithful, worshipping, and doing His work of service to other people when He comes.

The Second Coming is the time in which He will gather all those that believe in Him so they will live with Him forever. This will be the completion of our salvation. Those believers that have already died will be resurrected to join Him.

SECURITY (COMFORT, PROTECTION)

Ex 3:1-15; Ob 1:1-15; Jn 6:35-40; 1 Jn 5:1-15.

We seek security, and we do that in different ways and in different senses. We want it for protection, for feeling safe, but also we can feel insecure, and this causes different problems. An insecure person may do wrong things by going along with the crowd. Also, if you feel insecure, you may simply fail to do things that you should because you are afraid. One example is that before I received my call to go into the pastoral ministry I had a fear of speaking in public, like many people do. But I overcome that fear by trusting in God. I said to myself, "Lord, if you want me to do this then you will give me the strength to do it." And He did. You don't have to be insecure. Trust in God for He loves you. He cares for you. The only true security comes from knowing the living God. He is from everlasting to everlasting.

Commit yourself to Jesus. God has promised that Jesus will not lose a single one who commits themselves to Jesus (Jn 10:28). If you know Jesus, then you have eternal life (see Jn 17:3).

SELF-ESTEEM (HEALTH, Self-love)

Gen 1:27; Ps 8:1-9; Mk 12:31; Lk 12:4-12; Rom 12:1-8.

What opinion do you have of yourself? Do you think well or bad of yourself? A distorted self-esteem is bad, regardless of whether you have a high or low opinion of yourself. If it is too high, then it is a prideful attitude. If it is too low, then you cannot love God or others.

God created you. He loves you. Look at yourself in that light. You are indeed worth very much. God demonstrated that because He gave His Son for you. But don't elevate yourself above others. They are precious too.

Our true value comes from our relationship with Christ. We are only children of God if we receive Jesus. We cannot use the world's standards to judge ourselves. It is only God's standards that count.

SELFISHNESS (PRIDE, SIN)

Gen 4:9; Prov 11:26; 18:17; 28:1-13, 27; Zech 7:6; Mal 3:17-18; Mt 19:21-22; Mk 8:31-38; Lk 6:32-34; Rom 14:15; 1 Cor 10:24; Phil 2:4, 20-21; Jas 4:1-10; 1 Jn 3:17.

Selfishness affects more than the person committing the act. It involves those whom the consequences of the act also affect. It is also a poison that can affect the whole body.

Selfishness separates us from God and others because we are concerned about ourselves. It is a "me" attitude. *What's in it for me? What will I get out of it?* A selfish person is not concerned with helping others. However, they might if they will get some personal glory or benefit out of it. It is also very costly because it can cost a person his or her soul.

Jesus said in Matthew 10:39 that whoever loses his life for the kingdom's sake will find it. If we are selfish and try to hold on to things for ourselves, we will indeed lose everything, but if we give them up for Jesus, then we will gain everything.

SELF-RIGHTEOUSNESS (EXCUSES, HYPOCRISY)

Job 22:2-3; 33:8-9; Prov 12:15; 14:12; 20:6; 21:2; 26:12; 27:2; 28:13, 26; Is 5:21; 50:11; 64:6; Jer 17:5; Mt 7:22-23; 9:9-13; 16:6; 23:29-31; Lk 15:1-32; 16:14-15; 18:9-12; Rom 3:27; 2 Cor 1:9; 10:17; Gal 6:3.

The big problem with self-righteousness is that the person does not really think of themselves as a sinner. Thus, they cannot receive God's redeeming love because they don't confess their sin. They don't feel that they are sinners. Their religious acts are simply show. Their acts say, "See how good I am." In Matthew 6:5, Jesus speaks of the hypocrites that stand praying in public places so that they may show how religious they are. The self-righteous judge others as the hypocrite in Matthew 6:5 did.

Recognize what you are. You are a sinner and in need of God. Everyone needs God. Do not be a hypocrite. We cannot have self-righteousness. The only righteousness that we can have is that which Christ gives to us when we accept Him as Lord and Savior. That is the only righteousness that counts in God's eyes.

SEPARATION (Apart, DIFFERENCE)

Lev 18:1-5; 2 Ch 6:28-33; Mt 27:45-56; 2 Cor 6:14-18; 2 Th 1:3-12.

Separation means different things in the Bible. In one sense, it means to be apart or different. Israel was to be different from the other nations with all of their immoral practices.

In another sense, we are to be separate from the world so we do not engage in sinful activities. We are to do God's will and not the world's.

Occasionally we feel separated from God. In those times, let us pray to God so that our relationship can be restored. Do not worry about feelings because they change. Just trust in God.

Christ felt that separation on the Cross when He bore our sins. Eternal separation from God is hell. In Dante's *Inferno,* over the gates of hell are inscribed these chilling words: "Abandon all hope ye who enter here." Yes, to have no hope at all—that truly is hell.

SERVING (Assisting, HELP, MINISTRY)

Lev 25:39-41; 1 Sam 2:1-11; Prov 17:2; 29:19-21; Mal 1:6; 3:5; Mt 5:1-12; 8:9; 10:9-10; 20:20-34; 24:45-46; Lk 12:35-37; 17:7-9; Jn 13:16; Rom 7:1-6; Eph 6:5-6; Col 3:22-23; Tit 2:9-10.

Serving is one of the keys of the Christian life. Jesus gave the example when He washed His disciples' feet (see Jn 13:4-10). This was the task that was normally done by a servant. In Matthew 20:26-28, Jesus said that whoever would be great in the kingdom of God must be the servant of all. He also says the Son of Man (Jesus) came to serve, not to be served. Repeatedly, Jesus makes it clear that He is carrying out the will of the Father. In other words, He is serving the Father.

Let each of us open our eyes and hearts, examine ourselves, and ask God how we are to serve Him. Let Him use your talents and abilities. Let Him use you right now, where you are. You may have to go to school or something to prepare you for the task, but begin where you are.

Service is dedicating your life full-time. There are no part-time Christians. God may not have called you into the pastoral ministry or anything that is normally called "full-time" ministry, but whether you are an office manager, farmer, janitor, or anything else, you are full-time. You may never preach a sermon from the pulpit, but you preach from the pulpit of your life every day. You may never write a book on the Christian faith, but you are writing a letter that is read by the people who see you every day. You are a living letter. What does your letter say?

My prayer for all of us is that we will hear those glorious words of approval from our Master when He says, *"Well done, good and faithful servant"* Matthew 25:21.

SEX (ADULTERY, PLEASURE)

Deut 22:13-30; Prov 5:15-21; 6:20-35; Mt 5:27-30; 1Cor 6:12-20; 7:1-11; 1 Th 4:1-8.

Sex is a powerful drive and can be very destructive if misused. When it is misused, then it can lead to other sins. In the story of David and Bathsheba, it led to murder (2 Sam 11:1-17). It can disrupt relationships. A person may become unfaithful to a spouse. Promiscuous sex can lead to various diseases that are transmitted sexually. Sexual abuse of children is still another misuse of sex. Pornography is one way that this perversion is fed.

We must watch our thoughts, because that is where sexual sin begins, and also watch our deeds so that we are not led into sexual sin. In Matthew 5:28, Jesus says that whoever lusts after a woman in his heart has committed adultery with her already in his heart. The key here is lusting after the woman, and not just admiring a woman's beauty. Pray for strength to resist this temptation.

Sex is good if used properly, for God made sex. Sex within the bonds of marriage is for procreation, but also for expressing your love for one another. Keep it good and precious as it was meant to be and not a cheap or evil passion.

SHAME (Dishonor, EMBARRASSMENT)

Gen 2:8-25; Lk 9:18-27; Rom 1:8-17.

Have you ever been ashamed? Why? All of us have said or done things that we are ashamed of. How did you feel? You didn't feel very good, did you?

Sometimes it is because we have reacted in anger and lashed out without thinking. Perhaps a friend has let you down and you said something not very nice and you hurt them. Have you ever been ashamed of your Christian faith?

Something we should be ashamed of is our sin. When we sin, we are not living as God intended, and thus we should be ashamed because we are doing evil.

We need to be willing to confess our sins to God so that we might receive His forgiveness. Let us not try to keep secrets from Him because we can't, but let us give ourselves to Him totally.

Two things that we must never be ashamed of are Jesus Christ and the gospel. People will mock you, but they mocked our Lord too. They will try to make you feel ashamed, "You believe that?" Do not give in to such foolishness, for they are the fools. If we are ashamed of Jesus and deny Him before men, then He will deny us before the Father (Mt 10:32-33).

SICKNESS (HEALING, Illness)

Ex 15:22-27; Mt 4:23-25; 8:5-17; 25:34-45; Lk 10:30-34; Rom 8:38-39; 2 Cor 7:6; 12:9.

Sickness is a part of life. We do not get sick because we are evil. The Bible does not promise that the believer will be free of sickness. Committing sin can make you sick because of the consequences of that sin. One example is catching venereal disease as a result of promiscuous sex or a dirty syringe that was used in taking dope. Excessive drinking can lead to cirrhosis of the liver. Excessive anger can eat away at you and cause physical and emotional problems.

We are blessed today that we have a medical profession that helps us with health problems. One source we should not neglect is the body's own ability to heal. God created our bodies, and if we give them the right materials in our food, then there can be amazing cures. Even deadly things like cancer can be combated.

God has certain laws; these have a purpose. He is looking out for our best interests. By following those laws, a lot of disease can be prevented. Jesus demonstrated healing while He was here on earth, and we still look to God for healing.

SILENCE (Quietness, SOLITUDE)

Job 2:11-13; Ps 46:11; 50:16-23.

Silence is sometimes the only way that you can share another person's pain. Sometimes this is the best way to show them that you care and feel with them. Have you ever suffered a loss and there was someone with you that was giving you words of comfort, but they just wouldn't shut up? You didn't need that at that time. Many pastors have sat with a person whose loved one is very ill and maybe even dying and have known that all you can do is to be with that person and that is all they need right then. Your presence is enough. Actually, God is present in your presence.

We need to exercise silence with God also. We need to listen for His voice and worship Him in silence. God's silence is often simply His patience. He is waiting for the proper time or waiting for us to be still to hear Him.

SIN (EVIL)

Gen 2:17; 3:1-24; 6:5-6; 19:13; 20:1-18; Ex 2:11-17; Lev 4:1-12; Num 15:30-36; 32:23; 2 Sam 11:1-27; Ps 10:2; 25:7, 11, 18; 32:1-5; 41:4; 51:2-5; 139:1-24; Prov 22:8; Is 1:18; 6:5; 55:6-7; 59:1-2; Jer 17:9; Mt 1:21; 5:43-48; 6:12-15; 8:1-4; 27:45-56; Mk 3:28; 7:1-23; Lk 3:1-20; 12:1-12; Jn 1:29-34; 19:28-37; Act 2:38; 13:38-39; Rom 3:9-20; 4:7; 6:15-23; 1 Cor 6:9-10; Gal 6:7-8; Eph 4:32; Col 2:13; 1 Jn 1:5-10; 2:1-2, 12; Rev 1:5.

Many different things are sinful, but what is sin? Of course, some do not believe that there is such a thing as sin. Christian Science, for one, says that sin and evil are not real. Scientology is another belief system that says there is no sin. I would partially agree with them if there were no God. I would then say there are bad things that happen: murder, violence, wars, etc. However, there is a God, and there is sin. Jesus's death on the cross is the proof that there is sin, and this was the biggest sin that we as human beings could commit. We crucified God. That Jesus lived and died is a historical fact. There are nonbiblical references that confirm it. Anyone that says there is no sin is misguided, to say the very least. They are not "enlightened." It is difficult to refrain from using strong words, but I just pray that they will see the error of their ways. Jesus would want us to forgive them and not tar or feather them. If they want to deny that there is sin, then they have a big problem. Sin is a missing the mark, a disobedience of God. Sometimes sinful acts are unintentional. Then other sins are very blatant. There are sins of commission and of omission. Sin cannot be removed by any human effort because it is a crime that has been committed against God. Others may be involved, but God always is involved. Since this is an offense against God, only God could provide a cure for sin. As long as we are sinful we are separated from God.

Sin has widespread results, touching many others in various ways. It is just like the ripples on a pond. Sin creates a barrier between God and man. God is holy and abhors sin; thus, man cannot have a relationship with God as long as he is a sinner.

The Bible says that the wages of sin is death (Rom 6:23). Too often we take a light approach toward sin. We may think it is bad, etc., but it is hard for us to imagine how seriously God regards it. But when we look at His remedy for sin, then we see what an awful thing sin is. Christ died on the Cross for our sins. Christ underwent extreme agony. The Roman soldiers scourged Jesus severely. Sometimes people died from these beatings. It is hard for us to imagine what He went through. The very Son of God gave Himself for us. No heavier price could be paid. Our only escape from the punishment of sin is to accept Jesus Christ as Lord and Savior. Our sins are forgiven because of His death on the Cross.

How does His death atone for us? Because God is a God of justice, then sin has to be punished by death. But all the death of a human would accomplish is to pay for his or her sins. It would have no effect on anyone else. God is also a God of love, and in His love He provided a way that His justice could be satisfied and He could show His love. God Himself in the person of Jesus Christ died on the Cross. This is the only way that a death would mean anything. He took all of our sins upon Himself and died in our place. Our sins were nailed to the Cross so that through His death we could receive forgiveness for our sins. The barrier between God and man had been torn down. The relationship had been reestablished. And with our forgiveness comes the gift of eternal life.

If you have sinned, then confess your sin, repent, and trust in Jesus for the forgiveness of your sins. Then do not continue to walk in sin, but follow Jesus.

SINCERITY (HONESTY)

Jud 17:1-13; Ps 12:1-8; 32:2; Zech 7:5-14; Mt 15:7-20; 18:35; Rom 12:9; 1 Cor 5:8; 2 Cor 1:12; 8:8; Tit 2:7-8.

We've heard the statement, "It doesn't matter what you believe as long as you are sincere." This is nonsense. We would laugh if someone tried to apply that to the physical laws. "I don't believe in the law of gravity, so I can fly like a bird, or walk on water." When they try it, they will find that the law doesn't care if they believe in it or not. The law is still in effect, and the person trying to fly will not get off the ground, and the person walking on water will get his or her feet wet.

Sincerity, to have any value, has to be based upon truth. We can be sincere, but we can be sincerely wrong. Sincerity by itself doesn't make something right or wrong.

A Christian needs to be sincere; to do the right thing for the wrong reason is sin. A sincere Christian is attractive and draws people to God because we know that person believes in his faith. That person demonstrates something that people are looking for. We should be sincere in our actions, thoughts, and attitudes. Deeds begin in the mind.

SINGLENESS (Bachelor, Unmarried Woman)

Mt 19:1-12; 1 Cor 7:1-11, 25-40.

Should you or should you not get married? That is a question that has to be answered on an individual basis. Some should, and some should not. It doesn't mean that there is anything wrong with you if you do or you don't. If you are struggling over this, spend some time in prayer about it and go in the direction that God is leading you. Seek good counseling too.

For some people, because of their personality and commitments, it would be best for them not to marry. But the reverse is true also. Based upon who they are, the type of person that they are, then they should get married. In 1Corinthians 7:1-9, Paul gives his advice on the subject. He states that it is best not to be married; however, because of immorality, and these type of things then it is good to be married if that is what is needed for you not to engage in sexual immorality. Some people get into some troubles that they would not get into if they had a solid marriage.

If you are single, then use the time that would be devoted to a spouse and family to serving God. Find what is best for you and serve God in that state, whether it is married or single.

SLANDER (False Witness, LYING)

Ex 23:1; Job 5:21; Ps 41:6-9; 50:20; 101;5; Prov 10:18; Jer 6:28; 9:4; Rom 1:29; Jas 4:11.

God abhors slander. This is divisive. We are to love one another. We are to do good to our enemy, not deride him.

If someone slanders you, do not take vengeance or try to get even, but instead get even by doing good things for that person. Of course, don't think of it as getting even, but rather as responding to the love that God has poured out to you.

In Matthew 15:19, Jesus says that it is not what goes into the mouth that makes a person unclean, but what comes out. For insults, slander, and things of this sort proceed from the heart and out of the mouth. This is what makes a person unclean.

SLEEP (REST, Slumber)

Ps 3:1-8; 63:1-11; 121:1-8.

Sleep is needed for our body to regain the strength that it needs for everyday activity. Sometimes bad dreams, pressures, and anxieties make it hard to rest.

We need to trust in God. We are not to be anxious; God does not sleep, and we are in His care. Reflect on His care the next time you are sleepless.

SOLITUDE (Aloneness, SILENCE)

Mt 14:1-14, 22-33; Lk 4:38-44.

Solitude is important. Jesus found it necessary to have times alone with God. We need to make it important in our lives. Have times of prayer.

Solitude can be for times of grief or refreshment. There are times when we need to be alone. Don't neglect to have times of solitude.

SORROW (GRIEF, Sadness)

Jud 2:1-32; Lk 15:1-32; Jn 14; Rev 7:1-17.

We experience sorrow at the loss of a loved one. There is sorrow because we miss that person. For the Christian, this sorrow is also combined with joy. We are sad because they are gone, but we are glad that they are with the Lord.

Sometimes sorrow is a result of a deep conviction of sin and the repentance of that sin. Pray to God and lean on Him so your pain may be eased.

John 14 is a very good chapter to read. Jesus is comforting His disciples because He is about to leave them. In 14:1, He says, *"Trust in God; trust in me."* Then He goes on to say that in His Father's house there are many rooms and that He goes to prepare a place for them so they can be with Him. This is His promise to all who put their trust in Him.

SOUL (Being, Spirit)

Deut 6:5; Ps 56:1-13; Jn 10:22-42; Rev 7:1-3.

The soul is that inner most being that constitutes the real you. This soul cannot be touched by any human. The body can be killed, but only God has control over the soul.

Trust in Jesus for the protection that we need. In Him your soul is safe.

SOVEREIGNTY (Control, POWER)

Job 36:22-33; 37:1-24; 38:1-41; Ezra 6:1-18.

There is no greater power than God. The mightiest ruler simply has the power that God has granted to him. God's ways cannot be successfully opposed (but they are continually opposed). His power, might, and wisdom are beyond comprehension.

His sovereignty extends to His love. His love is eternal and all-powerful.

SPIRITUAL GIFTS (ABILITIES, Talents)

Rom 12:1-8; 1Cor 12:1-31; Eph 4; 1 Th 5:12-28; 1 Pet 4:10-11.

God has given each of us certain spiritual gifts that we are to use. There are many different gifts and they are important in building up the church. Various lists are given in the New Testament. In Romans 12, some that are mentioned are prophesy, serving, teaching, encouraging, contributing to the needs of others, leadership, and showing mercy. In 1 Corinthians 12, some more are mentioned: message of wisdom, message of knowledge, faith, healing, miraculous powers, distinguishing spirits, speaking in tongues, and interpretation of tongues. In Ephesians 4, he mentions some gifts that are actually offices in the church: apostles, prophets, evangelists, pastors, and teachers. This is just a partial list of gifts that have been given to us. Think of the special talents of people that you know, and that will give you an even larger list. One big one is the gift of hospitality. There are many people that cannot preach from the pulpit, but they can certainly open their home and serve people in that manner. (In the section on Hospitality, I give a personal example of a time when hospitality was shown to my wife and me when our daughter was very ill. It was a real answer to prayer.)

Do not belittle your gift. Some people have many and some have just a few, but don't look down on your gift and think it is not important. Nor should anyone look down on you and make you feel unimportant. God expects us to use our gift for His service. Paul gives the picture of the body and said that all parts are needed (1 Cor 12:12-21).

Paul had to settle a dispute that had arisen in the Corinthian church. There were some that spoke in tongues, and they looked down on those who couldn't speak in tongues and even questioned their faith. There are some today that claim that same thing. Paul spoke in tongues often, but he says that prophesy is the better gift, for it edifies the church. The gift of tongues only edifies the person speaking (1 Cor 14:4). Be faithful in your ministry and God will be faithful to you.

STATUS (Position, REPUTATION)

Lk 14:7-14; Jas 2:1-13.

What is your status? The world tends to be status-seeking, but this is not God's plan. Instead of seeking status, we are to seek to serve. Jesus says that whoever would be great must be the servant of all (Mk 9:35).

Be humble in your role. If you are to have a place of prominence, then God will call you to that place. In Luke 14:10-11, Jesus tells a story and says for us to take the lesser seat and if the host wants us to move higher he will tell us. Otherwise, we could be humiliated if we take the high place and then we are told to move to a lower one. He says those who humble themselves will be exalted. We must not judge on the basis of status, but extend your love to all.

STEALING (see THEFT)

STEWARDSHIP (see TITHING)

STRENGTH (ABILITY, POWER)

Gen 49:1-28; Is 40:25-31; Lk 4:1-13.

On whom do you rely to get your strength? What is its source? God has given us strengths, but sometimes we let these get in the way of serving God. We lean too heavily on our strength instead of relying upon God. We must always use our strength, but not when it would lead us in a way that is contrary to God. We must follow His lead and then use the gifts that He has given to us for the accomplishment of that task. Let us not glory in our strength, but glory in God's might.

What are the strengths of the Christian? We have none on our own. However, our strength comes from the Living God. Jesus says of Himself in John 5:19, *"I tell you the truth, the Son can do nothing by himself; he can do only what he sees his Father doing, because whatever the Father does the Son also does."* Thus, our strength has to come from God as well. He provides us that strength through His written word and through Jesus, the Incarnate Word, who dwells in us in the form of the Holy Spirit. There is nothing greater.

STRESS (Difficulty, Strain, WORRY)

Ex 16:1-12; Ps 62:1-12; Rom 5:1-5; Phil 4:4-9.

The pressures and tensions of the world can cause stress. How do you react when circumstances go bad? Do you complain?

There are various things that cause stress. Demands of the job can put you under stress. There is stress at home. One cause of stress is that several things are demanded of you at the same time or in a short period of time. Still another cause of stress is that bills can pile up so that you are under pressure to pay them and to get the money to pay them. Another example is that you have plans to do something, and then something is delaying the performance of that task. And you are wondering if the hindrance will be removed so that you can do the task. To make this clearer, I will give you a personal example. We had our car in the garage to have some work done on it. There was a delay in fixing it because a part needed to be ordered. My wife had to go out of town on business, so this delay was irritating and stressful. She needed to go, but had to wait for the car.

We need to lift up our situation to God in prayer. This won't make the situation go away, but it can help us deal with the situation, and we can receive some insight of how to relieve or lessen the stress. Call upon Him to see us through the situation. Know that His strength is all that we need. Stress may make you want to pull out your hair, but let His peace and love work in you. Do not dwell on negative or bad thoughts.

Paul is a good example of where an outward stressful condition does not need to cause inner stress. In Philippians 4:4, Paul says, "Rejoice in the Lord always. I will say it again, rejoice!" He was in prison when he wrote this letter, but he could still say rejoice!

STUBBORNNESS (Hardheaded, PRIDE)

Ex 8:1-19; Ps 81:1-16; Mk 2:18-22; Jn 20:24-31.

Are you stubborn? Are you hard to get along with? What do you think of stubborn people?

Stubbornness gets in the way of serving God. You may want to do it your way, but things have to be done God's way. Your stubbornness may make it hard for you to work with other people.

Do not let stubbornness prevent you from believing or prevent you from changing when change is needed. Stubbornness can make you think that you are right when you are actually wrong.

Examine your thoughts. If pride or stubbornness is preventing you from accepting and following God, then get rid of it immediately.

Stubbornness, when it is perseverance, is good. You are not letting fads sway you. Persevere in the Lord.

SUBMISSION (OBEDIENCE)

Lk 14:25-35;1 Cor 11:2-16; Eph 5:21-33.

What is submission? Often people have the idea of a doormat. This is not the biblical concept.

Our main submission, if we are Christians, is to Christ. We profess Him as Lord and Savior. He is Lord, and we are called to follow Him even to the point of death (Lk 14:27). We must submit to His Lordship. He is Lord and not we.

Submission is a matter of choice, rather than someone forcing another. One person is not superior to another. Each person was made in the image of God.

In a marriage, it means for a wife to follow her husband in leadership under Christ, and for the husband to set aside his own interests for the benefit of the wife and children. It is a mutual cooperation.

SUCCESS (ACCOMPLISHMENTS)

Josh 1:1-9; Ps 1:1-6; Jer 51:59-64; Mk 9:33-37.

What is success to you? What yardstick do you use? The world often thinks in terms of material possessions: money, house, cars, power, and possessions.

God does not use these standards. If we are faithful to God, then we are successful. We are on the winning team. God will subdue all opposition to Him. They are already defeated. In John 16:33, Jesus comforts His disciples and tells them that the world will give them problems, but don't worry, for He has overcome the world.

Being faithful to God does not mean that you can't or won't have money or other material possessions. It simply means that this is not the measure of your success. Your success is determined by how faithfully you serve the Lord. If you have wealth, then use it for God's glory.

SUFFERING (Affliction)

Mt 16:21-28; Mk 9:2-13; Lk 21:5-36; 24:46-47; Jn 6:51; 9:1-41; 10:11, 15; Rom 4:25; 5:6; 8:17-18; 1 Cor 1:17; 15:3; 2 Cor 1:7; 4:11-12; 5:14-15; Eph 5:2, 25; Phil 1:29; 3:10; Col 1:24; 1 Th 3:1-8; 2 Tim 2:12; Heb 9:28; 10:10, 18-20; 1 Pet 3:18; 5:10; 1 Jn 3:16.

We must remember that as Christians we are not immune to suffering. In fact, Christians in the past and sometimes today have to pay with their lives for their faith in Jesus. In Luke 14:27, Jesus says if we would be His disciple, then we must carry our cross. Thus, we can expect hardship.

Jesus's suffering shows that He understands our suffering. There is no suffering that you can experience that He has not experienced. He experienced the death of a friend (Lazarus), persecution, rejection, betrayal, friends falling away, a brutal beating by the Romans, and even death. Thus, He knows our pain. For that reason, He can be our source of strength when we experience suffering.

Sometimes we have to go through suffering in order to test our character, to find out what we are made of. This also can be a testimony. It shows that you are willing to stand up for your belief, and it shows the strength that God is giving to help you through the testing.

It is easy to follow Jesus in good times, but are you willing to follow Him when it is unpopular or involves suffering? As mentioned above, Jesus says that we must be willing to bear our cross (Mk 8:34). How strong is your faith?

TEACHING (GUIDANCE)

Deut 6:1-9; Jud 2:6-17; Mt 4:23-25; 7:24-29.

Teaching is an important function of the church. Jesus was the Master Teacher. He taught a lot by parables and stories, but His key teaching was by demonstrating the scripture in His living. He lived His teachings, and that is what made Him so effective and powerful a teacher. He wanted us to understand God's truth. The Christian faith is not a body of knowledge although it involves that. The Christian faith is a matter of coming to know God through Jesus Christ. It is a personal relationship with God.

Any good teaching relates life and truth. You teach your children love and other virtues by living those virtues. You demonstrate your beliefs to others by how you live.

TEMPTATION (Seduction)

Gen 3:1-7; 20:6; Ex 34:12; Deut 12:28-32; 2 Sam 11:1-27; 1 K 11:1-13; Prov 1:10; 4:14; 6:27; 16:29; 19:27; 28:10; Is 33:15-16; Mt 4:1-11; 5:19; 26:31, 41; Mk 4:15; 13:21-22; 14:37-38; Rom 7:5; 12:21; 14:13; 1 Cor 8:9; 10:13; 2 Cor 2:11; Gal 5:17; 1 Th 3:5; Heb 2:18; 4:15; 12:3; Jas 1:2; 4:7; 2 Pet 2:9, 18;1 Jn 4:4; Rev 3:10.

Temptation is attractive because it appeals to our natural desires, but its purpose is to lead us away from God. It leads us to serve ourselves instead of God.

Temptation itself is not sin. The sin occurs when we give in to the temptation. The first step is to recognize a temptation. Then we need to ask for the strength to resist the temptation. In some cases you may have to flee from it, like Joseph did from Potiphar's wife when she wanted him to sleep with her (Gen 39:11-14). You may not have to run, but if you're in a tempting situation, get out of it as soon as possible. Whenever it is possible, don't get into that situation in the first place. Say no to those things that are wrong. Even a petty temptation like a "white lie" can have dire consequences.

Temptation can lead from one sin into a worse and worse sin as did in the story of David and Bathsheba. The temptation of lust for a woman led to the murder of her husband (2Sam 11:1-27).

I would like to give a brief word to some young girls and guys here. In dating, a boy may try to get a girl to have sex with him by saying, "If you loved me, then you would." That is a temptation to do it. However, if your boyfriend tells you that, drop him like a hot potato. He wants to have sex, not love. If he really cared about you, then he would not try to get you to do something that is wrong. Guys, if you care about a girl, do not do that. Show her that you care and respect her.

TESTING (PROBLEMS, SUFFERING, TEMPTATION)

Gen 12:10-20; 22:1-18; 2 Ch 32:24-33.

We will be tested throughout our whole life so don't be surprised when these times come. Testing comes when we face problems. How will you deal with them? Will you crack under the pressure? Use the wrong means to get them taken care of? You will be tested when you suffer and when you are tempted.

Do not bemoan these times, but use them as times to rely and trust in the Lord for His strength. Stay faithful. Use your mind to think about the situation.

Tests are a means of making us stronger. They help to show our real character, to develop our faith. If you fail in a test, you can learn from that too. You can examine your failure to see why you failed and what you can do to be faithful the next time.

THANKFULNESS (APPRECIATION, PRAISE)

Ex 13:3, 8; 34:26; Lev 23:14; Deut 26:10; 1 Ch 16:4-36; Ps 48:11; 92:1-15; 98:1; 105:1, 5, 42; 106:1; 116:12-14, 17; Prov 3:9; Joel 2:26; Rom 1:18-23; Eph 2:1-10; 5:4, 19; Phil 4:6; Col 2:7; 4:2; 1 Th 5:18; 1 Tim 2:1; Heb 13:15.

We have so much to be thankful for. First, as Americans, we have countless freedoms and benefits that other people do not have. We should appreciate them and not take them for granted. Let us not abuse our rights and privileges either.

Then we have countless things to thank God for: for the planet that we live on, the air that we breathe, the food that we eat, the sun that shines down, for His mercy, His Love, the gift of His Son that gave us forgiveness of our sins, and for eternal life.

Let us constantly give Him thanks by word and deed. In John 14:15, Jesus said, *"If you love me, you will obey what I command."* Thus, this is a way to show our thankfulness. Respond to Him, remember Him, do acts of kindness to one another. Do this in a grateful response to His blessings, and not in an obligatory manner.

THEFT (Stealing)

Ex 22:1; Lev 19:11, 13; Prov 6:30-31; Jer 2:26; Mt 19:18; Jn 10:1; Eph 4:28; I Pet 4:15; Rev 9:21.

One of the commandments says that you are not to steal. There are a number of ways that we can steal. We can rob from our employer by not giving an honest day's labor for an honest day's wage, but if you are a Christian, God expects you to give an honest day's work for an honest day's wage. It is no excuse if every one else is just doing enough to get by. If you remember that God is your boss, then you will not try to steal from Him. We can steal by cheating on our income taxes (by using deductions that we are not entitled to, or not reporting income that we should).

There have been some big corporations that have been guilty of theft recently, and many shareholders lost a lot of money because of this. Greed is one of the sins behind theft.

Stealing can lead to other sins too. If a person is stealing from a bank or something, they may commit murder to keep from getting caught. Stealing may be a means of providing money for another sin, such as taking illegal drugs.

If someone steals from you, we are to forgive that person just as we would any other sin. Pray for that person. When we steal, let us repent of our sin and restore the property to its rightful owner.

Let us also not be guilty of stealing from God by not giving Him our best in time, talent, money, and service.

Another form of stealing that comes to mind is that some companies have stopped the pensions to their retired employees.

THINKING (Reasoning)

Prov 15:1-33; Mk 7:14-23; Rom 12:1-8; Phil 4:2-9.

We need to use our minds in the best manner that we can. Let us think about what we say so we do not speak rashly or too quickly. A thoughtless word can hurt very much and do a lot of damage.

An action begins in the mind as a thought. Thus, we should watch our thoughts. Think on good and positive things and do not dwell on negative things (see Phil 4:8).

Your mind is a precious gift; pray for God to help you use it wisely.

TITHING (GENEROSITY, GIVING, stewardship)

Gen 28:22; Lev 27:30; Num 18:21; Deut 14:22-29; Mal 3:10; Mk 12:41-44; Lk 11:42; 18:12; Heb 7:4-5, 8-9.

Tithing is to teach us what is important, to put God first. We are also reminded that all we have is a gift from God. Tithing is a biblical principle of giving one tenth to the Lord. People will argue over basing it on gross income or net income. But that is not the essential point of tithing.

We are really to give everything to God, and not ten percent. Anything less is unacceptable. If you would belong to God, then you must give Him all of yourself—your heart, mind, soul, and strength. Everything that we have is a gift from God. You may have worked hard for that paycheck, but it was God who enabled you to do that. We are only stewards of God. He has entrusted this planet, our gifts, and our very lives to us.

Monetarily, we only return a portion of this, but a tithe of your time or talent is not acceptable. Remember that we are not owners, and let us give to God's work from time, talents, abilities, and finances.

TOLERANCE (ACCEPTANCE, PATIENCE)

2K 10:16-36; Mt 5:27-30; Act 5:12-42.

How tolerant are you? How tolerant should you be? As Christians, we are not to tolerate sin; it must be removed from our lives. We need to be open to other viewpoints, but if those other viewpoints would lead people into sin, then we cannot tolerate those viewpoints. However, let us make sure that our own viewpoint is not contrary to God's will.

Sometimes we may not be sure of a teaching. In that case, we should take a wait-and-see attitude. If it is of God, then it cannot be overthrown, but if it is of man, then it cannot stand.

In today's society, there is a cry for tolerance; however, too often that is a one-way street. Christians are expected to be tolerant of other faiths, but Christianity is discriminated against. There is a strong intolerance of the Christian faith.

As Christians, we should not discriminate against others, but we do have to be intolerant to be true to our faith. In John 14:6 Jesus says, *"I am the way, and the truth, and the life. No one comes to the Father except through me."* There is no other way. Christianity is not one of many ways to God, it is the only way. Christ alone is THE WAY. How do I know that? He said so.

Christianity is exclusive in that there is only one Way and that is Jesus Christ, but it is inclusive in that all are invited.

TRINITY (GOD, HOLY SPIRIT, JESUS CHRIST)
Mt 3:11; 28:19; Mk 1:9-13; Lk 1:35; 3:22; 4:1; Jn 1:32-33; 14:16-17; 15:26; Act 2:33; Rom 1:3-4; 1Cor 2:10-11; 8:6; 2 Cor 3:17; 13:14; Gal 4:4, 6; 1 Tim 3:16; Tit 3:4-6; 1 Pet 1:2; 3:18.

The trinity is the doctrine that there is one God but in three persons. These three are one. There are not three Gods. God is one. There is God the Father, God the Son, and God the Holy Spirit.

Various images have been used to try to picture it. Water can be solid, liquid, or a gas, but it is still water. Then we say that one person has different titles. A person can be a man or a woman. That man can be a father, husband, uncle, brother, teacher, or any number of other things; but it is still the same person in each case. The same is true of the woman. She can be a mother, wife, aunt, sister, secretary, or any number of other things; but she is still the same person. We can't explain the Trinity. We simply have to accept it.

TROUBLES (see PROBLEMS)

TRUST (CONFIDENCE, FAITH)
Gen 30:1-24; Ex 14:1-31; Prov 3:1-8; Rom 3:21-28.

Trust is an important trait. We want friends that we can trust. Our friends want to feel that they can trust us. Trust is something that is earned. We earn it by being trustworthy. We are given an occasion in which we must be trusted, and then we show that we can or cannot be trusted by what we do in that situation. It is not always easy and sometimes you will fail. When you do, don't try to hide it, but confess to that person and do small acts that show you can be trusted.

Sometimes trust involves patience. We must depend upon God to act in His time, for He is faithful and always keeps His promises. Trust takes courage sometimes. The circumstances may be working against you, but you still need to rely upon God.

Decision making is still another time in which you need to exercise trust. Trust in God to help you make the right decision.

Give yourself completely to Him. There is no other place that you can place your trust and it will not fail. Only God is always faithful. In God, you are in the hands of a loving Father. You are secure. Nothing can take you out of His hands if you have received Jesus as your Lord and Savior (Rom 8:38-39). You are a child of God.

We must always know that God can be trusted. He is faithful. Over and over we see that He has kept His promises. There are no promises that He has not kept. There are some that have not been fulfilled yet, but He has broken no promise.

TRUTH (BELIEF, Fact, FAITH)

Deut 32:4; Job 14:1-22; Ps 33:4; 40:10; 51:6; 57:3, 10; 85:10-11; 96:13; 100:5; Prov 12:1-28; 16:13; Is 65:16; Mk 15:1-15; Lk 9:28-36; Jn 8:30-47; 14:1-14; 16:13; 17:17, 19; 18:37-38.

What is truth? That is a question that has been asked through the ages, and it is the question that Pilate asked of Jesus.

There are different kinds of truth, or truth in different areas. There is social truth. This is the type that a society has developed. It involves what is appropriate to wear, hairstyles, and things of this sort. These change and are often called fads. Types of music that are popular are still other things that change. A society does have morals, and some of these change also. The morals of one society can also be quite different from the morals of another society.

Unlike the world, God's truth does not change. Often people want to say that there are no absolutes, that everything is relative, and if there were no God then that would probably be true. But because there is a God and He never changes, and He is the one that determines truth, then we can say His truth never changes.

God's word is truth. Jesus spoke the truth and lived the truth. Jesus said, *"I am the truth"* (Jn 14:6). Thus, when we know Him we are set free (Jn 8:32). We are set free to live our lives to their fullest potentials and not be encumbered by a load of sin.

UNBELIEVERS (Agnostics, Non-Christians)

1 Sam 8:1-22; Ps 26:1-12; 78:19-22, 32; Is 53:1; Mal 1:2, 7; Mt 10:14-15; 13:13-14; 21:32; Mk 9:24; 16:14, 16; Lk 12:46; 16:31; 18:8; 19:41-42; 22:67; Jn 4:48; 5:38; 8:24, 45; 17:16-19; 20:27; Rom 3:3; 1 Cor 1:18; 2:14; 2 Cor 6:14-18; I2 Th 3:2; Tit 1:15; Heb 3:12; Jas 1:6-7; 1 Jn 5:10, 12.

There should be a significant difference between a Christian's life and that of the person that does not believe in Jesus. Outwardly there are many non-believers that live quite moral lives, but they still need Jesus. Does the world see a difference in your life?

We must have a loving, caring attitude toward unbelievers, but we must not lead a sinful lifestyle. Some religions are very hostile toward nonbelievers and even kill them. It is our hope that by showing love to people and living a Christ-like life, they will come to accept Jesus as Lord and Savior.

UNDERSTANDING (Knowing, OBEDIENCE)

I Ch 15:1-15; Ps 147:1-6; Mt 17:14-23; Mk 4:1-25.

Understanding is important, but it cannot be the most important part of our faith because there is much that we are not able to understand. "For my thoughts are not your thoughts, neither are your ways my ways, declares the Lord. As the heavens are higher than the earth, so are my ways higher than your ways and my thoughts than your thoughts" (Is 55:8-9).

God does not expect us to understand everything, but He does expect us to obey Him. He expects us to trust Him.

By trusting and obeying Jesus Christ, our understanding of life, of ourselves, and of God will grow.

UNFAIRNESS (Injustice)

Gen 31:1-13; Jud 11:1-10; Job 14:1-22.

There is much injustice in the world. You will be treated unfairly, but do not return injustice with injustice.

Trust in God, and show love for even those who persecute you. God has an eternal solution. Unfairness will be done away with. He has given us the opportunity through His Son Jesus to live forever with Him.

UNITY (FELLOWSHIP)

Ps 133:1; Mt 23:8; Jn 6:22-59; 17:6-21; Act 4:32; Rom 11:1-24; 14:19; 15:5-6; 1 Cor 1:10; 2Cor 13:11; Phil 1:3-11; 2:1-11; 3:16-17;1 Pet 3:8.

In John 6:25, Jesus says that He is the bread of life. He also talks about eating His flesh. This was a hard saying for some to accept. Jesus was emphasizing that we must accept His sacrifice of Himself on the Cross for our sins, believe in His resurrection, and follow His teachings and devote ourselves to Him.

Jesus wants us to be united as one, just as He and the Father are one. We do this by supporting each other in love and prayer. Do not gossip or do negative things toward one another.

Unity indicates the importance of being with other believers. Unity is not fully realized yet. The church is still divided, but let us do our part in bringing that unity closer to a full reality.

As the words of that song go, "They will know we are Christians by our love." In John 13:34, Jesus gives a new commandment. He says, *"Love one another. As I have loved you, so you must love one another."* Let us daily live by the words of that song and this new commandment.

UNSELFISHNESS (SELFISHNESS)

Rom 12:10; 15:1-3; 1 Cor 10:24, 33; 13:4-5; 2 Cor 8:9; Phil 2:3-4; Jas 2:8.

The world is very selfish although there are many unselfish people in it. Many people are out for number one. Often they do not care who has to be hurt in order to get ahead in life or to get what they want.

Christian love is not selfish (see Phil 2:4-5). Sometimes Christians are selfish, but when that happens they are following the world and not their Lord. In 1 Corinthians 13, Paul describes the characteristics of love. Christian love is concerned about the other person and that is for all people, not just your friends. Jesus said to love your enemies (Mt 5:43). "Love one another," is the new commandment that He gives in John 13:34. In Matthew 22:37-39, He tells us to love God and to love our neighbor as ourselves.

VALUE (Worth)

Ps 8:1-9; 113:1-9; 139:1-24; Mt 13:44-46.

What is valuable to you? Why? Are you of value to yourself or to anyone else? Unfortunately, many people do not think that they are worth very much. However, you are worth very much, and do not let anyone tell you that you aren't! Do not tell yourself that, either.

How valuable is Jesus? He is the only begotten Son of God. In Philippians 2:5-6, we are again reminded that He is, by nature, by essence, God. In John 1, He is called the *Logos,* "The Word." That Word is God. In the Greek text, the passage does not say that He is a god (like some sects would say), but it uses the definite article, so the text reads "the God" and not "a god."

A human being is very valuable in God's eyes, for we are made in His image. Remember that and do not put yourself down or let someone else put you down. You are precious. You are loved. We need to remember that in our treatment of others and in our treatment of ourselves. We should treat all people in that manner, and not just those that are wealthy but the social outcasts also.

God demonstrated how valuable we are by giving us His only Son for our salvation. No greater love could be shown. Let us respond to this great gift by loving God and others. In John 13:34, Jesus gives us the new commandment to love one another. In John 14:15, He says that if you love Him, you will obey His commands.

VIRTUE
Phil 4:8; 2Pet 1:3.

The Christian is to be like Christ and practice those virtues that we see in Him. Some of those virtues that we see are purity, honesty, love, boldness, compassion, perseverance, mercy, forgiveness, patience, prayerfulness, obedience, unselfishness, godliness, generosity, integrity, submissiveness, kindness, and any number of other positive traits. We are not perfect, but by walking with Him, we can grow in that likeness. We will grow in the virtues that should be a part of our life. It is a process. Practice the golden rule, which, said in a different way, is *Do those things to others that you would like to be done to you.* You want to receive love so give love. You want to receive compassion then give compassion, etc.

VOWS (COMMITMENT, PROMISE)
Gen 28:20, 22; Lev 5:4-6; Job 22:27; Ps 22:25; 50:14-15; 61:5, 8; 65:1; 66:13-14; 76:11; 116:14; Prov 20:25; Ecc 5:4; Mt 5:33-37; Jn 2:9.

We should be careful what we promise. God expects us to keep our word. It hurts a person's testimony if they make promises and do not keep them. However, sometimes we make a promise too quickly, and then something unexpected happens that makes us break that promise. Try to make peace and gain the understanding of the person with whom you had to break the promise. Do this quickly so trust is reestablished. How much would you trust someone who continually breaks their promise to you? Often parents do that to children. The child comes to think that the parent does not love them that much if they continually fail to keep their promise. The other commitment is more important. Don't do that to your children. Occasionally you do have to break a promise. But only do it if it is essential, and do not make a habit of this. Let your child feel that you are a person of your word.

God is faithful to us. He always keeps His promises. The Bible is full of His promises and we see many fulfilled ones. We see no unbroken ones. We do see some that are not fulfilled yet, but there is not a single broken promise.

WAITING (Delay)
Gen 8:6-16; 29:15-30; 1 Sam 16:19-21; Ps 27:1-14; 40:1-4; Mt 24:32-51; LK 15:20; Act 1:15-26; 2 Th 3:6-15; 2 Pet 3:8-9.

Do you find it difficult to wait? Are you impatient? When I rode the bus to work in Chicago, I saw a lot of people that found it hard to wait. They would continually pace back and forth and look at their watch. They weren't still a minute.

Waiting isn't easy and often we think, what is the delay? What's happening? We have an appointment at a certain time and we're there, but we are still waiting. If you want, you could ask why there is a delay, but don't be rude.

Sometimes we have to wait for God to respond. In those times, let us remember that He will respond in His time. Sometimes the delay is because the situation is not ready, and sometimes we are not ready to be used by God.

Waiting shows the importance of something. It is sad that often people will stand in line for hours and even in cold weather for a concert or something of this nature, but they would not think of doing that in going to church. The waiting shows that it is important to that person.

Are we willing to wait and work toward the objective? Is this something that we need right now? Is it something that needs to be done now?

While we are waiting for the achievement of our goal, we are to be doing the will of God. Waiting is not an idle time.

WATCHFULNESS
Ex 34:12; Deut 4:9, 23; Josh 23:11; 1 K 8:25; Ps 39:1; 119:9; 141:3; Prov 4:23-26; Mt 6:1; 18:10; 25:13; 26:40-41; Mk 4:24; Lk 11:35; 1 Cor 10:12; 16:13; Eph 5:15; 1 Th 5:4, 6, 21; Heb 2:1; 1 Pet 4:7; 5:8; Rev 3:2-3, 11; 16:15.

We are to be careful in our Christian walk. There are things that we should do and things that we should not do. Let us follow the example of Jesus in our deeds, actions, and thoughts. We are watchful in a calm, natural manner. We are watchful to see that we are walking with God, and that we are not taken in by false doctrine or fads of the times. Not like a frightened animal that is watching for predators, nor watching and examining with intensity lest a detail slips by.

We also need to watch for His return. We don't sit down and wait for it because only the Father knows the date. But we are to be faithful and carry out His work of ministering and serving others. In Matthew 25:13, Jesus gives the parable of the wise and foolish virgins. The point is to be ready, for you do not know when the Master is coming.

WEAKNESSES (Failures, LIMITATIONS, SIN)
Rom 14:1-23; 2 Cor 12:1-10; 1 Jn 3:1-11.

All of us have strengths and weaknesses. We need to develop our strengths and be on guard in the areas in which we are weak; and if we can develop those areas in which we are weak into a strength, then let us do that. Let us use our strengths to encourage another person. We can even make use of our weaknesses by demonstrating that we have need of God in our life, and let another use their strengths to encourage us.

We need to let God's strength come into our lives through prayer, worship, Bible study and devotions, and trust. Rely upon His strength. Paul spoke of His thorn in flesh and in 2 Corinthians 12:10, he says, *"When I am weak, then I am strong."* God's strength is made strong in our weakness.

WEALTH (ABUNDANCE, ETERNAL LIFE, MONEY)

Jer 9: 23-24; Mt 19:16-30; Mk 10:17-27; Lk 12:13-34; Jn 8:12-30.

Wealth can be a blessing or a curse. If a person lets that wealth take the place of God, if that becomes the ruling passion for him or her or, in other words, that becomes that person's god, then wealth is a curse. And that person is to be pitied, for that person will lose everything. In Mark 8:36, it says, *"What good is it for a man to gain the whole world yet forfeit his soul?"*

Wealth can be a tremendous blessing if it is used in the right way and not selfishly. It can be used to benefit people and do a lot of good things.

Material wealth is not true wealth. Material wealth can do some great things, but it is spiritual wealth that is the true wealth. True wealth is accepting Jesus as Lord and Savior of your life. In Matthew 13:46, Jesus gives the story of a man finding a pearl of great value, and he sells all that he has to possess it. This is what the kingdom of God is like. This is what we must do. We need to give everything we have to possess it. That everything is our very life. Give yourself to Him and lay up treasure in heaven (Mt 6:20-21), and you will possess everything that really matters. Material wealth will fade away and can be stolen, but not the treasure in heaven, not your relationship to Jesus Christ.

If you have been blessed with abundance, then use it to help other people. Use it to glorify God. Do not be a slave to your wealth.

WISDOM (KNOWLEDGE)

1 K 3:1-28; Ps 107:43; 111:10; 119:97-112; Prov 1:1-7; 3:13; 7:2-4; 12:1-8; 19:8, 20; 23:12, 23; Ecc 8:1-8; Mt 7:24-25; 11:19; 25:1-3; Lk 2:33-40; 1 Cor 3:18; 13:11; 2Cor 8:7; Eph 5:15-17; Jas 1:2-8.

What is wisdom? Wisdom is more than knowledge. All of us have heard and may have even experienced the "educated fool." Wisdom is putting knowledge to proper use. It is right and proper discernment, practical judgment. If you know what is right to do, and you do that, then you are exercising wisdom. Wisdom comes from applied knowledge. Where do we get wisdom? True wisdom comes from God.

In Psalm 111:10, it says, "The fear of God is the beginning of wisdom." Living and thinking in accordance with God is the wisdom that God wants us to have. See things from His perspective and make your plans accordingly.

Study His word for knowledge and wisdom. Spend time in prayer. Converse with His dedicated servants and learn from them.

WITNESSING (Telling)

2 K 3:20; Jon 3:1-10; Mt 28:16-20; Act 1:1-11.

Witnessing is vital because that is the way that everyone became a Christian. The gospel was shared to you by someone. We must share and want to share that same message with others. Witnessing is introducing someone to Jesus Christ. If Jesus means so very much to you, then shouldn't someone else know Him too? In Matthew 28:19 is the great commission in which Jesus tells His disciples to go and make disciples of all nations.

In witnessing, we never know who will respond, so we must not prejudge and exclude anyone. We should also not be obnoxious in our witnessing. "You're going to hell if you don't repent, you dirty, rotten heathen." That doesn't sound like Jesus is in that person's heart. Demonstrate that Jesus is real to you is the best way to witness. Tell them your story in simple terms. For some, it was a quite dramatic event, and for others, it was a more gradual thing.

What are you witnessing to? I was not there when Jesus rose from the grave, but there were many that were. I accept their testimony. Then another vital part of my belief is that Paul was originally an enemy of the Christian faith. He thought the Christians were leading people away from God so he was persecuting them. Then, on the road to Damascus (see Act 9) to arrest some Christians, Paul had a vision in which He meets the Risen Lord, and Jesus tells Paul that he is persecuting Him. This would be a big shock to someone. He thought he was doing God's work when in fact He was persecuting God. The scripture says that Jesus is God, and a mere man could not do the things that He did. Another part of our testimony is that this good news has stood the test of time. A lie falls apart, but truth stands. Then the final part of my testimony is that I came to the point that I believed that I was a sinner. I needed a Savior, and I found Him in Jesus Christ. I feel that He has come into my life. I can walk with Him and talk with Him. A song that has a tremendous message says that *"Because He lives I can face tomorrow."*

WOMEN (HUMANNESS, IMAGE)

Gen 2:18, 21-22; 3:16; Prov 11:16, 22; 12:4; 14:1; 18:22; 21:9; 31:10-31; 1 Cor 14:34-35; 2 Tim 3:6.

A woman is created in God's image and is not inferior to man. She was not an afterthought. In fact, God felt that the woman was needed in order for man to be complete (see Gen 2:18). Men and women need to treat each other as equals. In marriage there is a oneness between the man and the woman. The two become as one flesh, but neither loses his or her identity. A man and a woman have different roles, but the same goal. We are to serve God.

Jesus did not belittle women or treat them as second class. The early church had some women that served in some very important roles in it. In 1 Corinthians 14:34, Paul commands for the women to be silent in church. This was because this was causing a disruption in the service. They sat on opposite sides of the room and were asking their husbands questions. Paul is saying to ask their questions at home.

The traditional role was for the woman to be in the home, but that has changed considerably. The women who are working should not disparage those who are housewives. That is a very important role. No one should make fun of it or belittle it. On the other hand, those who work should not be disparaged by those in the home. They are doing important work also. The key is to serve God where you are at, and to influence those around you. In the home, you have children and a spouse. On the job you have coworkers, and if married, you have a spouse and perhaps children also.

Touching on something that was said above: women not speaking in church? We would lose a lot if that were adhered to. Women play a very important role in the life of the church.

WORDS (Communication, CONVERSATION)

Ps 19:1-14; Prov 13:1-6; Mt 12:33-37; Col 4:2-6.

We need to watch our words so that they are pleasing to God. Words can bring joy and be the source of love, but they can hurt and be a source of division. Do not gossip or flatter. Think before you speak.

Sometimes it is best to be quiet. If your words will hurt or will tear down, then be quiet. Don't say that angry word (then you won't have to regret it later and it will not add fuel to the fire). But as Proverbs 15:1 says, *"A gentle answer turns away wrath, but a harsh word stirs up anger."* Our words can draw people to or repel them from Christ. Let any praise be honest praise.

We need to keep our word so we will be known as reliable people. Our actions must back up our words.

Be kind, patient, and loving in your words. Let your words build up. Let them give comfort. Use your words to praise God.

WORK (EFFORT)

Gen 31:22-35; Ex 16:13-36; 35:4-35; Ruth 2:1-13; 2 K 10:30-36; Lk 19:11-27; Jn 3:22-36; Eph 6:5-9.

Work is an important part of our lives, and we are to take it seriously. Do you enjoy your work? Many people do not for quite a number of reasons. Do not hate your work. If you have to find different employment, then do so. We are to be hard workers, doing our best at our job. Use the skills that God has given to you.

Just as we are to work hard, we are also called to rest from our work. Don't be a workaholic. There are some that work several jobs or work long hours. They claim that they are doing this for their family, but they don't have any time to spend with their family. Thus, they are really hurting the family. Sometimes they do this because of pressure on the job, but that has to be resolved so that you do have time for your family. In addition to work, we have to have some time to rest and worship God.

WORLD (CREATION, MINISTRY)

Mt 5:13-16; Jn 17:6-19; Rom 18:8-28.

Jesus has told us to be the light of the world (Mt 5:14). How we live is an influence upon those around us. He wants us to make a difference in the world.

God created the world. He gave it to us to live on. We should take care of it as faithful stewards. We are to have respect for it. We are to do good. Today, there is pollution and the consuming of our natural resources. We need to use the resources at hand to conserve our natural resources rather than using them up. Let us take advantage of the sources that are actually free, such as solar energy and wind power.

WORRY (Anxiety, FEAR)

Ps 37:1-11; 46:1-11; 121:1-8; Is 26:3-4; Mt 6; Lk 12:22-28; Jn 14; Phil 4:4-9; 1 Pet 5:7.

Are you worried, or do you ever worry? A truthful answer is yes. All of us worry from time to time, some people more so than others. We need to keep our worries to a minimum. We need to rely on God. John 14:1 is a great passage. Jesus says do not worry, *"You believe in God believe also in me."* Let us remember that things are in His control. In John 10:28-29 is another great passage. Jesus says that no one can be snatched out of His hand, and in the next verse, He says that no one can be snatched out of the Father's hand. We are not asked to understand a situation; we are only asked to trust.

Worry can be harmful to your health. In Luke 12:22-31, Jesus tells us not to worry. Our Heavenly Father knows our needs. If He has provided for the birds of the air and clothed the lilies of the valley, then how much more will He take care of you. He also points out that your worry cannot add one second to your life. Too often we worry about matters that are out of our control. If it is in your control, then God simply expects you to do your part. Let us pray instead of worrying.

WORSHIP (ADORATION, PRAISE)

Ex 3:1-6; 34:8; Lev 7:28-38; Num 28:1-8; Ps 27:4; 29:2; 35:18; 63:1; 81:1-16; 84:1-2; 95:6; 100:1-4; 103:1-4; 138:2; 149:1; Hab 2:20; Mt 2:1-12; 17:1-8; 18:19-20; Lk 4:8; Jn 4:23-24;1 Cor 14:26-33; 1 Tim 2:8; Heb 12:28.

What is worship? How should we worship? It is much more than the one or more hours that a person spends at church on Sunday.

Worship is an encounter with the Living God. It is not a dull ritual as some would think of it. Anyone with that attitude is not worshipping. It is a real and vibrant encounter. If the things that we do in a worship service degenerate into a ritual, then we must take the steps needed to get back to the original meaning and the original life of that ritual. We need to establish a fresh contact with God.

We must be prepared when we come to Him. Give Him our total being in worship: heart, mind, and soul. Give Him your best. Praise Him continually by the life that you offer up to Him. Worship in your daily living. Remember His greatness, His mercy, and His love. Confess it by your acts and relationships.

We must worship in the right spirit, for we are to worship in spirit and in truth. Do you worship God, things, the world, or Satan?

Worship should be done in harmony. The believers are to be built up. Worship is not a performance. Sometimes people come and expect to be given something. Worship is receiving, but it also involves giving. As has been said above, you must give of yourself. You must participate. Worship is not a spectator sport. It is not something that the pastor, choir, and other leaders are doing to entertain you; it is a participation of all of God's people. If you don't give of yourself, then you are not going to receive anything.

There are many styles of worship. You need to find the style of worship that best fits who you are. One type involves a lot of emotion. There may be the speaking in tongues, people shaking from receiving the Spirit, clapping, dancing in the aisles, and emotions expressed in many different ways. Then, on the other end from the very emotional type, is a very formal type of worship. This type appeals to the intellect as opposed to the emotions. Then there are all those types in between. *Find the balance* that you need to express your personality, your faith. **Find a type that means something to you**. What I dislike very strongly is for a person of one type of worship to belittle another type. "Those are Holy Rollers; they run up and down the aisles, roll in the aisles, and act like a bunch of crazy fools." or "Everyone is dead in that church. The Spirit sure isn't at work there."

How dare we judge the way someone worships God. But what is even worse is that some churches feel that they are the only true church. You have to belong to that church in order to be saved. This of course is not true. Let us thank God that the person is worshipping God. God works among His people in different ways. Just because it is not the way that you worship, and you do not care for that style, does not mean that it is not meaningful to someone else. Don't feel that your way is correct and a different way is not correct. It is just as bad to say, "Come on, boy, raise the hands." As it is to say, "Don't raise your hands in here. Don't do something, just to go along with the crowd. Do what is meaningful to you, but don't disrupt a service either."

WORTH (see VALUE)

Topics

Being A Christian

Introduction

(This topic is from one of my earlier writings for a men's study group. The material here presents what it means to be a Christian in different areas. Some questions are posed to start your thinking. I hope that you will mediate on the areas in more depth. Ask yourself, where am I? I have changed it a little, and of course, this all applies to men and women alike. I hope this might help you identify your strong points and weak points and as a result help in your Christian growth).

In life there are ups and downs. When a person becomes a Christian, often the person feels that things will be smooth sailing now, but very often things become even more difficult. One reason is that Satan tries to discourage the new Christian. I think a large part of the problem is that we struggle with turning complete control of our lives over to God. There's a voice that whispers to us that says that God wants us to think and to develop our potential. Or, to put it another way, there is that voice that questions God: "Did God really say, 'You must not eat from any tree in the garden?'" (Gen 3:1). Satan would have us question God. Did He really say that? It is true that we are to develop our potential, *but we are not to be independent of Him.* We can only find our full potential when we rely upon God. We are created by Him. (Gen. 1:1) We are to be dependent upon Him. He gave us life, and He gives us the things that we need in order to maintain that existence. Thus, to try to live independently from God is foolish and impossible. It can't be done. Part of developing to your fullest potential is to recognize your need and dependence upon God. You need food. You need God.

In this, I want us to think of different areas and attempt to answer questions. For this to have any value to you, you must give your honest answers. Then you can judge yourself and see what areas you need to work on. You can do this in a group of friends that you trust or by yourself. Share what you feel comfortable in sharing, but by all means take this home and study, meditate, and pray about the goal of becoming a person that follows God in a more complete manner.

As we think of various religions, there are various paths and goals. Some use meditation to become at peace with their inner self. Many of them have various steps. In short, if I do these things, then I can go to heaven or whatever they call it and get that inner peace. The goal of Hinduism is to be absorbed into the Brahman—this is the ultimate reality. Hinduism has the belief in reincarnation. Your caste or station in life is determined by the kind of life that you lived in your prior life. In Buddhism, the goal is to end suffering, which is a craving for the satisfaction of the senses. This suffering can be overcome by following The Noble Eightfold Path. Following this eightfold path involves meditation.

This is just a sketchy view of Hinduism and Budhism and in no way am I trying to spell out the details of these religions. I only want to make one point. These religions have *man* attempting to reach a higher stage. The believers are doing certain works to attain their goal. For the Christian, salvation is a result of *God's* work and not man's. God has taken the necessary step to reconcile man to God and man to man. Works are vital and important, but are a result of salvation, not a means to it.

What is it that the Christian feels that God requires of him or her? This is the central question that we want to discuss. Of what does Christianity consist? Is it a set of moral ethics or a value system or a lifestyle? It is all of this, but it is much more. How would you describe it to a seeker? What distinguishes it from any other religion?

Another important thing that we must remember as we try to analyze what it really means to be a Christian is simply this: A Christian is someone who is imitating Christ. Let us look at some different areas. In Mark 12:30-31, Jesus quotes from a passage that is found in Deuteronomy and Leviticus. "Love the Lord your God with all of your heart and with all your soul and with all of your mind and with all of your strength. The second is this: 'Love your neighbor as yourself.'" What does this mean in these areas?

I

Personal

1. *As you pass through this life, what do you see? What does Jesus see? Is it just work, toil, problems, pain, and frustration? Do you approach things with a positive attitude? Do you see the opportunities?*

   Jesus walked this earth as one of us. He saw hurts, pain, frustrations, evil, and a number of other things. He reached out in compassion. He saw needs and ministered to them. Do you see the possibilities or just the problems? Jesus saw the problems, but He was here to meet those problems to save us. Jesus saw a people that needed God. In Matthew 23:37, He says, *"O Jerusalem, Jerusalem, you who kill the prophets and stone those sent to you, how often I have longed to gather your children together, as a hen gathers her chicks under her wings, but you were not willing."* He saw God at work. He is God at work. Too often we don't see God, and Jesus would say to us, *"O you of little faith."* He said that often to His disciples. Often, we may wonder how Jesus could see all of the evil that He saw and say, "I have come to redeem them," or, *"I have overcome the world."* He did and could because He knew that there is not anything or anyone with greater power or greater love than God. Because the Father has love for us, Jesus does so also for they are one in the Spirit. It was out of love that the Father sent the Son (Jn 3:16).

2. *What kinds of things frustrate you or irritate you? Think of the little things and think of the big things. Why are you frustrated?*

   Sometimes a word said at the wrong time or in the wrong way frustrates us. You are cut off in traffic. Maybe you feel that you were overcharged. Maybe it is the burden of debts. Maybe your team that you play on or watch loses. There are just all sorts of things, but don't let them get you down. Maybe pause and have a little laugh if it is not serious. In any case, take your frustrations to God in prayer, in reading the Bible. Let Him help you. Rely on His strength.

3. *How do you react to criticism?*

    Sometimes I say to myself, *If you think that you can do a better job, then do it yourself or shut up.* We need to do something, and not just criticize. It is true that sometimes people who are doing nothing are the first to find fault. We need to look at the criticism and see if it is justified. If so, then let us correct the error. If the person is criticizing out of jealousy or some other reason, then let us pray for that person and also take steps to mend the broken relationship. One way would be to say, "You're right. Would you work with me to help correct this?"

4. *What gives you joy and pleasure?*

    Jesus and the Heavenly Father rejoice over the repentance of each lost sinner (see Lk 15:10) just as we rejoice when we find something that was lost. Is our joy and our pleasure in material things and blessings? We need to be thankful for them, but let them have their proper place in our lives. Let our pleasure and joy be in the higher things.

5. *What do you do for entertainment? Would the Lord approve of your reading matter? What about your music?*

    If you feel ashamed of what you like for entertainment, then there must be something wrong with it. Do you watch television? Some people feel that is wrong and, with a lot of what's on television, I would agree. However, there are good programs too. Some of today's music is nothing but filthy language. That is wrong. Let your music speak to you and lift you up. Music can bring back memories too. Let it. I still enjoy the kind of music that I sang in the barn as I was growing up on the farm. What about your reading material—is it uplifting? Today, many magazines and other media use sex to sell. You know what I mean: a buxom young woman in a very revealing outfit is holding toothpaste or something or draped over a car. "Shine-O gives you that smile he can't resist." Or, "Hey, guys, she uses Shine-O, shouldn't you too?"

    Let your reading feed your mind and soul with the proper thoughts and not be a source of exciting the senses. Don't let someone else make you feel ashamed of what you like, but make sure that it is of a good nature.

6. *What are your dreams, your hopes, and ambitions?*

I would encourage you to dream big, for our God is big. *"Jesus looked at them and said, 'With men this is impossible, but with God all things are possible.'"* (see Mt 19:26). Dream of how you can help God carry out His work. I hope to do more for the church. I would like to see Trinity Baptist Church grow in numbers and in spirit. God offers His salvation to all. Be sure your dreams involve helping others and serving God. Let us remember Jesus's words of Mark 8:36, *"What good is it for a man to gain the whole world, and forfeit his soul?"*

7. *How well do you communicate with others?*

Communication is important. I don't communicate with others as well as I should or would like. Good communication involves a desire to want to communicate, a willingness to listen to others even if they have different opinions from yours, to consider those other opinions, and to respect them and to learn from them.

Do you communicate with God, or is it a one way conversation—all yours?

The Christian must not only converse with other believers, but also with God.

8. *How do you relate with other people, especially those that are different from you?*

There are different types of people. Some are very outgoing and relate very easily to a large number of people. Others have more difficulty in doing this. If you are of this type, then start with a small group and extend your circle of friends. If you are an outgoing person and are aware of some people that have difficulty in making friends, then be a friend and introduce them to others.

We must reach out to other people that have different ideas, come from different backgrounds or races. We must not reject anyone. We may be against their views, lifestyles, ideas etc., but we must not reject the other person.

9. *What kind of person are you?*

Some people are easygoing. Others are very formal. Some people are very picky and detail-oriented people while others are much more casual and don't sweat the small stuff. There are introverts and extroverts. There are the perfectionists. There are fun-loving people, serious people, and considerate people. Some people are easy to get to know and others are very difficult to know. There are people of all kinds. Whatever your type, serve God. Be someone that people want to know, for in that way you are reflecting Jesus as your Lord. People wanted to know Him.

10. *What kind of people do you like?*

Most of us like people that have similar interests as we do. We want to be comfortable around the other person. They are not busybodies. They are a good friend. Stop and think what you consider the characteristics of a good friend. A good friend is certainly one that you enjoy spending time with. That person can be trusted and you will share confidences with him or her. A good friend does not betray your confidences. A good friend encourages you but will try to dissuade you when you want to do wrong or think wrong. Of course, the only friend that will never let you down is Jesus Christ.

11. *What is important to you?*

Different people stress different things and demonstrate a thing's importance by the time that they spend on that thing. Money, prestige, and power are important to many. For the Christian, we need to place God first in our life. Jesus gives some strong words in Luke 14:26, "*If anyone comes to me and does not hate his father and mother, his wife and children his brothers and sisters—yes, even his own life—he cannot be my disciple.*" This shows us the position that God must have. He must be first even over our own life.

He must be very important, but too often He is not as important as He should be. He is not ruler of our life except in name. When this is true, then we must repent and strive to make Him central.

Another important thing to all people is the need to be loved. We need to feel that someone cares. We are not alone. We can be surrounded and feel that no one cares or we are unloved. The church must reach out in real love. We must show that we really care. Jesus gave us a new command (Jn 13:34), "*A new command I give to you: Love one another. As I have loved you, so you must love one another.*"

12. *Have you ever asked, what in the world am I doing here? What do you feel your purpose in life is?*

At the end of our life, we want to feel that we counted and that we made a difference. The Christian is to glorify God, so we have to answer the question of what it means to glorify God. In the song "Amazing Love" there is the phrase, "In all I do, I will honor you." We honor God by returning the love that He shows to us to others. We honor Him by being obedient (Jn 14:15). If your faith is real, then you honor God. A hypocrite dishonors God.

13. *How do you give criticism?*

We mentioned that some give it in a cruel manner. It is a gibe. It is a teardown. The Christian needs to give it in the spirit of building up.

14. *What use do you make of your talents and abilities?*

Each of us has talents that God expects us to use. We need to use them to develop them. This provides a blessing both to the giver and to the receiver. Many people that have made hospital visits have often said, "That person blessed me more than anything that I did for them." There are ministries for all of us. One example is that when our daughter was in the hospital we drove sixty miles one way to see her. This got to be too much so we rented a hotel room for a short time. This got to be expensive. Then, as an answer to prayer a person used the gift of hospitality. She opened her home to us so we could stay close by the hospital. These are the type of deeds we need to do.

I would encourage you to develop and use the gifts that God has given to you. You will bless others and you will be blessed too.

II

Work

A large part of our day is spent in work. This probably takes up the majority of our day. If a person is retired, then some other form has to take up this block of time. It might be part-time work, engagement in a hobby, volunteer work at church, or on the mission field—either at home or abroad. Something has to take up this time. Too many people stop working and have nothing to do so they die. For the retired person, I would say, "Take advantage of this retirement and work for the Lord."

1. *How do you act at work with your fellow workers, those over you and under you, the people with whom you come in contact in the course of the business day? What is your attitude?*

   We need to be helpful with our fellow workers. They need to see the spirit of Christ working in and through us. We should not cheat others. We need to work with a cheerful spirit. Be concerned about people's needs and problems. An attitude of concern and love should be evident. Practice the golden rule.

2. *In traveling to and from work, how do you conduct yourself, whether it is driving or riding on public transportation?*

   If someone cuts you off in traffic, honks his or her horn, what do you think and feel? Unfortunately, in today's society, sometimes that is the prelude to a release of violent anger and rage. This is termed road rage; people have even been killed in this senseless fit of anger.

   Be courteous and don't let things irritate you.

3. *What are the problem areas at work?*

Sometimes there are unethical practices that are carried on by the business, or by people, in trying to get ahead. Maybe you are used or taken advantage of; there can be discrimination and harassment. Sometimes the problems can be so severe that your job is threatened. If you work with the public, sometimes the people that you are dealing with may cause problems, tensions, and stress.

4. *Do you enjoy your work?*

Many people do not. If possible, we need to make our work enjoyable. One way of doing this is by regarding it as a ministry. Honor God in doing it to the best of your ability. In some cases, you may have to find another line of work. God does not expect us to live a life of drudgery, of discouragement, of disappointment, and discontent. In Christ, we are not victims of our circumstances.

5. *Do you regard it as a ministry?*

Even the most menial task can be a ministry and should be approached in that way. Dedicate it to the Lord.

6. *Is work robbing you of your family or causing problems in other areas of your life?*

Sometimes a person becomes so wrapped up in his or her job that the family is neglected. Sometimes it pushes God aside. The work may be good and important and necessary, but it should not be at the expense of the family, nor cause other problems. Even a pastor, in dealing with his congregation, can be guilty of this. The pastor spends so much time with his congregation that he neglects his family. This is also not sending the proper message to people in his congregation, for some of them may neglect their family also.

7. *What does it mean to serve God in your position, in the work that you are doing right now?*

It means to make God real to people. It is to demonstrate His love by word and deed. It is to allow Christ to work in and through you. It is to carry out your tasks with the sense that the Lord is your real boss. It is Him that you are striving to please.

III

Family

Your family is your closest group. We, as the church, need to be an extended family.

1. *How do you relate to you wife, your husband, your children, your in-laws, and other relatives?*

   Husbands and wives need to share with each other: dreams, goals, frustrations. Support each other. The husband is not a dictator or a tyrant. He should carry out his role in the household in love and in the fear of the Lord just as the wife needs to carry out her role. They are a team and need to work together. She is not a second-class person. The husband needs to let his wife and his children know that he loves them. Together they should raise their children to know the Lord, encourage them, support them, and direct their paths.

2. *How well do you listen to those in your family?*

   Unfortunately, parents do not always listen to their children as well as they should. And man and wife do not always listen to one another either. Some divorces could be prevented if people simply listened, for if there was genuine listening, the differences would be recognized and often corrected before they are beyond repair. Listening is a neglected art. Listening shows concern. You want people to listen to you, so listen to others.

3. *What are the goals in the family?*

For many people, money and prestige are primary goals. The husband can become a workaholic, claiming to be doing this for the sake of the family, but he is really doing it for himself and is destroying the family. The children and the wife do not want the things that he is giving them as a substitute for love. They want him. They want a father. The wife wants a husband. There can also be a churchaholic. This is an individual that is so involved in the activities of the church that he or she neglects the family and its needs.

4. *What are some problems in the family?*

Money is a primary one. Another problem is differences in religious beliefs—for example, perhaps one is a believer and the other isn't. There can be favoritism. Thus, the disciplining of the children is still another problem. Physical abuse and sexual abuse are some more problems. Unfaithfulness is still another. Dividing up household activities can be still another.

IV

The Christian Faith

1. *What do you feel is the easiest thing about being a Christian?*

    To become a Christian is probably the easiest, for it is simply a recognition of your need for a Savior and accepting Jesus as Lord and Savior. In fact, sometimes it is too easy in the minds of some. They feel that they have to do something to earn their salvation, but there is nothing that they can do. Salvation is in Christ alone; it is a gift of God (Rom 6:23).

2. *What do you feel is the most difficult part of being a Christian?*

    To live the life that Christ wants us to live and to live up to His standards is very difficult. Growing can be difficult also since it involves moving out of our comfort zones. It involves action and decisions. We must want to grow. We must help each other grow. Another difficulty is that sometimes we are called to difficult situations. Moses was called to free His people and He did not want to. There are people that are called to leave their homes to go to foreign mission fields. We must be obedient. Matthew 16:24 says that we must take up our cross and follow Jesus.

3. *How would you describe the Christian faith to a seeker?*

    You are a sinner. This means that you have rebelled against God by desiring to do your own will instead of God's will. There is nothing that you can do to become right with God. However, God so loves you that He has provided the only way that your sin can be forgiven and you can be at one with Him and with other people. You can find the peace with others and with God that you desire. That way is through Jesus Christ, who died on the cross for your sins. By repenting and confessing your sins and accepting and following Jesus Christ as Lord and Savior, you are making a complete about-face, and instead of going away from God, you are walking with God (see Rom 10:9). (This is what a person has to come to accept before they become a Christian. A person has to feel that he or she is a sinner and needs forgiveness. Then they must learn that Jesus offers them that forgiveness).

4. *What distinguishes Christianity from other religions?*

Christianity is exclusive. It is not one of many paths to God. Christianity claims it is **the only way** to God. In John 14:6, Jesus says, *"'I am the way and the truth and the life. No one comes to the Father except through me."* Christianity's assertion of exclusiveness is based upon Jesus's own statement. He is the one that says there is no other way. In Acts 4:12 is the further assertion made by the disciples, "Salvation is found in no one else, for there is no other name under heaven given to men by which we must be saved."

Another distinction is that Jesus is God in man—God Incarnate. He is all God and all man.

A third distinction is the resurrection. Jesus overcame death. He rose from the dead. Buddha and Mohammed cannot claim this.

5. *Of what does Christianity consist?*

Christianity is relational. It is not just a set of ethics. The basis of pleasing God is not a set of acts, works, or deeds. In 1 Samuel 15:22, Samuel indicates that the Lord regards obedience better than sacrifices. The deeds we do are a result of accepting Jesus and following Him, not a way to Him; the deeds or Christian ethics are an outgrowth of one's relationship with God. Christianity is based upon a loving, holy, and righteous God. God took the steps to restore the broken relationship between Himself and man and the broken relationship between man and man. Mankind had rebelled against God and then went his own way.

The resurrection is the heart of Christianity. On the Cross, God restored this broken relationship. His justice was satisfied, and His love redeemed mankind. It has been said that no one, not even God Himself, can substitute Himself to heal the evil that has been done to me. The fallacy of this is that in every offense, God is the One who is wronged and not just you. Every crime is against God, first and foremost. Thus it is only He, and He alone, that can forgive and heal that gap that has occurred.

The heart then of the Christian faith is relational in that this is the core. As has been said, Christianity involves ethics, a lifestyle, a philosophy, and all of that, but this is not the heart of it. The heart is relationship—your relationship to God. Reconciliation between man and man and God and man is simply the establishment of a relationship with God. It is a walk, a communion with the Living Lord. This is how we should look upon it. It is not the adherence to teaching. The teaching explains our relationship but it is not the relationship. I am a child of God (Jn 1:12). The heart of Christianity is being. Any doing comes as a result of being, as a result of who we are.

6. *How are you using your time, talents, possessions, and abilities for God?*

Everything that we have is a gift from God. It is easy to squander time, etc. Often we see stories about this on television. A spirit of a dead person looks at his or her life and sees missed opportunities. In the New Testament, there is the story of the rich man who dies and goes to hell and begs to have someone go and warn his brothers so that they do not come there. He is told that if they don't believe Moses and the prophets, then neither will they believe someone who returns from the dead (see Lk 16:23-31). Jesus returned from the dead, yet many still do not believe.

When a loved one dies unexpectedly, we think, *If I had only said this or done that.* Let's not live a life of regrets. Use your time. Use your opportunities. Say the word. Do the thing.

Also, we have talents and abilities. Are we putting them to use for God? If you have the gift of speaking, then speak. Of hospitality, then use that gift. Our possessions need to be put to the best possible use. Be generous.

7. *What does worship mean to you?* (see Worship)

For some, worship is a duty or obligation, a chore to be endured. It is a performance that is put on by the minister, the choir, and other leaders. If I go to church faithfully, then I will earn my little gold stars that I need to get into heaven. This is an exaggeration, and the people that act this way really are not consciously thinking in this manner but their attitude and unconsciousness is.

Worship should really be an opportunity in which you actively participate. You are responding to God's love for you. It is a time of renewal and refreshment, a time for learning, for equipping, for strengthening, for meditation, for thanking and praising God for the wondrous things that He has done and how wondrous He is, just to mention a few of the things it involves.

8. *What role has the Bible in your life?* (see Bible)

For some, the Bible is a law book. But does the Bible speak to you? It can, if you allow the Holy Spirit to speak from its pages. This is one way God reveals Himself to us. It is amazing how all of these different books that compose the Bible and were written over a long stretch of time have a common theme. The Old Testament points toward Jesus, and The New Testament describes His ministry. It is also wonderful to see how God is working through various events. Joseph was sold into slavery and goes to Egypt. He is falsely accused, and then is thrown in prison, but later he is raised to power. This enables him to bring his whole family to Egypt to escape the famine. (Gen 37-48). The people are later treated as slaves, but they learn how to govern themselves. God is constantly at work in misfortune and is preparing them for what is ahead. The Bible reveals God to us. We cannot know anyone, especially God, unless that person reveals himself or herself to us.

9. *What is truth for the Christian?*

There are various ideas about truth. Today, many people feel that there are no absolutes. What is right for you may not be right for me. But the Christian says there are absolutes. Unfortunately, even among Christians, there is a division about truth: gay rights and abortion, to mention just two. This division hurts our witness.

In science, truth is something that explains or corresponds to reality. It is held until there is contradictory evidence. Then a new truth is formed that takes this new evidence into account. This is objective truth. In Christianity, there are objective truths. The Ten Commandments are some examples of objective truth. But the essential part of truth in Christianity is not objective but a relational truth.

Jesus said, *"I am the way, the truth . . ."* (Jn 14:6). He is a person pointing to the correct relationship with God. The Ten Commandments are laws and are objective, but the heart of the commandments is relational. If you keep the letter of the law but not the spirit of the law, then you are actually breaking the law. One example of that was that when the religious leaders accused Jesus of doing wrong by healing on the Sabbath. In Matthew 12, He says several things about this. He says that He is *"Lord of the Sabbath,"* and in verse 11, he says that they would take a sheep out of a ditch. Then in verse 12, He says, *"How much more valuable is a man than a sheep! Therefore it is lawful to do good on the Sabbath."*

There are many truths of Christianity that we could mention. There is only one God (Deut 6:4); He is the Creator (Gen 1:1). He provided for our salvation through His Son, Jesus Christ (Jn 3:16). God's Spirit is at work today. God is a loving God. He is love (1Jn 4:8). He provides eternal life for all who repent of their sin and accept and follow Jesus as Lord and Savior.

10. *What does it mean to glorify God? Why should we?*

To glorify God is to give Him honor and praise, to recognize who He is, and to acknowledge that He is worthy of praise because God is good. When we stop and think about His goodness, His mercy and love, then of course He should be praised. There is none other that is worthy of praise. None can compare to Him.

11. *What are some ways or things in which we can glorify God?*

To obey Him, to worship Him, to respond to His love and goodness are some ways to glorify Him. We glorify Him for He is worthy of it, but also in order for us to be fully human, we must do it. Giving love to others is still another way. Just as a little child can give honor to his or her parents by the things just mentioned and by living a life that is pleasing to the parents, so we can honor God by living a life that is pleasing to Him.

Bible

What is the Bible to you? For decades, it was the best-selling book and each household would have more than one copy, but it is not a well-read book. Some feel it is outdated and boring. One example of it being boring is the genealogies of strange names. I will admit that parts of the Bible are not that exciting, but it does have value. Others think of it as a bunch of unconnected stories: David and Goliath, the fiery furnace, etc. Many of them would question if these stories are real.

Is the Bible true? Fulfilled prophecies are one source that proves the Bible is true. Still another source of verification of the truth of the Bible is that many of the writers of the Bible were brutally martyred in defense of what they had written. Why would a person die for something that they know is not true? They wouldn't. You will die for something that you believe to be true. But this is not a matter of belief. They knew that what they had written was either true or not. They could have denied the writing and their lives would have been spared. There is archaeological evidence also. For example, in Exodus we have the story of the crossing of the Red Sea by the Israelites, who were pursued by the Egyptians. That account tells of the drowning of the Egyptians when the waters closed over them (Ex 15:19). Archaeology has discovered chariot wheels imbedded in the coral at the bottom of the Red Sea. These are just some of the attitudes that people have toward the Bible. Too many people do not see the Bible as it truly is. Then there are some that want to understand the Bible.

The Bible (here again I am simply talking about the Old and New Testament and not any others) is a library of sixty-six books. There are thirty-nine in the Old Testament (Genesis to Malachi) and twenty-seven in the New Testament (Matthew to Revelation). These books were written over a span of several centuries (from approximately about 2000 BC for the oldest Old Testament book to about AD 95 in the New Testament), and has about thirty different authors. However, before I go too far, we should raise the question of who is really the author of the Bible. Yes, a number of different men wrote it down, but these men only wrote down God's revelation to them. The real author of the Bible is God. This is why we call it God's word. God, by His very nature, can only be known if He reveals Himself to us. And this is what the Bible is about.

With its diversity in time and writers, as has been mentioned, it might be questioned if it has continuity. The Bible does have a central thread running through it. It may not be that apparent at first notice, but it is there upon study. That thread is that in the Old Testament, it looks forward to the coming of a deliverer. Sometimes this is a nation, at other times it is a remnant of the nation, and sometimes it is a person. The Jews called this person a Messiah. Then, in the New Testament, the Messiah comes in the person of Jesus Christ, the Son of God. This deals with His life and teachings and that of His disciples and the early church.

For the Christian, the Bible is God's written word to His people. It contains history, poetry, wisdom, and prophecy. In 2 Timothy 3:16, we are told scripture is "useful for teaching, rebuking, correcting, and training in righteousness."

Let's take a brief tour of the Bible. The first five books of the Bible are called the Torah (these are the books of the Law). In Genesis, we have the story of the beginning of things. Genesis 1:1 says, "In the beginning God created the heavens and the earth." It goes on to record the creation of all things. (See Creation in Topical section for a discussion of this). Then it records the fall of man (Gen 3) and the first murder and the promise of redemption. Further sin by man leads to his destruction by a flood (Gen 6). Noah and his family were spared in order to continue the line of mankind. Then we have God selecting Abraham to carry out His plan of redemption through his line (Gen 12). Abraham is the father of the people of Israel. The Israelites were God's chosen people because He revealed Himself to them, but they were also to be a light to the nations (Is 42:6). Through them, all nations were to come to know the Lord and thus be blessed. Unfortunately, they did not always realize this and did not always practice it.

Exodus describes the people's deliverance out of slavery to the Egyptians by Moses. They are given the Ten Commandments at Mt. Sinai, but have to wander in the wilderness for forty years because of their disobedience. Finally, they come into the Promised Land.

Leviticus gives laws for the people concerning holiness and worship. Numbers recounts the wandering in the wilderness. Deuteronomy also recounts the wilderness journey.

The next twelve books, Joshua through Esther, are books of history. After the death of Moses, Joshua became the leader that led the Israelites to conquer much of the Promised Land. Canaan is called the Promised Land because this is the land that God promised to Abraham and his line. Judges were raised to help the people solve some of their problems. The people came to demand a king, as other nations had, so Saul became the first king. After David's reign, the kings that followed were mostly bad. We see them obeying God and serving Him for a short time, and then later falling into idolatry and being punished for their sin. It is a rise and fall over and over again. The nation is even split into two. After the return from Babylonian captivity, Ezra tells the rebuilding of the temple that had been destroyed. Nehemiah recounts the rebuilding of the walls of Jerusalem.

The next five books of the Bible, Job through Song of Solomon, are the poetic and wisdom literature. Job asks the question of why. The man Job follows God but has to endure much suffering, so he asks *why*. The Psalms are hymns and prayers, some of which were used in public worship. They cover a wide range of emotions. The book of Proverbs gives advice on probably every area of life. Ecclesiastes states that the life without God leads to a meaningless life and one of despair. Song of Solomon is a poem about romantic and physical love.

The last section of the Old Testament, Isaiah through Malachi, has the prophetic books: the major and minor prophets. When kings ruled Israel, God spoke to the people through the prophets. Sometimes they did give some predictions about future events (Isaiah 42 is fulfilled by Jesus), but their main function was to call the people back to God and away from their sin. They gave warnings of what would happen when the people sinned. They admonished the people to repent of their sin.

In the New Testament, the first four books, Matthew, Mark, Luke, and John, are called the gospels. Gospel means good news. They present the same information but address different audiences and from a different perspective. The good news is the proclamation of God's salvation from sin. The gospel accounts tell of Jesus's birth, His life, teachings, ministry, His death and resurrection. The book of Acts could more accurately be called the acts of the Holy Spirit. Here we see the Holy Spirit at work in the early church. Then we have the epistles that address various problems in the early church. Finally, there is the book of Revelation, which talks, about the end of the earth.

The Bible shows God at work with His people. It is amazing how He uses various circumstances. One example is that the Israelites were slaves of the Egyptians, but in that slavery they were under Egyptian control and learned some important rules that they would need in order to govern themselves.

Another example is that Joseph was sold into slavery by his brothers. Then he was falsely accused by Potiphar's wife and he was thrown into prison. In prison, he interpreted some dreams, but he was not remembered when one of the men was released. However, later, when the pharaoh had a dream that no one could interpret, he was remembered. He correctly interpreted the dream—that there would be seven years of plenty followed by seven years of famine. He was in put in charge of storing up grain during the plentiful years and distributing the grain during the lean years. He was second only to the pharaoh. He brought his family to Egypt where they were treated well until he died. But it was amazing how all of these hardships put Joseph in the place that he needed to be and throughout all of his hardships he was faithful to God (Gen 37-47).

The supreme example of God using terrible events is in the crucifixion. Jesus came and ministered to people, but he was hated and put to death on a cross. Satan appeared to have won. But God used that death on the cross to defeat Satan, to defeat sin. Jesus provided the salvation that God had promised.

People interpret the Bible in various ways. A couple of things that need to be remembered: as scripture is being interpreted, the context of the passage needs to be considered, and there are some things that are not to be taken literally. Some of these are easy to see. In John 6:51, Jesus says that He is the Living Bread, or in John 10:7, Jesus is the gate (or door) for the sheep. Obviously these are symbolic, for He is not bread or a gate, but a living Person.

Many people agree with what they like in the Bible, but reject the parts that they don't like or disagree with. Some feel that the writers of the books of the Bible put in their own biases and consequently we should ignore what our "enlightened senses" tell us. This is dangerous, and you may as well reject all of scripture, for you are setting yourself up as a higher authority than the Bible. What is the basis or foundation for these "enlightened senses"? What is the authority to which you are appealing?

The proper study of the Bible is to approach it with an open mind. Do not have a prejudice for it nor against it for either one can prevent the Bible from speaking to you. Approach the study of the Book with an honest attitude. You should approach it with reverence, again despite your belief or disbelief of its statements, for it is discussing important matters. It should be read in a systematic manner rather than haphazardly—reading a page here and another there or opening the book and pointing to a page for your inspiration. You might point to the passage where it says, "Judas went out and hanged himself."

The Bible places a demand upon you. A response is expected if you read it with any depth. A cursory and flippant reading is the same as no reading at all. One response is that if the statements are true, then they are to be obeyed. The study of the Bible involves reading, thinking, analyzing, and coming to a point of knowledge.

The Bible has something to say on the problems of life. This is what the topical concordance of this book was about. It lists various subjects with some scripture to start your thinking on various topics.

Why read the Bible? It is not out of date as some would claim. It deals with the same problems that we are dealing with today. To live correctly, I need a proper foundation. There are all sorts of theories that are proposed, but only Jesus's word is the solid foundation that will not fail. Jesus's disciples said to Him, "'Lord, to whom shall we go? You have the words of eternal life'" (Jn 6:68). This is the faith that we need to have. We won't find what we need or what we are looking for anywhere else.

The Bible is not a magical book, but it is a book of life. It can give you strength, peace, comfort. It can give you the words of eternal life. It is the written word and reveals Jesus Christ, who is the Living Word.

Some people think it is wrong to question the Bible, but God is not afraid of any legitimate search. If you search with a closed mind and refuse to accept anything that is contrary to your belief, then that is not a legitimate search for truth. But if you search the Bible with an open mind, then you will find the truth. Many skeptics have investigated the Bible and have met the Living Lord on its pages. Jesus says in John 14:6 that He is the truth. Therefore, any legitimate search will lead you to Him, not away.

God

Let us tackle this idea of god for a moment. You will notice I used the small g at this point. Down through history and in various cultures, there is the concept of gods and goddesses. Some of these were very capricious in nature and, if nothing else, very human in some of their folly. If a god or goddess granted you your wish, it may not be what you wanted. In Greek mythology is the story of Eos, goddess of the dawn. She made the wish that her lover, Tithonus, never die. This was granted, but her lover continued to age instead of maintaining his youthful form. The Greek and Roman gods and goddesses in particular were capricious.

There was animism, in which there were gods in rocks and trees, etc. The various gods were used to explain things. For example, when violent things happened in nature, that meant that the gods were angry. Why this belief in the supernatural, which some would regard as mere superstition? As for the Christian, I would say it is in the very core of human nature because Christianity believes that God created us. He placed a hunger there for Him.

What is your concept of God? Of course, many people do not think that there is a God. They claim not to accept things that cannot be proven by the rational senses. Yet their very assumption is based upon an assumption that is not verifiable but has to be accepted for them to proceed. Then the very system that prides itself upon discovering truth by the scientific method—science itself, palls when we get into delving into such matters as atoms and subatomic particles. One principle that is popular is the Heisenberg principle of uncertainty, which states that a particle's position and motion cannot be determined at the same time because the observation of it affects the particle. Even wilder in the quantum theory is the idea held by some scientists that an electron, for example, does not actually exist until it is observed. Gravity itself, one of the first forces to be explained mathematically, is coming under new examination as to its nature. In Einstein's special theory of relativity, he gave his definition of gravity, but that is now being questioned by some scientists.

All I want to point out here at the moment is that the scientific system, as it delves further and further into things, realizes that there is very little that we really do know. Thus, we all operate on a "faith" basis. It just depends upon what you have faith in. As I have said earlier in this book, it takes much more faith not to believe in God than it takes to believe in God. If you do not believe in God, then you are saying that all this complexity in the universe, the physical laws that are necessary for the existence of life, etc., and all that are merely the result of chance. I will politely say I do not see how you can believe that and call yourself a rational person.

Some in the scientific world would like to dismiss the idea of a Creator as being unscientific, but this violates the principle of objectivity in the scientific method. A Creator cannot be comprehended, but a Creator can certainly be apprehended. An example of the arbitrariness of these men is this: an electron is materially inconceivable, but this electron is used to light our cities and do numerous other things. It is accepted, but a Creator is rejected.

I would like to take this just one step further (and I hope that I do not lose you here) for my own pondering and to show any skeptics reading this that Christians are not afraid to ask such questions. As I consider the universe and how vast it is with all of the worlds, first I am awed, but then I wonder how can there not be intelligent life on some distant world? Of course, I really don't know and can only go on what I believe. One source is the Bible, and I do not see how other intelligent life would correspond with what is there. At this time, I don't see the possibility of two intelligent life forms meeting due to the vast distances between planets of another solar system and ours. At this time, that is an impossibility; however, if that should ever happen, I am convinced we will gain some knowledge that enlightens our own faith. The Bible really does not say that there isn't intelligent life on other planets. We just assume that there isn't. However, there really isn't any point for it to address that question anyway. One example of making the Bible say what it doesn't is in the idea of the earth being flat. Galileo was persecuted by the church when he proposed that the earth is round and circled around the sun. This idea did not contradict any biblical truth, but contradicted man's thinking at that time.

God is the God of the universe. If there is other intelligent life, then God is their God also. Again, in my purely rational moments, I ask, *how can there be a God?* And when I think about it some more, I conclude, *how can there not be a God?*

In philosophy, there are various arguments that are proposed for the existence of God. One is the teleological argument. This is the argument from purpose. For example, a watch presupposes a watchmaker. There is some merit in this. As I look at the order in nature, the laws at work, life, the complexity of some things, for me it takes a tremendous amount of faith, an unreasonable amount of faith, to believe that this is merely the result of chance. You can look in a philosophy book for the various arguments. No argument is going to convince anyone of the existence of god, or God, if they do not want to believe. In philosophy, some of the gods are merely cold, impersonal ideas, such as the ground of being. They are simply there to explain something. They don't have anything to do with us. And this is how some feel—that there is a god but that He is not interested in our affairs. This is Deism. Some view god as some invisible power. Still others say god is in everyone. This would be a pantheistic view. In my own mind, as I have just stated above, there has to be a god. And all of these views are inadequate. We were created because we did not always exist. Let us call the One that created us the Designer. The Designer created everything in the universe and all of its complexity. This naturally raises some questions. Why did He create? What is the nature of this Designer? What relationship does He have with His creation? We know that He set up a system that keeps it going. We also know that we have minds that think. This Designer cannot be inferior to us in any way. He has to have an intelligence and power that goes beyond our imagination. It seems a little hard for me to imagine that this Designer does not have an interest in His creation. The universe displays orderliness, not chaos. As I consider the nature of this Designer, some impersonal concept such as Ground of Being cannot account for what I see. Think of the personal traits of a human being and our emotions. These were put into us. For me, the best concept of this Designer is the God of the Bible. This seems the most rational. God, to be God, can be inferior to no other god or even the concept of any other god. There are many concepts, but the true God has to be superior. He takes in all of the characteristics of the Designer. Isaiah 55:8-9 states it this way: "'for my thoughts are not your thoughts, neither are your ways my ways,' says the Lord. 'As the heavens are higher than the earth, so my ways are higher than your ways and my thoughts than your thoughts.'" The Designer, to be truly God, has to match this statement. Therefore, this Designer is God and He alone is God. This is God the Father, God the Son, and God the Holy Spirit.

It is difficult to get an adequate picture of God the Father (as I mention under the subject Jesus Christ). Every picture I can imagine is wrong. God is Spirit (Jn 4:24) and that is accurate, but how do you picture a Spirit? We should add to this also that we are made in the image of God (Gen 1:26, 27). This implies more than just the moral characteristics that we normally associate with the idea of the image. This also implies that we have a spiritual body. God has a spiritual body. God is not some big ghost. In Luke 24:39, Jesus appears to the disciples after the resurrection. He lets them know that He is not a ghost. He has flesh and bones (Naturally, these are spiritual flesh and bones). In Jesus Christ we can think in human terms (see Jesus Christ). In Jesus, He tells us what the Father is like. Think of the Father as being like Jesus and also think that He has a spiritual body as opposed to some formless blob.

There are other questions that need to be raised. We can't picture Him, but how powerful is He? How big is your God? We limit God very often. Sometimes we run ahead and try to do God's job for Him and as a result mess things up. Abraham and Sarah are a good example of this (Gen 16:1-4). Instead of waiting for God to fulfill His promise of a son, Hagar was used to provide a son. Thus, as a result, there is enmity between the sons of Isaac (the promised son) and the sons of Ishmael (Hagar's son) to this day. If they had only waited, so much suffering would have been avoided. We need to expect great things from God, for with God all things are possible (Mt 19:26).

God's ways are higher than our ways, and His thoughts are higher than our thoughts (Is 55:8-9). There are many problems that we cannot resolve. Why is evil permitted? How can God allow some of the very terrible things to happen? We don't know, but the most terrible thing that could happen—the death of God—was permitted and even ordained. That death of God was the death of His Son Jesus on the Cross. As a result of that terrible event, a complete transformation occurred between the relationship of God and man. There was reconciliation. But we don't see any purpose in any of these other terrible events—for example, the extermination of millions of Jews. We only see a lot of suffering. Satan says, "See, God does not care. If He cared, this would not have happened." But we know that God *does* care. We can only trust in Him.

Under the subject of creation, we mentioned that man cannot create anything. All man can do is take the things that are already here and work with them, change their form, but he cannot create. Only God can and does do that. God also creates out of nothing. In the same manner, God is the only one that can heal. No doctor has ever healed a single person. God works through doctors. The way a person is healed is by giving the body the things that it needs: A person has lost a lot of blood so they are given blood. They are given things to combat infection. The doctor provides all of that to the body, and then the body takes what it needs and works according to the laws that God has dictated to it to produce the healing. This is not belittling the doctor. The doctor did a very important and needed task; otherwise, the person might have died. However, I just want to emphasize here that sometimes we rely too much on the doctor and medicines when there are better remedies. There are things in nature that do amazing things. This is not surprising since God made the body and God made the plants.

We noted above that Jesus Christ is central to our understanding of God. Jesus told His disciples that by seeing Him they had seen the Father (Jn 14:9).

I accept that there is a God, a Heavenly Father, who cares for each of us on the basis of Jesus's word, life, death, and resurrection; and also on the apostle Paul—he was a bitter enemy and persecutor of the Christian faith, but was confronted by the Living Christ. Further comments about this are in the section on Jesus Christ. I also believe that I have met the Risen Lord and that He dwells in each believer.

Life after Death

There are different views on this topic. As has been said before, there is the belief in reincarnation, in which a person is reborn as a new person after they die. If they led a good life, then they are born to a higher caste but, if not, then they are born to a lower caste. This is not the Christian's viewpoint.

Another view is that we are absorbed into that great ground of all being.

Still others feel that when you die that is it. There is no life after death—that is simply wishful thinking. Again, that is not the Christian viewpoint.

The Christian viewpoint is that there *is* life after death, and this is real life and not an absorption into some great cosmic something. We talk of heaven as having streets of gold and pearly gates. But it isn't this. These are just more images to tell us it is very beautiful and wonderful. We have said earlier than you cannot explain in words the beauty of a beautiful sunset to a person that is blind all of their life. They cannot conceive of color. In the same way, a person who came from heaven would not have the words to describe its beauty to us.

Just as we really cannot picture God, *so, too* the nature of life after death is difficult to imagine. I understand this life, but what is that next life like?

Again, let us use a metaphor to try to look at it. A person is a small embryo that develops into a fetus inside its mother. The fetus is very restricted in space. Its nourishment is derived from the mother. It is in a dark environment. I believe we get the general picture. This is life for that fetus.

Then the fetus is born, and there is a baby. No wonder the baby cries at birth, for it is a painful awakening and the baby is in alien surroundings. The fetus had no idea of this. Much of it is the same. In both cases, it was in the same dimensions of space and time, but the space was much more limited. Just look at the fetus and then the baby and then the young person and then the mature person. The life before birth is alike and yet very different.

In the same way, life after death will be the same in many ways, but different in many ways. I cannot imagine the differences, and that is frightening because it is unknown. However, do not be frightened. As I said earlier, I do not like to think in terms of streets of gold because it is not that. Rather let us think in terms of the best that we can imagine. There is no sickness, sorrow, death, and pain (see Rev 21). The beauty is unbelievable. Life after death is a better type of life.

We mentioned a few wrong ideas above that are common, such as literal streets of gold. However, another would be the cartoon image of a person floating on a cloud, playing a harp. I do not think anyone takes this seriously, but it does portray an image. That image is that heaven is boring. I will sing praises forever. I believe that is true, but not in a literal way. Heaven will be joyous. There is no sickness, evil, or anything bad of any kind. We need to think of it as life in a new dimension. There is a variety of activity. There is relationship. My worshipping, singing, and everything that I am doing forever *is* a living experience. I am not bowing, singing, or anything of this sort. It is **LIFE!** It is the life that God made us for and that we have desired all of our time here on earth. Everlasting life is everlasting life. Yes, we sing of His praises, but one type of praising and singing is by the life that we live. I have said this badly, but think of it as life at its fullest and most complete.

We are told in the scripture that we will have resurrection bodies (see 1 Cor 15:35). In addition, in Luke 24:39, Jesus appears to His disciples after His resurrection. He assures them that He is not a ghost. He says that He has flesh and bones (These would be spiritual flesh and bones, whatever they are). Jesus came into a locked room so that indicates that there are no physical barriers. Again, we cannot explain this resurrected body, but we simply need to accept it. In 1 Corinthians 15:36-38, Paul writes that when we sow a seed, that seed dies and then new seed is born out of that death.

As we said above, some have said that there is no life after death. The Christian believes that there is life after death because of Jesus's testimony. He said so when he walked this earth. In John 11:25, Jesus says, *"I am the resurrection and the life. He who believes in me will live, even though he dies; and whoever lives and believes in me will never die."* Jesus is identifying Himself with God. That is the significance of the I AM. In John 10:17-18, Jesus indicates the Father gave Him the authority to lay down His life (to die voluntarily), which He did willingly and no one took it from Him (He was not a victim. He was in control.), and to take it up (to rise from the dead). Therefore, because He is raised He has the power over death and will raise (from the dead) everyone that believes in Him. Then in John 14, He tells

His disciples that He goes to prepare a place for them, so that where He is they can be with Him also.

As I think about life after death, it is like my thoughts on God. I wonder how it can be true. But at the same time, I know that it is true. My reasoning is this: (1) if there is a God, and I believe there is and (2) that He made us in His image and (3) as John 3:16 states, *"For God so loved the world that he gave his one and only son, that whoever believes in him shall not perish but have eternal life."* This indicates God's great love for us and states that there is life after death all of which I believe is true, then (4) if all of this is indeed true, it follows that there has to be life after death. Jesus's sacrifice would mean nothing if there is no life after death. He would be a liar also since He said there is.

I cannot believe that God who did all of the above could allow you to be a conscious being one moment and then a moment later, at death, you are nothing. Consciousness is completely gone. You are extinguished. It is not some kind of sleep. There is nothing. **That is true if there is no God.** However, we can rejoice that there is life after death. How do I know? As the words of that hymn say, **Because He lives!**

Summary

As we said in the beginning, it is easy to live the Christian life on Sunday when you are at church with other believers. However, the real test comes the moment you walk out of the doors of the church building. How do you live the rest of that day and the rest of the week?

In this little book, I have presented some topics that we meet every day: change, loneliness, death, purpose, love, etc. We encounter some of these things each day as we try to live the Christian life. I hope that this topical approach is helpful and that you look to the Bible for the material that you need to live by. Make the Bible a vital part of your whole life: body, mind, heart, and soul. Then you will be able to live this life the way that God wants you to and the way that you want to. This is the secret to Christian living seven days a week.

There is a lot of junk out there. Many people are really messed up. However, if you let Jesus into your life, then you can get rid of that junk. Some people think that they are smarter and superior to Jesus, but no one comes even close to matching His teachings and life. I challenge you that whenever someone says, "Follow my philosophy (teaching, religion, or whatever)," compare that person and his or her teachings with Jesus Himself and His life and teachings. If you do, then you will see that He alone is worthy of being followed. When many of the followers of Jesus left Him, Jesus asked His disciples, in John 6:67, if they would leave Him too. In verse 68, "Simon Peter answered him, 'Lord, to whom shall we go? You have the words of eternal life.'" If you reject Jesus, you will not find the answer anyplace else.

I want to repeat because this is so important. Read and study the Bible to give your heart, mind, and soul (your inner being) the nourishment that it needs. God made us, for we are created in His image (Gen 1: 26). He is the manufacturer, and He actually owns us too.

The fact that we are made in His image has various ramifications. It indicates that we are very important, but also indicates that we have a purpose. Life is not meaningless. We are created to have fellowship with God. This is why we have that longing in us. We have a need to love. Humans must have love. They have to give it and receive it in order to be complete. Unfortunately, too often we try to satisfy this hunger in us by other means such as drinking, drugs, sex, etc. But He does not impose that ownership upon us. Instead, God has given us free will. With that free will, we can choose to obey Him or go our own way. The choice is up to us. It amounts to a matter of choosing eternal life, which is life with God, or eternal punishment, which is separation from God.

One purpose of this book is to try to give the reader some biblical information on various topics to stimulate his or her thinking and to direct the reader to find some answers to questions in the Bible. At the same time, this book is written for those who have not accepted Jesus Christ as Lord and Savior but are seeking the truth. If you seek the truth, you will find Jesus because He is the way, the truth, and the life (Jn 14:6). And in John 8:32 Jesus says, *"Then you will know the truth, and the truth will set you free."*

Each one of us needs to make many different kinds of changes. An important part in making changes is to correct our thinking. However, we have to do more that consciously make up our mind that we are going to do something. All of us know that New Year's resolutions do not last very long. We said something about this in the topic on change. We have to get down to the subconscious level in order to make changes. We reprogram our computer. Our basic beliefs have to change.

Visualization and use of imagination are helpful along these lines. We are familiar with athletes improving their performance by using their imagination and visualizing what they want to do.

I read a story once—I do not if the story is true—that Jim Thorpe was on the boat to go to the Olympics. His fellow athletes were exercising and doing different things to get ready for their event. One of his teammates asked Jim, "Aren't you going to practice?" So Jim got out of his deck chair, went to one of the decks, and drew a line on the deck. Then he paced off a distance of almost thirty feet and drew another line. He studied it for a while and then sat back down. At the Olympic Games, Jim jumped that distance, but had his title taken away because they claimed he was not an amateur. But he accomplished his goal.

Under Habits, it was mentioned that we need habits to keep our minds busy. Be sure that you have plenty of good ones: habits that bless you and those around you. Habits that show you are a child of God.

All of us are sinners and have fallen short of the glory of God (see Rom 3:23). God has given His Son for our salvation so that all who believe in Him may have eternal life (Jn 11:25-26).

Confess your sin, seek forgiveness, and give forgiveness, as it says in the Lord's Prayer.

The last two thoughts are in 2 Corinthians 5:17, "Therefore, if anyone is in Christ, he is a new creation; the old is gone, the new has come!" and in Romans 12:2, "Do not conform any longer to the pattern of this world, but be transformed by the renewing of your mind. Then you will be able to test and approve what God's will is—His good, pleasing and perfect will."

Therefore, be the new creation that comes from knowing God, be transformed by the renewing of your mind, and have the mind of Christ in you.